T0384526

JUST FOLLOWING ORDERS

How can obedience and carrying out orders lead to horrific acts such as the Holocaust or the genocides in Rwanda, Cambodia, or Bosnia? For the most part, it is a mystery why obeying instructions from an authority can convince people to kill other human beings, sometimes without hesitation and with incredible cruelty.

Combining social and cognitive neuroscience with real-life accounts from genocide perpetrators, this book sheds light on the process through which obedience influences cognition and behavior. Emilie Caspar, a leading expert in the field, translates this neuroscientific approach into a clear, uncomplicated explanation, even for those with no background in psychology or neuroscience. By better understanding humanity's propensity for direct orders to short-circuit our own independent decision-making, we can edge closer to effective prevention processes.

Emilie A. Caspar is a professor at Ghent University, Belgium, specializing in social and cognitive neuroscience. She is one of the few neuroscientists worldwide working on the topic of obedience and she has received many awards for her research, which combines neuroscience with field interviews involving former genocide perpetrators.

JUST FOLLOWING ORDERS

Atrocities and the Brain Science of Obedience

Emilie A. Caspar

Ghent University, Belgium

Shaftesbury Road, Cambridge CB2 8EA, United Kingdom

One Liberty Plaza, 20th Floor, New York, NY 10006, USA

477 Williamstown Road, Port Melbourne, VIC 3207, Australia

314–321, 3rd Floor, Plot 3, Splendor Forum, Jasola District Centre,
New Delhi – 110025, India

103 Penang Road, #05–06/07, Visioncrest Commercial, Singapore 238467

Cambridge University Press is part of Cambridge University Press & Assessment,
a department of the University of Cambridge.

We share the University's mission to contribute to society through the pursuit of
education, learning and research at the highest international levels of excellence.

www.cambridge.org
Information on this title: www.cambridge.org/9781009385435

DOI: 10.1017/9781009385428

© Emilie A. Caspar 2024

First published 2024

Printed in the United Kingdom by TJ Books Limited, Padstow Cornwall

A catalogue record for this publication is available from the British Library

Library of Congress Cataloging-in-Publication Data
NAMES: Caspar, Emilie A., author.
TITLE: Just following orders : atrocities and the brain science of obedience / Emilie A.
Caspar.
DESCRIPTION: New York, NY : Cambridge University Press, 2024. | Includes
bibliographical references and index.
IDENTIFIERS: LCCN 2023052631 | ISBN 9781009385435 (hardback) | ISBN
9781009385411 (paperback) | ISBN 9781009385428 (ebook)
SUBJECTS: LCSH: Cognitive neuroscience. | Obedience.
CLASSIFICATION: LCC QP360.5 .C357 2024 | DDC 612.8/233–dc23/eng/20231229
LC record available at https://lccn.loc.gov/2023052631

ISBN 978-1-009-38543-5 Hardback

Contents

Figures

Preface

If someone had told me a couple of years ago that I would find myself at the age of 33 talking to, testing, and interviewing genocide perpetrators in Rwanda and Cambodia while pursuing a career in neuroscience, I would never have believed them. It is fascinating to look back and see where life has taken you when you decided to take the opportunities that arose. Many of the studies conducted with the populations mentioned in this book, such as the military or the genocide perpetrators, are mostly the result of chance meetings with the right people, not something that I had planned at this stage of my career.

Admittedly, I have always been interested in criminal behavior and eager to understand why people choose to conduct violent acts against others. As part of this quest, while I was working on my PhD in neuroscience, I also completed a two-year course in forensic sciences and forensic psychiatry at the Université libre de Bruxelles in Belgium. Forensic psychiatry was of deep interest to me because it offered insight into the research conducted on individuals – sometimes with highly psychopathic or narcissistic personality traits – who committed atrocities. However, I never thought that I would have the opportunity to do such research myself. And at no point did I think my research interests might take me to Rwanda or Cambodia.

It started in 2016, when I published a seminal study on how obeying orders impacts brain functioning in a high-impact scientific journal. I had developed an experimental study where I ordered people to administer electric shocks to each other to see how frequently they would comply with my orders and to study what happened in their brains. This work received a high degree of media coverage across the world, with many interviews. In one of these interviews with a journalist for BBC Future, I talked about my work and what it takes to stand up against authority. I also mentioned my scientific dream to be able to develop programs targeting individual responsibility to prevent atrocities from being committed on the grounds of obedience. Spoiler alert: I am still unfortunately very far from succeeding, but I remain hopeful. I did not know at the time, but this specific interview was about to unexpectedly and positively influence the trajectory of my career.

The idea of conducting field research actually followed the BBC interview in 2018, when I received an email from Georges Weiss, the director of the nonprofit organization Radio La Benevolencija Humanitarian Tool Foundation. Radio La Benevolencija is a Dutch NGO that develops radio soap operas and educational programs, targeting citizens from vulnerable societies to recognize and resist hate speech and manipulation to violence. Georges reached out to me after reading that interview, as he considered that we were sharing some strong humanitarian values and ideologies. The headquarters of Radio La Benevolencija are located in Amsterdam, and I was a postdoctoral researcher at the Netherlands Institute for Neuroscience at the time, so we went for a hot chocolate (for me) and a coffee (for him).

In Rwanda, Radio La Benevolencija is famous for having created *Musekeweya* (which can be translated as "New Dawn"), a radio program broadcast throughout the country, whose messaging is based on the academic research of Erwin Staub, an emeritus professor of psychology at the University of Massachusetts who wrote a book on the origins of genocide and other group violence. *Musekeweya* is a radio drama that tells the story of people living in two villages in Rwanda situated in opposite hills with marsh land in between. As the quantity and quality of land available is limited, disputes between the two villages developed over the years. These disputes are exacerbated by the fact that the two villages have different ethnic identities. By displaying the stories of different characters in those villages, *Musekeweya* seeks to explain how group violence can escalate and how to actively prevent it.

Georges told me that they were looking for scientists to help them test their interventions aimed at reducing group conflict, be it in Rwanda or elsewhere. The approach was very interesting because, unfortunately, it is not that frequent that stakeholders try to validate the efficacy of their interventions by collaborating with (neuro)scientists.

When he talked to me about Rwanda and the genocide, my mind started racing. I was already studying how obedience influences cognition, but I was far from thinking about going into a country where a genocide had actually happened relatively recently. I had not yet considered meeting with real perpetrators at that moment, and I was instead focusing only on university students who have a very limited experience of the disastrous consequences of obedience. As I will explain later in this book, in neuroscience, we are not really taught about the fact that we can recruit populations in other countries and contexts. During our education and from the huge majority of the scientific papers we read, we hear mostly about studies conducted on university students. Thinking differently requires stepping outside the box and entering into the unknown.

After meeting with Georges, I decided to go to Rwanda to study the question of obedience. Over the years, many colleagues have asked me how I thought conducting such neuroscientific projects in Rwanda was actually feasible or a "good idea," in their own words, considering no one had done this before. Honestly, I don't really remember; there is a sort of "black hole" between conceiving that idea and its conceptualization. But certainly, I do not regret seizing this opportunity as it ended up being an incredible scientific and human adventure.

Uniquely, the research I present in this book has thus been conducted in the lab *and* in the field, presenting a new and necessary perspective on how obeying orders affects our cognition in such a way that we could commit acts of violence against others.

Like previous scholars, I have observed a form of "violence" in laboratory contexts under orders, with striking results. Over the last eight years, I have given 45,000 orders to individuals to administer a real painful electric shock to someone else. Only about 1,340 orders were refused (roughly 2.97 percent). In other words, only about 54 individuals out of 1,500 refused an order to hurt another person – although they did not necessarily refuse every order they were given.

When I started working on obedience and designed this experiment that was about to attract massive media coverage, I really thought that no one would ever agree to administer a real and painful shock to someone else, especially not for a monetary reward as small as €0.05 per shock. In addition, the majority of the people I tested knew the experiments of Stanley Milgram, a famous scientist in social psychology who studied destructive obedience in the 1960s and the 1970s. So why would they obey orders that involve inflicting real physical pain on someone else?

The capacity for humans to obey orders, even atrocious ones, does not have to be proven anymore. As Howard Zinn famously pointed out in his book published in 1997, "Historically, the most terrible things – war, genocide, and slavery – have resulted not from disobedience, but from obedience."[*] Many societies rely on hierarchical institutions. Without a strict organization in which citizens follow the rules mandated by societal representatives, humans would probably not have achieved such an advanced degree of networking and interaction. However, the dark side of obedience results in societies being able to orchestrate the extermination of entire populations. Sadly famous examples include the Nazi genocide (1939–1945), when the Nazis exterminated millions of Jews and other ethnic minorities, as well as those they considered to be pariahs, such as homosexuals, Roma and Sinti, communists, or disabled persons. Another example is the Khmer Rouge army, led by Pol Pot, which exterminated between 1.7 and 2.2 million Cambodian citizens who were perceived as enemies or opposed their values and political vision between 1975 and 1979.

But such examples have been observed not only in soldiers given orders in the context of genocidal wars. Numerous historical episodes have shown that civilians are also capable of atrocious acts against other groups while following figures of authority. As an example, the genocide against the Tutsi in Rwanda in 1994 included a high number of civilians who joined the Interahamwe militia, the Hutu militia often cited as being responsible for the genocide, even though they had never killed anyone before.

But how have such terrible events been successfully instrumentalized, and how did the orchestrators of such violence convince civilians to join their campaigns?

---

[*] H. Zinn. *The Zinn Reader: Writings on Disobedience and Democracy.* (Seven Stories Press, 1997), p. 420.

Answering the *How* is one of the main objectives of this book. Across its chapters, I will delve into qualitative interviews conducted with former perpetrators in Rwanda and Cambodia, alongside an examination of experimental research in psychology and neuroscience.

I first considered dedicating the present book to the "Righteous." The Righteous are individuals who were able to resist propaganda and save threatened human beings from extermination during genocides. However, dedicating this book only to the Righteous would be too reductionist. Plenty of rescuers worldwide died before being recognized as Righteous. Others refused to accept any credit for their heroic actions and are thus not officially recognized. Further, plenty of brave acts have been conducted worldwide by human beings without any official status and in contexts other than genocides. Resisting immoral orders is not only important during extreme examples such as genocide, but also in daily actions. For instance, resisting the pressure of your boss to discriminate against people when hiring, or speaking up and intervening to protect the victims of acts of bullying, harassment, or discrimination, are also examples of brave resistance.

This book, therefore, is dedicated to every single human being who once, no matter the context, refused an immoral order despite the consequences associated with this decision. Motivated by the diverse concerns and questions that I regularly receive from people from various parts of the world who are in distress, I hope this book will be a source of inspiration and answers.

Acknowledgments

This book and the scientific studies reported would never have been possible without the help of a number of people and institutions.

I would first like to thank the professors who supported me during my doctoral studies and my postdoctoral positions. Professor Axel Cleeremans, director of the Center for Research in Cognition and Neuroscience at the Université libre de Bruxelles (Belgium), has supported me since the very beginning of my academic career, by accepting me as a PhD student. He granted me the invaluable freedom to cultivate my independent thinking and research, allowing me to develop my unique line of scientific investigation. I am eternally grateful for this exceptional opportunity. During my doctoral studies, I was fortunate to work under the guidance of Professor Patrick Haggard from University College London (United Kingdom) for a year and a half. His mentorship was instrumental in developing my seminal study on obedience to authority, which laid the foundation for my entire research trajectory. I am deeply thankful for the countless meetings and hours devoted to refining this paradigm. Additionally, I extend my sincere appreciation to Professor Christian Keysers and Professor Valeria Gazzola for hosting me as a postdoctoral researcher for two transformative years at the Netherlands Institute for Neuroscience (The Netherlands). Their expertise in human behavior and the neural underpinnings of empathy for pain proved invaluable in shaping and guiding many of the experiments I conducted.

The guidance, support, and mentorship of these professors have been pivotal in my academic growth and achievements. Their belief in my potential has been a driving force in propelling my research forward.

I am truly fortunate to have had the privilege of working with such outstanding scholars.

Throughout the years, I have also received support from stakeholders working in different institutions and organizations worldwide, without whom I would never have been able to recruit the populations I mention in the book. I would like to start by expressing my deepest gratitude to Georges Weiss, the director of Radio La Benevolencija Humanitarian Tool Foundation. Georges gave me the idea to initiate research activities in Rwanda, which probably would never have crossed my mind otherwise. We have worked together on other projects not directly mentioned in this book, and I have always appreciated his extraordinary enthusiasm. For research with the military, I warmly thank Professor Lieutenant-Colonel Salvatore Lo Bue from the Royal Military Academy in Belgium, who helped me gain access to this rare population. For access to prisons in Belgium, I must thank Karim El Klimchi, as well as the many prison directors for authorizing our access with all our electronic equipment and assisting us with the recruitment of inmates. In Rwanda, I received assistance from Professor Darius Gishoma and Dr. Clémentine Kanazayire from the University of Rwanda, as well as from people working for Prison Fellowship Rwanda, including Félix Bigabo, Silas, and François. In Cambodia, I was aided by Ratha Seng from the National University of Battambang, and I also received support from Youk Chhang, the director of the Documentation Center Cambodia, as well as from the local directors of three local centers across Cambodia: Ly Sok-Kheang at the Anlong Veng Peace Center; Seang Chenda at the Kampong Cham Documentation Center; and Pheng Pong-Rasy at the Takeo Documentation Center.

I am also really grateful to all the interns, master's thesis students, research assistants, PhD students, and postdocs who have helped in the data collection for some of the projects mentioned in this book. More specifically, I would like to thank my colleagues and co-authors for their invaluable feedback and support throughout the research conducted on obedience to authority. Their expertise, whether in study design, data collection (or acquisition) or data analysis, and insights greatly contributed to the development of the studies. In chronological order: Julia Christensen, Frederique Beyer, Kalliopi Ioumpa, Nicolas Coucke, Nicolas Bourguignon, and Antonin Rovai. Some of them have become good friends and I would like to further express my gratitude for the joyful time we spent working together. I also would like to thank Alison Mary for providing feedback on one of the chapters.

I would like to express my sincere gratitude to the many institutions and scientific organizations for their generous funding that supported the research presented in this book: the Fonds National de la Recherche (FRS-FNRS, Belgium), the Fonds Wetenschappelijk Onderzoek (FWO, Belgium), the BIAL Foundation (Portugal), the Marie Curie Actions (European Commission), the Francqui Foundation (Belgium), the Evens Foundation (Belgium), the Université libre de Bruxelles (Belgium) and Ghent University (Belgium).

My relatives also greatly contributed, directly or indirectly, to this book. Guillaume Pech, my life partner, offered me the greatest support I could have imagined. Despite having to work on his own research, he nonetheless accompanied me in Rwanda and in Cambodia in order to provide technical and emotional support during the research activities. I also would like to thank my mother, Anne Hauzeur, who has shown me her passion for science since I was a child, and my grandmother, Hendrica Cramer, who shared with me her humanitarian values.

I also need to express my gratitude to my closest friends, for their support throughout the years: Katarzyna Suchanecka, Sarah Miller, Jennifer Michiels, Laurène Vuillaume, Lola Seyll, Juliane Farthouath, Irene Cogliati Dezza, Anna Atas, Aurore Bouyer, Pedro Alexandre Magalhaes de Saldanha da Gama, Albert De Beir, and Whitney Stee.

I also want to warmly thank Janka Romero, the commissioning editor who assisted me in the crucial initial steps of the book, as well as Emily Watton, the commissioning editor, and Lisa Carter, the content manager, who were present during the final stages of the book's development, as well as Rowan Goat, Joon Moon, and David Repetto from Cambridge University Press. I would also like to extend a special thanks to Elena Abbott, who helped me structure the book. Her enthusiasm and unwavering positivity during our conversations were truly invaluable in this process.

And of course, I thank my cats, Newton and Euclid, for their company during the writing process, even though their form of support mostly consisted in sleeping next to me. Just like Jane, Sky, and Napoléon, my rabbits, who thankfully did not eat the pages while I was reading and correcting the book proof.

Introduction: Understanding Genocide as a Means to Prevention

I N JANUARY AND FEBRUARY 2023, I was in Cambodia working at the National University of Battambang. I was staying in a small hotel not far from the city center, where one of the workers was a French immigrant who decided to stay in Cambodia more than a decade ago. He married a Cambodian woman, had children with her, and spoke the Khmer language fluently.

One day, he said something that really stuck with me. Referring to the Cambodian genocide that unfolded between 1975 and 1979, he said, "You know, these people, they are so nice, so kind by nature. How can you explain that they started killing each other like that?"

While researching this exact question, I discovered that, for many, the answer they would probably give is that they were simply following orders.

Around the world, the phrase "I was just following orders" is used in every conceivable context to justify why people do things that can aptly be described as "bad," "immoral," or "illegal." I have heard this simple sentence so many times now that it is like an incessant chorus playing in my head.

Indeed, the "just following orders" argument has been used across many documented wars and genocides throughout history in different countries, on different continents, and with people from very different cultures. What accounts for the fact that this justification is used so consistently across time and place? Could it be that it reflects, at least in part, a reality in perpetrators' brains – a reality of how we perceive ourselves that might be shared across all the members of our species? Moreover, does obeying orders alter our natural aversion to hurting others? From an evolutionary perspective, such a finding would probably make sense. After all, following rules is part of the blessing and the curse

1

of being hyper-social animals, which enabled us to overcome many obstacles, but also led to committing atrocities.

Human behaviors are incredibly complex to study and understand, and can be influenced by a plethora of factors, ranging from our biology and our genetics to social, economic, cultural, and historical factors. This is certainly the case for a phenomenon like genocide.

Genocides do not happen suddenly. They happen because of a number of events, circumstances, and individual decisions that played out over many years. The genocide in Rwanda, for example, arose in a context of economic difficulties and political instability exacerbated by past and ongoing ethnic tensions. Following the colonial period in Rwanda, first under German and then Belgian rule, the Tutsis – a minority ethnic group – were often favored by colonial policies, which resulted in disproportionate access to wealth, better jobs, and educational opportunities compared to the majority Hutus and other groups. When Rwanda gained its independence in 1962, the Hutus became the leaders and frequently portrayed the Tutsis as the reason for every crisis. In 1993, the Radio Télévision Libre des Milles Collines (which can be translated as Free Radio and Television of the Thousand Hills), which was supported by the government, started to broadcast hate propaganda messages against the Tutsis and to dehumanize them. It was reported that the Tutsis were planning to kill the Hutus and take over the country. In April 1994, after a plane crash resulted in the death of the Hutu leader of the government, President Habyarimana, the Tutsis were blamed, and a genocide was launched against them. In only three months, about 500,000 to 600,000 individuals were murdered.[1]

A somewhat similar pattern played out in Cambodia against any individuals perceived as not part of the Khmer Rouge ideology. Influenced by the communist ideology and by their willingness to create a classless agrarian society, Saloth Sâr (best known as Pol Pot) and the Khmer Rouge took power in Cambodia in 1975. These events followed years of instability after both a civil war and the Vietnam War. Immediately, the Khmer Rouge set about radically reorganizing Cambodian society. They forced people who lived in urban areas to work as farmers and split up families. They turned the entire country into a huge rice field that had to produce three tons of rice per year, according to the leaders' plans. Their plan was inspired by the "Great Leap Forward" campaign of Mao Zedong, former President of

China, who pursued the total collectivization of agriculture. In the new society of the Khmer Rouge, individuals were given roles based on their gender and age. Opponents and intellectuals – or sometimes simply individuals wearing glasses[*] – were killed or re-educated. Every person who complained, did not work hard enough, refused a forced marriage, did not produce enough rice, met in groups, revolted, or was denounced as a traitor (whether true or false) was tortured and/or killed. Mass graves popped up everywhere in the country. In four years, a quarter of the Cambodian population was killed by the Khmer Rouge or died because of starvation or disease. This so-called "auto-genocide" ended in 1979 when the Vietnamese army took over the country.

The Nazi genocide, too, unfolded in the wake of longstanding instability for which a part of the population was designated guilty. The end of World War I left people in Germany, already traumatized by the war, in a situation of high insecurity. The Treaty of Versailles (June 28, 1919) set up a peace settlement that drastically impacted the economy of Germany. The Treaty required Germany to disarm, to lose territories, and to pay reparations to several countries. The cost of those reparations is estimated to be equivalent to $442 billion in 2022. The German population was hungry and desperate, which gave Adolf Hitler and the National Socialist German Workers' Party significant popular support. His party blamed the country's instability on the Jews, the Roma, and people with physical or psychological disabilities. Despite being in a modern and educated society, the Nazi leaders were able to convince the population that those undesirables had to be "exterminated."

The three above-mentioned examples are a simplistic résumé of very complex situations, with each of them deserving more than a single book to be fully understood. No single discipline alone can explain how and why they emerge, and how and why they unfold the

---

[*] It is often heard that "those wearing glasses were killed" during the Khmer Rouge regime. However, it is essential to note that simply wearing glasses did not guarantee a death sentence, nor was it an official rule under the Khmer Rouge regime.[2] While such incidents did occur, they were primarily a consequence of the Khmer Rouge targeting intellectuals as dangerous individuals. Thousands were killed merely because they had an education or belonged to a higher socioeconomic class, rather than having a rural background. Individuals wearing glasses were more likely to be associated with a higher social status, making them susceptible to being controlled or targeted by the regime.

way they do. An interdisciplinary scientific approach is necessary. For instance, psychology may focus on individual traits and mental health. History may delve into previous group conflicts. Politics may examine the political situation in the country. Sociology may examine the group and the social environment. Anthropology may help us understand why a specific group is targeted.

And brain sciences, wich are the main focus of the present book, can study the brain structure and functioning.

Trying to understand how genocide and mass atrocities can happen thus has enormous complexity. On the one hand, we have collectively recognized that being under the immediate threat of physical harm – such as torture or death – is a mitigating circumstance when obeying an order to kill another person.[†] But, clearly, many people have taken part in mass-exterminations without the existence of such threats. Wars and genocides involve the participation of thousands and thousands of individuals, with a plethora of factors explaining their group and individual actions. Our role, as scientists, is to help identify the processes that lead to such acts of destruction.

Crucially, understanding and studying the factors that explain mass atrocities does not excuse the actions of the perpetrators nor does it diminish their individual responsibility, an aspect that will be explored in more depth later in the book.

Rather, identifying the neural mechanisms associated with the execution of atrocious acts out of obedience has the potential to raise hopes of developing efficacious interventions to prevent blind obedience, even if there is still a long way to go. Unfortunately, however, when interventions are planned to prevent some behaviors or to promote some behaviors, the neural level is currently barely considered, except in some recent disciplines such as neuromarketing. This means that even if some changes are observed as a result of the intervention, no one really knows how those changes occurred and if some aspects of the intervention should be more emphasized to produce a greater behavioral change.

[†] International Military Tribunal at Nuremberg, No. 21948–04-09, "The Einsatzgruppen Case, Case No. 9, United States v. Ohlendorf et al., Opinion and Judgment and Sentence" (1948), 480, accessed June 8, 2016.

In neuromarketing, the one contemporary exception to this generalization, it is widely assumed that consumer behaviors are driven by subconscious motives that questionnaires cannot detect. The discipline thus uses more objective methods such as brain scanning and physiological tracking. Neuromarketing has certainly proven its efficacy at influencing people's behaviors. It stands to reason, therefore, that neuro-based interventions could be similarly helpful for changing people's harmful behaviors towards others.

In the case of obedience, however, the question remains: Should such interventions target empathy and compassion, or rather target individual responsibility for one's own actions, or even other mechanisms? By using more objective and precise methods – by understanding how our brain processes the information in situations of obedience – we may be able to find strategies to help people resist blind obedience.

THE ROLE OF NEUROSCIENCE

I am sometimes contacted by people searching for answers to what happened to them or their families during wars or other events, hoping to find an explanation thanks to neuroscience for what they had to endure. Obtaining answers is clearly a critical part in the healing process. Unfortunately, the answer is not simple. Many biological, societal, cultural, and historical factors have been explored to explain how and why atrocious acts are perpetrated. Neuroscience, however, has only recently begun to address this question and may provide novel and complementary information. The objective of this book is thus to bring a new element into the equation by looking at the structure and function of the brain in relation to obedience and the perpetration of violence.

Notably, neuroscience is not a miracle solution to understanding genocides or other mass atrocities – as mentioned, a single discipline could not boast of having the answer to such a broad and complex question. However, in this book, I explain what is happening in the brain of individuals who have accepted and followed orders to hurt another person, and I offer significant insight into understanding how they can perpetrate the cruel acts they do. Moving beyond previous books and scientific research on obedience, this book thus seeks to understand immoral behaviors out of obedience to authority at a deep and individual level – that is, at the neural level.

Any decisions we make, any actions we perform, originate in the brain. The brain is a complex structure composed of trillions of neurons that produces our thoughts, our feelings, our decisions, our memory, our senses, and that regulates our body. While a high range of environmental and social factors can modulate how our brain processes information and computes decisions, the brain is nevertheless the central processing system. To generate actions, the brain continuously processes all the information received from our environment as well as our past and present experiences to compute a decision, which is then sent to our muscles to make us perform movements. Thus, to have a more complete overview and a better understanding of how people can commit atrocities when they obey orders, neuroscience has significant learning to contribute.

The most common approaches to neuroscientific research rely on physiological measurement, especially neuroimaging. Two crucial dimensions in neuroimaging are space and time, which provide insights into where and when brain activity occurs. Magnetic resonance imaging (MRI) is conventionally used to reveal with a very good spatial resolution the anatomical structure of a region of interest (the "where"). It is used not only when there is suspected brain damage, but also when medical doctors want to ensure that your foot is not broken or see if there are any tumors, cysts, or other anomalies in your body. fMRI, or functional magnetic resonance imaging, is an MRI technique that specifically measures blood oxygenation. Thinking, speaking, or moving involves specific parts of our brains, whose neurons suddenly demand more energy to fire. This request for local energy increases the blood flow roughly 4 to 6 seconds after a neural activity – especially the oxygenated blood in this region. While these changes are captured spatially by the MRI scanner, however, the lag between the targeted neural activity and the increase of blood flow prevents MRI scanners from providing a good temporal resolution of brain functions.

This is where electroencephalography (EEG) and magnetoencephalography (MEG) come in. These technologies offer a very good temporal dynamic of brain functions (the "when"), although they have a weaker spatial resolution. When clusters of neurons fire because we are thinking, speaking, or moving, an electrical current is conducted to the scalp

through tissue, cerebrospinal fluid, and the skull. With electrodes posi-
tioned on the scalp, this current is recorded with a millisecond precision.
Unfortunately, however, the specific source of this activity is much more
difficult to determine, partly because the scalp has spread the electrical
information. For instance, while the spatial resolution for fMRI is typically in
the range of 1 to 2 millimeters (sometimes even less), it is typically around 2
to 3 millimeters for MEG and around 7 to 10 millimeters for EEG,[3] resulting
in differences of hundreds of thousands of brain cells. Being able to
position the electrodes of the EEG directly inside the cranium at the
surface of the brain allows a better spatial resolution, but such methods
are reserved for animal studies or patients already undergoing surgery.

There exist many more techniques in psychobiology and neuroscience, such as facial electromyography, galvanic skin responses, heart rate
monitoring, neuropharmacology, neuromodulation, and lesion studies.
Some of those methods will be approached in the different chapters,
when necessary. However, in the present book, most of the studies
mentioned will be based either on (f)MRI or on EEG.

A central premise of this book is that when human beings perform
actions, they are the only ones making the decision to follow or not follow
an order, especially without the presence of immediate threats, as mentioned earlier. Thus, a crucial aspect of conducting this research is reiterat-
ing again and again that uncovering the neural mechanisms explaining how
people can commit atrocious acts out of obedience does not offer an excuse
or an escape door for people trying to justify their actions. Although
obeying orders may be considered a factor diminishing one's own accountability in the eyes of the law, we should never forget that deciding to follow
an order does not fully remove the agency of perpetrators. In fact, throughout history, several examples have demonstrated that people sometimes use
the excuse of obeying orders to commit even more terrible acts.

During the genocide against the Tutsi in Rwanda, for instance, some
of the cruelest acts ever recorded in the history of humankind were
observed. Perpetrators did not simply obey the order to kill other
human beings. They went further by conducting atrocities and acts of
torture that are beyond imagination and went beyond murder. Even
though obedience can be blind, it is also, often, cruel. Further, history
is filled with examples of individuals who have taken enormous risks to

save others, even strangers, as we will see in the book. Obeying orders may thus not be the only option.

NEUROSCIENTISTS ALMOST NEVER MEET NON-WEIRD POPULATIONS

If you come from a Western, Educated, Industrialized, Rich, and Democratic society, you are probably WEIRD.

In 2020, Joseph Henrich, a US anthropologist, published *The WEIRDest People in the World: How the West Became Psychologically Peculiar and Particularly Prosperous.*[4] He conducted a very detailed analysis on how WEIRD people have their own culture, their own way of thinking, their own way of behaving, and how this brought the West to conquer most of the world in 1500 CE.

Because the West has been able to develop critical scientific knowledge due to its development, many scientific disciplines are WEIRD-centered. For instance, almost all the questionnaires used in sociology or psychology have been developed and validated on WEIRD samples. They were written by WEIRD researchers, with their own WEIRD culture and education. They have put into the questionnaires their own WEIRD definitions, their own WEIRD conceptions of life.

Neuroscience is no exception to this WEIRD-centrism. And the availability of neuroscientific technologies exacerbated the phenomenon. Neuroscience relies on very recent technologies that can cost several million euros and are used by people who have received a very long and specific university training. These technologies are clearly not available in many places on Earth. As a consequence, most WEIRD researchers recruit participants predominantly from their own WEIRD societies, often university students, who are convenient to test due to their easy accessibility. These researchers then draw conclusions about the human brain based on this limited sample.

This is of course highly problematic. First, the WEIRD do not represent the majority of the population on Earth. In 2008, Jeffrey Arnett, a US psychologist, calculated that roughly 95 percent of participants recruited in published behavioral research are from WEIRD societies.[5] However, the WEIRD population represents only 12 percent of the entire human population. No need for a degree in mathematics to understand the problem. Nowadays, additional societies across the world have started to also acquire neuroscientific equipment and are running neuroscientific studies. This is notably the case in China or Japan, for instance, where there are numerous teams of active neuroscientists. Yet the huge majority of the world is still excluded. A team of researchers indicated that, in 2016, just 3 percent of the submissions to a famous journal in social neuroscience were from Central and South America, South Asia, Africa, and the Middle East.[6]

Second, we know that our social environments can strongly shape our brains. Recent findings in neuroscience, for instance, showed that our sociocultural environments influence neural activity during different cognitive, affective, perceptual, or attentional tasks.[7,8] This makes it difficult to know whether neuropsychological functions discovered in WEIRD populations extend to "all human brains" or are culture specific. Not extending research to non-WEIRD populations is thus a terrible flaw in neuroscience. And this is the case for all disciplines.

Furthermore, I firmly believe that remaining solely within a laboratory setting and testing convenience samples is insufficient to fully understand the motivations behind genocide perpetrators and mass atrocities. While lab studies are critical for understanding how obedience alters our natural aversion to hurting others, how can we develop theories about obedience if we never talk to people who have been in the situation? How can we fully understand human behaviors without also conducting interviews with people to learn about their subjective experience?

These questions also supported my decision to undertake the highly unusual step in neuroscience of going into the field. I now travel the world with my portable electroencephalograms and my audio recorder as a means to better understand human behaviors. I also wanted to meet genocide perpetrators and talk to them, to try to understand them. I was – and I still am – convinced that it is only by considering what people have to say, and what we understand from the brain, together with contextual factors, that we will obtain critical answers as to why atrocities are conducted on the grounds of obedience.

Yet conducting field research in neuroscience is clearly a challenge, for many reasons. When I started to consider doing such research – in Rwanda first, and then in Cambodia – my colleagues largely told me that it was totally unfeasible. I did not obtain some research grants specifically because reviewers on the scientific panels evaluating my projects considered that they "raised deep concerns regarding feasibility."

The challenges were, indeed, many: transporting the neuroscientific material to these destinations, recruiting populations that may be hesitant to meet or talk to strangers about the atrocities they committed, asking them to wear an electroencephalogram on their head while most of them had never seen electronic devices before, testing in dusty and uncontrolled environments, the list goes on. This is why such field research in neuroscience is extremely rare, with only a handful of researchers in the world doing it.

Part of this book's objective, therefore, is to detail how such projects were conducted so that we can begin to see more of them in the future. I will thus hereafter briefly describe some critical steps to consider.

In many countries around the world, the methods used in neuroscience do not exist, so it is necessary to send research materials by plane. The simplest way would be to put the material in the luggage. However, everyone probably knows how risky it is to do this. A survey published in 2006 indicated that about seven bags are lost on every jet.[9] Another recent investigation further reports that the chances of seeing your bags lost by the airline companies are drastically increasing.[10] As I did not want to be part of those terrible statistics, especially when I transport such an expensive and precious cargo, I did not even consider putting the material in my luggage. Even though I have many insurance policies, if my cargo got lost, I would spend months dealing with administrative paperwork and miss out on important research activities. Rather I use the system of diplomatic bags to ensure that my boxes of material arrive safely at the closest embassy I can find – although this process is significantly more expensive.

Neuroscientists also like very clean and controlled environments to conduct their study: a proper experimental room, with electricity, no surrounding noises, no visual distractions. In the field, you are unlikely to find such five-star testing conditions. Dust on your apparatus, goats, chickens or dogs passing by, children staring at what you are doing all day long, noisy crows on the metal rooftops, heavy tropical rains are but a few of the testing conditions one might encounter. I usually prioritize buildings with electricity, at least, to ensure that my batteries will last for the entire day. In many villages in Rwanda, inhabitants did not have electricity in their houses, so we found ourselves testing in churches or bars. In Cambodia, we also tested in the backyard of a small shop, surrounded by rice fields. To minimize visual distractions, we find ourselves tapping into our very basic carpentry skills, building walls out of wood or whatever materials we can find around.

Then, we must explain to the local population what an electroencephalogram is and convince them that it will not hurt them. Many of the individuals we recruited have never used a keyboard in their entire life or even looked at a computer screen. And here we come with a weird contraption to put on their head that makes them look like an alien. Understandably, most of them are afraid because they think it will hurt them, alter their health, or that we could read their mind with it. Simply saying that it is a safe and non-invasive technique is not sufficient to reassure them.

For presenting the electroencephalogram and the computer tasks, we must therefore use very simple language. Usually, we use as an example the situation where someone has a temperature, and you put your hand on their forehead to feel if the temperature is too high or not. We then explain that the machine does the same, it is only touching their head to record what their brain can reveal to us, and not injecting something or reading their mind. We sometimes even make a demo where one of us wears the electroencephalogram in front of them to show that it is entirely safe.

And finally, we must always remember that we are guests in a country with a different culture, history, and sensitivities. When conducting neuroscience research with such populations, particularly those who have endured the trauma of genocide, we must approach the study with deep understanding and respect for cultural differences and sensitivities. These populations often bear the weight of profound experiences that have shaped their collective and individual psychologies in unique ways. Cultural norms, beliefs, and the societal impact of such catastrophic events play a significant role in how these communities perceive, interpret, and engage with scientific research. It is crucial to recognize that standard methodologies and interpretations, often developed in WEIRD contexts, may not be directly applicable or appropriate in these diverse settings. Therefore, collaboration with local individuals is crucial, as they provide invaluable insights necessary to contextualize research within their specific cultural and historical landscape.

Clearly, field research in neuroscience is a challenge, but it is worth it to avoid WEIRD-centered conclusions about the human brain and to help humanity to understand non-WEIRD history and phenomena.

CONDUCTING INTERVIEWS AS A RESEARCH METHODOLOGY

This book combines scientific research in psychology and neuroscience with interviews conducted with the perpetrators of genocide. As previously mentioned, combining interviews and experimental approaches is a powerful way to better understand mass atrocities.

Interview-based qualitative studies of perpetrators are important to understand how genocides or other mass atrocities can develop in our societies. Academics can indeed develop lab experiments or make in-depth analysis of demographic data or of historical precedents. However, we will never fully understand the implication of our results if we also do not speak with the persons who committed such atrocities. This approach helps to integrate theory, practice, and real-world cases, providing a more comprehensive view of the bigger picture. They are all critical if one wants to have the most complete overview possible of the problem. Undoubtedly, staying in an office or in a lab is not sufficient.

Shedding light on the subjective experience of perpetrators when they conducted atrocities is thus a necessary step towards a better understanding of such events. But trying to understand the behaviors of genocide perpetrators is not always well received by the general public. Popular culture generally describes perpetrators as psychopaths, cold-hearted individuals, or monsters who experience pleasure when they see their victims suffering. Although it may be the case for some of them, the reality is much more complex and troubling. In fact, such a simplistic view denies all the factors that can lead regular people to become perpetrators of horrific acts.

A specific personality trait, psychiatric condition, or neurological malfunction cannot simply be the cause. One cannot say that all the individuals who participated in the Nazi genocide had brain damage or were psychiatrically ill. Neither can one say that the hundreds of thousands of Hutus who participated in the genocide against the Tutsi in Rwanda had similar issues. In Cambodia, every adult was assigned a role in the Khmer Rouge's novel society (i.e., Palm unit, mobile units, soldiers, teachers, medical unit, prison guards, cadres, etc.). Refusal meant being considered as a traitor and risking being killed – thus participation was in the majority of the cases not the result of psychopathy or "being a monster." It is clearly difficult to think about ordinary people turning into evil perpetrators, but this is the task of those who seek to understand genocides.

The disturbing truth is that perpetrators are not that different from the rest of us. Past research, for instance, failed to observe that Jihad members planning terrorist attacks had any mental health problems.[11] Actually, most of them were educated, married, and had children. They felt lonely and isolated and were willing to join a group movement that shared a strong connection with their own values, but they were not suffering from psychiatric illness. Hannah Arendt, a famous political philosopher and survivor of the Nazi genocide, has already concluded that Adolf Eichmann, one of the main organizers, was not a monster. She saw him, rather, as a bureaucratic clown at the service of the Führer and sharing his ideology.[12] As Jewish survivor Elie Wiesel stated: "It is demonic that they were not demonic."[13]

Interviews conducted with genocide perpetrators have not been frequent. Some authors have argued that the rareness of interviews with genocide perpetrators is in part due to the psychological difficulties associated with hearing unspeakable atrocities while trying to understand the decisions of the perpetrators. It is something that cannot be improvised; it requires deep psychological and emotional preparation.[14] For sure, reading or hearing stories where perpetrators blindly attacked individuals in a church with machetes,[15] how others threw babies into trees to kill them, how some raped young girls and then cut open their bodies and ate their livers[16] is emotionally very difficult. Recitals of atrocities committed in wars and genocides can be appalling to hear. Academics or journalists choosing to interview genocide perpetrators must be prepared to preserve their own psychological wellbeing. Not everyone is willing or ready to hear such stories.

Moreover, it is important to acknowledge that interviews present methodological challenges, an aspect which can also reduce their reliability. Indeed, one of the main challenges is that the results are not objectively verifiable.[17,18] As the interviews rely on what the interviewees agree to share, some of the responses can be, consciously or unconsciously, false, distorted, attenuated, or incomplete. Furthermore, many former genocide perpetrators suffer from psychiatric diseases such as post-traumatic stress disorder[19,20] or addiction.[21] For instance, during our interviews, a former genocide perpetrator in Rwanda was completely drunk. It is a very frequent problem because abusing such substances helps perpetrators numb themselves to what they did. Admittedly, alcohol in this case was making the interviewee very talkative. But are his words reliable enough to be integrated into the interviews?

For instance, even if some individuals have been judged for their crimes, they may also keep hidden other crimes in order to prevent future or additional conviction in court. Others may deny their crimes as part of a psychological process aimed at rebuilding a positive image of themselves. Others again may distort their responses or find external causes to attenuate their responsibility. People are usually ashamed or want to forget what they did. In Cambodia for instance, only five people have been brought to trial for the decimation of a quarter of the Cambodian population by the Extraordinary Chambers in the Courts of Cambodia (ECCC, 1997–2022). Thus, almost none of the killers have been officially recognized or sentenced. Most of them have decided to never tell anyone what they did to avoid revenge or prosecution.

Analyzing qualitative data is also tricky because researchers have to avoid putting their own subjective appreciation of the data into the analysis. In psychology, a common method that we used as well to prevent the issue of subjective perspective is to analyze qualitative interviews as follows: the main researcher first classifies each answer into different categories based on what is reported in the interviews. Then, several independent judges are given the responsibility to read all the answers and to indicate in which category or categories they belong. The answers of those different judges are then combined, and the majority determines the final classification.

But overcoming the above-mentioned obstacles is worth it: interviews are a rich source of information. They provide insights from the persons themselves into how killings were perpetrated and why.

Yet finding and interviewing genocide perpetrators is extremely complicated, for several reasons. First, most of the time, the events happened decades ago, as it is difficult – sometimes almost impossible – to reach the perpetrators during the ongoing events or rapidly in their aftermath. As a result, perpetrators may not be alive anymore. Second, for many of the recent or ongoing genocides, the political situation in the country is such that the genocide is either largely denied or the ongoing nature makes it almost impossible to conduct interviews with the individuals involved.

There are, however, genocide perpetrators who are still alive and who are living in countries where the genocide is officially recognized, thus allowing interviews. This is the case for Rwanda and for Cambodia. However, the perpetrators of these genocides are growing older. In Cambodia, the Khmer Rouge indoctrinated thousands of children in their early teens and taught them to follow any orders to kill without hesitation.[22] Even considering the youngest children at the beginning of the genocide in Cambodia, the youngest "perpetrators" are nowadays at least 55 years old. This is already quite old for a country where the life expectancy is estimated to be 70 years old according to the World Bank.

In addition, knowing who a "real perpetrator" was is complex in Cambodia. Members of the Khmer Rouge also lost many family members because of starvation, or because they suddenly became considered as traitors by the organization and were imprisoned and tortured, even killed. They may also have been killed during the "year of revenge" that happened after the end of the genocide. In Cambodia, it is considered that the perpetrators also largely suffered; they are thus considered "survivors," and even "victims," as well as perpetrators. With only five individuals brought to trial for the entire genocide, with many perpetrators already dead, and with those still alive preferring to remain silent, it is very hard to estimate how many people participated in the killings and "extermination" process.

With all this in mind, it is incredibly difficult to find in Cambodia people officially recognized as genocide perpetrators and have them agree to talk and reveal their innermost thoughts and feelings.

After the genocide against the Tutsi in Rwanda, a court-based justice process commenced, but there were so many potential perpetrators that it would be impossible to prosecute everyone, and the process would have taken many decades to complete. The perpetrators would have died awaiting trial in their cells and prisons were already overcrowded. The Rwandan government thus instituted the Gacaca courts in 2002 to try the perpetrators of the genocide.[23] Instead of using professional judges, trials were conducted by laypeople in the form of a community court. Those recognized as "upright" were placed in the roles of judges and the entire community was invited to participate. The lay judges had to listen to everyone, determine who did what, and give the appropriate punishment. These Gacaca courts have enabled the identification of genocide perpetrators on a mass level.

It is still a matter of debate, however, just how many individuals took an active part in the genocide in Rwanda. Past research suggested that between 14 and 17 percent of the adult male population of Rwanda took part in the genocide, which represents between approximately 175,000 and 210,000 participants.[24] After the Gacaca courts, it had been suggested that the number could actually be between 600,000 and 700,000 participants, but those numbers also involve those who were looting or being present at roadblocks.

CONDUCTING THE INTERVIEWS

In August 2021, when I flew to Rwanda with my partner Guillaume for research activities in neuroscience and to interview perpetrators, we were told that we would not have access to the prisons for the interviews because of the drastic increase in the number of Covid cases. My colleagues and contacts in Rwanda told me that it would probably be better to conduct the interviews in 2022. However, as I was already there and because of the unpredictability of the evolution of the Covid-19 pandemic that hit the world, postponing the interviews until the following year would actually not have been a safer option. But trying to find former genocide perpetrators by myself outside of prisons would have been almost impossible. People tend, understandably, to avoid talking about what they did during the genocide, especially to strangers.

I was not deterred. For the research activities we had to conduct in Rwanda, I fortunately was in contact with Prison Fellowship Rwanda, a local NGO whose aim is to foster psychological healing after the genocide as well as reconciliation between former genocide perpetrators and survivors. As Prison Fellowship Rwanda accompanies former perpetrators during their prison sentence and after, they thus know who has been officially recognized as a former perpetrator of the genocide. And since my planned research activities in neuroscience already involved recruiting them, I agreed that the interviews could also be conducted on former perpetrators released from prison. The approach worked.

The day we were to conduct the first interviews and experiments, we woke at 5.30 AM; I do not quite remember the day of the week. We had to quickly pack our material, which consisted in roughly 30 kg of equipment, including two electroencephalograms, four laptops, electrodes, electronic-based gel, and of course, the precious questionnaires and the audio recorder for the interviews. We charged all the electronic equipment in the car, took our two research assistants with us and started driving in the direction of an eastern province of Rwanda, which we understood was just over an hour away from Kigali.

We had to hurry because the curfew due to the Covid pandemic started again at 8 PM. Believe me, you do not want to be out past curfew in Rwanda. One of our research assistants told us that if you are caught twenty minutes after the curfew time, you have to pay a fine of 150,000 RWF (the equivalent of $150), you have to sleep in the stadium in Kigali, and your car is confiscated for five days. In addition, the journey time of 1.1 hours suggested by online maps was purely theoretical. There is just a single road with tarmac in the direction of the eastern province, with a single traffic lane in each direction. And on that single road, there was a never-ending parade of very old and slow trucks. Thus, the return journey time was regularly more like four hours leaving us with only a few hours to conduct our research activities and the interviews.

In the first reconciliation village we visited, we met with François, a representative of Prison Fellowship Rwanda. Reconciliation villages exist in different provinces of Rwanda and are supported by Prison Fellowship Rwanda. In those villages, survivors and perpetrators live side by side as neighbors. People get to decide whether or not to live in these villages. If they do, they are provided with material to build new homes, critical for people in a low-income country. Being part of those reconciliation villages also involves participating in sociotherapy sessions and activities aiming to rebuild some sort of relationship between victims of the genocide and former perpetrators.

François came to meet us as soon as we arrived in the village. We were driving a big four-wheel-drive car in a rural village of Rwanda made up of mud houses with straw roofs. We were unusual visitors and were of course spotted from afar. François was dressed very elegantly, with classic long pants, a shirt, and a V-neck sweater. Like many Rwandans born before the genocide, François had learned French and appeared to be quite happy to practice with us.

After installing the equipment in the church, which had been converted into an experimental room for the occasion as it was the only building around with electric plug sockets, I went for a small walk with him. He explained to me what happened to him and his family during the genocide. During our conversation, we suddenly crossed the path of an old man who barely looked at us. François calmly told me, "You see this man, he killed 13 people during the genocide," and then he continued his story.

I must admit, I felt a small chill run down my spine. In the past, each time I had met with perpetrators, I met them in prison. Information about their crimes was expected. This was not my first time in Rwanda, and of course I was there to meet with them. But even though I had taken the time to get used to the idea that I would cross paths with many of them, I was really not expecting François' announcement, delivered so casually.

I asked François if he thought that this man would agree to be interviewed regarding what he did during the genocide, especially by a stranger. He told me that he would certainly be open regarding my questions during the interview. Being part of the reconciliation village involves having publicly recognized one's crimes during the genocide and being ready to discuss them openly during the sociotherapy sessions.

In the end, this man was one of the first we spoke to among many perpetrators living in the village.

In Cambodia, I faced many hurdles before actually finding a way to conduct interviews with former Khmer Rouge members. I contacted several associations, but either they never responded or refused to help, because "it took too many years to gain their trust and they did not want them involved in any research projects." I almost gave up several times because it actually sounded unfeasible. As a last resort, I contacted Georges Weiss, the director of Radio La Benevolencija, who told me that perhaps the Documentation Center Cambodia could help.

The Documentation Center Cambodia (or DC-Cam) is a non-profit organization for whom one of the main missions is to collect testimonies from the survivors of the genocide. I contacted its director, Youk Chhang, to explain the project – even though I had no idea if it would be yet another flop. But Youk did reply to me after only one day and offered an online meeting.

He told me that the question of obedience to authority was crucial because the huge majority of former Khmer Rouge used it to explain that they followed orders and perpetrated killings. He, too, wanted to understand this phenomenon better. He nonetheless told me that the electroencephalogram sounded intimidating to him.

DC-Cam has several centers across the country, working with survivors of the genocide – both "victims" and "former Khmer Rouge cadres." Youk put me in contact with the local directors of those centers: Dr. Ly Sok-Kheang at the Anlong Veng Peace Center (in the north); Mr. Seang Chenda at the Kampong Cham Documentation Center (in the central part of Cambodia); and Mr. Pheng Pong-Rasy at the Takeo Documentation Center (in the south). I thought that the interviews would be complicated, as I was told so many times that the survivors rarely talk about what they did. That aspect, however, proved less difficult than expected. Since DC-Cam has been in operation for more than twenty years, they have gained the trust of the survivors who then agree to talk to them about their experience during the genocide. However, talking about their *experience* does not mean talking about what they *did*, as we will see in Chapter 1.

The electroencephalogram did prove to be a complicated part of the process. Some directors were very reluctant to use it as it was totally new to them. One even refused at first, saying that for cultural reasons, he did not want the survivors to be involved in computer tasks. Beyond convincing the potential participants, we thus also had to explain everything to the directors of the centers. It was clearly a historical encounter between neuroscientists and the local population.

The organization of villages in rural Cambodia is also quite hierarchical. Before being able to meet the villagers, we had to meet the village chief. On most occasions, the day before starting data collection, we thus drove into the different villages to meet the village chief or the deputy village chief. Upon their approval, we were authorized to meet villagers to explain the project.

The testing in Cambodia was much more complex than in Rwanda because if one participant was unhappy with the electroencephalogram for some reason (e.g., too long, not happy to sit for 40 minutes in front of a computer, did not like to look at a computer screen), we were very likely to lose the entire village. Each day was thus totally unpredictable. We nonetheless managed to obtain interviews with about sixty former Khmer Rouge and were able to analyze their reports.

THE PRESENT BOOK

In this book, I offer insight based on my years of neuroscientific research combined with first-person interviews with the perpetrators of violence in Rwanda and Cambodia. What I have found is that the activity in some brain regions – although critical for understanding the pain we cause to others and our responsibility in the act – is reduced when people obey orders compared to when they are acting freely. In other words, when people accept and comply with the orders of someone else, they do not fully take the measure of the consequences of their action. Their brains do not process the information as it should.

Is such a result consistent with what genocide perpetrators report when asked why they participated in the massacres? Could it be critical to understanding why mass atrocities are conducted on the grounds of obedience?

These are questions I explore in the chapters to come.

Even though the majority of the book focuses on the situation of obedience to authority, I wanted to offer a broader perspective on the very complex question of participating in mass atrocities. Obedience represents merely one, albeit intricate and critical, determinant in the multifaceted dynamics characterizing such events. But other determinants should not be overlooked. In some chapters, I will thus also take the time to explore other equally important mechanisms at play, such as dehumanization or intergroup prejudice. I will also delve into the brain mechanisms involved for those giving orders, as they are a crucial part of any hierarchical system and bear critical accountability for atrocities committed. An entire chapter will further be dedicated to the psychological and neurological consequences of conflicts, wars, and genocides for both victims and perpetrators. Understanding and gaining knowledge of what happens in the aftermath of such events is important for understanding how a society can ever recover from such atrocities.

The book is written to be understandable by a broad audience. However, readers may find some sections more complex than others.

I therefore provide a general conclusion at the end of each chapter, summarizing the main message of each chapter.

CHAPTER 1. This book starts by listening to individuals who took part in a genocidal process in order to understand how mass atrocities can take shape in our societies. Chapter 1 analyzes the many interviews I have conducted with former perpetrators of the genocides in Rwanda and Cambodia. For a deep understanding of what happened in their minds during the killing acts, we must dive deeply into their own words and perspectives.

A critical question I asked in this research was, of course, why individuals perpetrated the crime of genocide and/or why they did not stop working for the regime. Interestingly, in Rwanda the majority of perpetrators share the same phrases and explanations about why they killed, almost as if they had learned what to answer. Sentences such as "The reason why I did it was because of bad government that trained us to kill Tutsis," "I followed orders," "The bad government is responsible," and "I am not responsible as I obeyed orders of the government" were almost systematic. Indeed, claims that they were simply following orders of the "bad government" is a very common justification that a huge majority of the perpetrators reported in my interviews.

In the case of Rwanda, one might consider that since perpetrators had been in prison together and were talking to each other, they may have constructed a sort of common narrative to justify their acts and defend themselves during the Gacaca courts. But in Cambodia, the same justification was also used, again and again. None of the respondents admitted doing anything bad during that period, neither former soldiers nor those transporting prisoners to be killed. Yet all the respondents who agreed to answer this question said that they had to obey orders. It thus appears that obedience to orders strongly influenced their individual actions during the genocide.

CHAPTER 2. This chapter explores past experimental research to explain how obedience is studied in a lab context, as a foundation for understanding the neuroscientific research that followed. Experimental research, largely headed by the highly controversial work of Stanley Milgram, famously showed that humans can potentially kill another individual for the sake of the experiment they are involved in, even if they can hear the screams and pleas of the other person. These experiments showed that under certain circumstances, a majority of individuals could be coerced into inflicting harm on others at levels generally deemed unacceptable, even without any tangible social pressures such as a military court or job loss.

Critically, Milgram's studies on obedience, as well as the variants that have been conducted since, only allow us to study if, in a given situation, an individual will obey the injunctions of an authority figure. Milgram's studies were thus important for exploring situational factors that support obedience. However, no previous studies have allowed us to understand *how* it is possible that people commit atrocities when they follow orders. *How* can humans turn evil just when they follow orders while they would not act in such a way if they had not been incentivized by an authority figure? *How* does the simple fact of obeying orders have such an influence on people's behaviors?

"How" is a critical question but, strangely, one that has been largely avoided by experimentalists within the scientific community for decades. However, as this book shows, answering *"how"* is critical to better understanding human nature and trying to prevent future atrocities. Chapter 2 thus shows how human obedience is captured in an experimental set-up, showcasing that a different research methodology can help us understand *"how"* on a neurological level. By understanding the mechanisms of obedience, we will be better armed to prevent destructive obedience.

CHAPTER 3. This book then moves into the neuroscience research that allows us to understand better how obedience can alter behaviors. To understand how humans can commit atrocities when they obey orders, I had to target neurocognitive processes that are usually involved in moral decision-making. One of the most essential cognitive components for making decisions is the feeling that you are the author of your own actions, and thus responsible for the consequences. Academics have called this subjective experience the sense of agency. If you do not feel you have agency over your actions, you are less likely to feel responsible for the consequences of your actions. This reduction of responsibility can influence your decision to make good or bad actions, to decide between acting righteously or not.

We should in theory be able to recognize equal agency and responsibility for all the actions that we conduct. Yet this is not necessarily the case.

When people obey orders, they are undoubtedly the authors of their actions. Yet, as we see in Chapter 3, there are many social situations which diminish our sense of agency and our feeling of being responsible for the consequences of our actions, including the situation of obedience to authority. As this chapter shows, obeying orders impacts the sense of agency and the feeling of responsibility at the brain level. Further, working and living in some highly hierarchical and sometimes coercive social structures, such as the military, can also impact the sense of agency when people make decisions. It thus appears that hierarchy is a powerful facet of reduced feelings of responsibility and agency in individuals.

CHAPTER 4. Other critical neurocognitive processes involved in decision-making are moral emotions, notably the empathy we may feel for others, and how guilty we feel regarding our decision to hurt them. Humans, like other mammals, have the capacity to feel what others feel. They have empathy. Empathy is a capacity deeply engrained in our biology and is explained by shared neural activation when we both suffer or witness another human suffering. This innate capacity to feel empathy for others, be it for their pain or emotional states, is a critical cognitive and affective process that prevents us from hurting others.

In the case of obedience to authority, our inner aversion to hurting others should prevent us from obeying even when ordered within a hierarchical setting to hurt other human beings. Yet, as we will see in Chapter 4, complying with an order may alter this inner aversion. The research results showcased in this chapter suggest that our brain reduces the processing of the pain of others when we follow an order.

Moreover, when we transgress social norms, for instance by hurting someone physically or emotionally, we usually experience a feeling of guilt. Guilt is a powerful emotion because if you feel guilty about an action, it is less likely that you will repeat the same action in the future. You may even be willing to make amends and beg for pardon. Yet, I observed that activity in guilt-related brain regions was reduced when people obeyed orders compared to deciding to perform the same actions but freely. Chapter 4 thus illuminates how moral emotions are impacted when we follow orders – even immoral ones.

CHAPTER 5. While the first four chapters focus on unraveling the neural mechanisms at play for those who have obeyed orders and perpetrated violence, Chapter 5 turns to those who order the act of violence. Even if they do not execute the action themselves, they also bear responsibility for the violence that occurs under their command. Indeed, the behavior of those in positions of authority has a significant impact on the behavior of those below them, and understanding how authority is wielded and how decisions are made by commanders is essential to understanding the dynamics of obedience. By focusing not only on those receiving orders, but also on those giving orders and on those transmitting orders, researchers can gain a more complete understanding of the factors that influence obedience and develop strategies to promote more ethical and responsible behavior at all levels of the hierarchy.

Neuroscience research has revealed that giving orders also impacts the way the brain processes information and behaviors. In different studies, we observed that giving orders leads to a reduction of the sense of agency and moral emotions towards the pain of victims. Further, the chapter shows that being in an intermediary position, by simply *transmitting* orders received, can lead to a drastic increase in destructive obedience. Chapter 5 thus reveals how hierarchical situations can actually be very dangerous and how they can open the door to atrocious actions.

CHAPTER 6. Wars and genocides only bring desolation. Chapter 6 is about how surviving wars and genocides impacts mental health and can lead to feelings of revenge, which in turn may constitute a risk for future atrocities.

We often think about the dramatic psychological consequences for those who survived extermination programs or those who witnessed their families and friends being killed or mutilated. The strength that is necessary to survive such events and to overcome the psychological distress is enormous. Massive psychological trauma leaves a long-lasting imprint on individuals, who may suffer notable life-long post-traumatic stress disorder (PTSD) symptoms. Moreover, the effects of the trauma can also extend to the following generations.

Importantly, the psychological disaster observed in the aftermath of a war or a genocide does not only touch the victims, their relatives, or their descendants. It also has disastrous consequences on the mental health of those who commit acts of atrocious violence and their descendants. In Rwanda, many former perpetrators, as well as their children, suffer from mental health issues, such as PTSD and addictions. For instance, the generation of children born after the genocide is called the "forbidden generation," because instead of going to school and growing up as children, they had to rebuild the country, they had to take care of the land when their fathers were sent to prison for their crimes. They also have to carry a strong feeling of their parents' guilt as a family burden. Military veterans or military still active who have witnessed or perpetrated an act in combat that transgressed their moral values can also develop moral injuries, which may involve a persistent sense of guilt, shame, regret, remorse, depression, self-loathing, apathy, contempt, cynicism, or resentment, as well as PTSD.

Chapter 6 argues that in order to stop the cycle of conflicts, we must also understand how both victims and assailants are impacted at the psychological level by their respective experience, and how to help them overcome their demons.

CHAPTER 7. The final chapter adopts a more positive tone by focusing on disobedience and on people who risked their lives to save others in adversity. Several stories can actually be found of people who courageously rescued those in danger. In 1994 for instance, a pastor named Gratien Mitsindo refused to give up on more than 300 Tutsi he had hidden despite facing the Interahamwe, the Hutu militia responsible for the genocide in Rwanda. "I was determined to save the lives of the people I hid, and I was prepared to pay any price to achieve that," he said.[25] Pastor Gratien Mitsindo has been officially recognized as a "Righteous Among the Nations." While such stories receive universal praise, such highly altruistic behaviors are rare, and the history of nations is instead plagued by immoral acts of obedience that have caused the loss of countless lives.

Even though such stories are rare, history has fortunately shown that some individuals do resist the social constraint of receiving orders when their own morality is of greater importance than the social costs associated with defying orders. By presenting sociological, psychological, and neuroscience research designed to better understand the profile of those who risked their lives to rescue strangers in times of war, this chapter asks what makes this small subset of the population react differently than others and what hope it can bring to interventions designed to help people resist hate propaganda.

As this chapter shows, even if rescuers are few, they offer a glimmer of hope to show that all human beings potentially have the power to overcome hate.

A SINGLE LIFE MATTERS

Together, these chapters support my argument that obeying orders impacts the functioning of the brain, which helps to explain how people can commit atrocities when obeying orders.

But as mentioned in the Preface, neuroscience is not a miracle solution. Even if we arrived at the point of understanding perfectly why people comply with immoral orders at the deepest levels, it is highly unlikely that we would be able to prevent "everyone" from complying with such orders. It would be utopian to think that there is a simple switch to determine when one should follow a rule and when not. Furthermore, the concept of morality, particularly what is deemed "right" or "wrong," shifts dramatically during wars and genocides. This adds a layer of complexity to the already challenging question of moral behavior under extreme circumstances.

But neuroscience definitely has to take part in this line of research, as all the information surrounding us is processed by the brain. It is the brain that uses this information to compute a decision, and it is the brain that sends the command to our muscles, making us act. Neuroscientific research can help identify individual differences in neural functioning that may contribute to differences in how we process (dis)obedience. This knowledge can be used to develop personalized interventions that take into account an individual's unique profile.

Even if the approach works for only a very few people, even if it helps save just a single life, then that research is worth it.

CHAPTER 1

Listening to the Perpetrators of Genocide

Amarangamutima ntayararimo wagiraga amarangamutima abandi bakabikubuza wakoraga icyo bagutegetse, nta marangamutima yarahari bwari ubwicanyi gusa ntayandi marangamutima iyo watinyukaga kubi- kora ubwo wabaga ubigiyemo nyine ntakandi kazi wakoraga kandi.

There were no emotions, you were not allowed to have emotions, and you were supposed to do what you were told. There were no emotions, it was about killing and whenever you started killing, it would become your full-time job, you wouldn't have any other occupation.

Interview with former genocide perpetrator P171, Rwanda,
August 2021; translated from Kinyarwanda

In 2018, while attending a scientific conference in Krakow in Poland, I visited the memorial of Auschwitz-Birkenau. The Auschwitz concentration camp has become the symbol of the atrocities conducted during World War II (1939–1945), as it is estimated that 1,100,000 people died in this camp. As I was working on obedience to authority, I wanted to have a better view of the camps and of what happened during the Nazi genocide. Of course, as powerful as visiting this historical site is, it is impossible to fully comprehend the suffering that happened there. But it is important to remember what humans are capable of in certain circumstances.

The visit started in the original concentration camp, Auschwitz-I. Before entering the camp, we had to pass under the iron sign that spanned the main entrance bearing the slogan "*Arbeit macht frei*," which literally means "Work sets you free." The Nazis wanted to justify the existence of their labor camps, but the sign was ironic because in the huge majority of cases, only death could set people free.

Some of the barracks have been transformed into exhibition rooms, where thousands of the belongings that the Nazis stole from those who were brought to the camp are on display. Before entering the rooms, the guide reminded us that each of those items belonged to a human being. A person who had a family, friends, and dreams. In the first room we saw thousands of shoes piled up, forming a small mountain. There are so many that they are just impossible to count. In another room, we saw additional mountains of objects, such as suitcases, glasses, kitchen pots, etc. Again, thousands of them. The last room is even more horrific. It contains the hair that the Nazis cut from the persons who were delivered to the camp. Hair from men and women, gray hair from elderly people, and also, recognizable in the mass, hair from children. It is estimated that 7 tons of hair were found in 1945 when the camp was liberated. The Nazis cut the hair to dehumanize them, but also for the textile industry.

In the second camp, Auschwitz II-Birkenau, where the biggest gas chambers were actually located, we walked along the rail track, which transported people to their death. At the end of the rail track, near the main gas chambers, small identical stones are exposed. Each stone has an inscription written in a different language. I looked around until I could find one written either in French or in English. I eventually found the stone where the text was written in English:

> For ever let this place be a cry of despair
> And a warning to humanity, where the Nazis murdered
> About one and a half million men, women and children,
> Mainly Jews from various countries in Europe.
>
> *Auschwitz-Birkenau*
> 1940–1945

A warning to humanity.

If only.

It is estimated that at least 262 million people were murdered by governments via genocide, massacres, mass murders, and intentional famines in the twentieth century alone. It was the bloodiest century in human history. Even if people claimed "Never again" after the Nazi genocide, many more events happened after that and are still happening in the twenty-first century, again and again.

Still, even in a history plagued by wars and acts of destruction, recognized genocides are not that frequent. In Article II of the Genocide Convention adopted by the United Nations General Assembly on December 9, 1948 a genocide is defined as "any of the following acts committed with the intent to destroy, in whole or in part, a national, ethnical, racial or religious group, such as

(a) Killing members of the group;
(b) Causing serious bodily or mental harm to members of the group;
(c) Deliberately inflicting on the group conditions of life calculated to bring about its physical destruction in whole or in part;
(d) Imposing measures intended to prevent births within the group;
(e) Forcibly transferring children of the group to another group"

The genocide caused by the Nazis between 1941 and 1945 and the mass killing of Tutsis and moderate Hutus in Rwanda in 1994 were rapidly categorized as genocides by the countries where the atrocities happened. On June 7, 2013, nearly forty years after its perpetration, the National Assembly of Cambodia made it illegal to deny the Khmer Rouge regime's atrocities, thus officializing the genocide committed by the Khmer Rouge between 1975 and 1979. More recently, in 2021, Germany officially acknowledged committing genocide during its colonial occupation of Namibia in the early twentieth century.

However, there are many more examples in human history that could easily fit within the definition of a genocide, even though some are still denied or largely intentionally diminished, especially by those accused of having participated and by their allies who stood by. This is the case for instance with the mass killings of Armenians by Ottoman Turks between 1915 and 1922, during which an estimated 90 percent of the Armenian population died.[26] Or the genocide in East Timor during the Indonesian occupation between 1975 and 1999 that led to the deaths of between 100,000 and 300,000 persons. Or the famine in Ukraine caused by the Soviet army between 1932 and 1933, which caused the deaths of between 3.5 and 5 million people.

The list is longer, as I have only mentioned a very few examples. And such events continue to happen worldwide: the jihadist group Islamic State killing Christian, Yazidi, and Shia minorities in Iraq and Syria is a contemporary example, as is the mass killing of Rohingya people in Myanmar and the credible cases of forced sterilizations, labour, rape, and torture of Uighurs in China, to name but a few.

Why have so many people on Earth and across the centuries been – and still are – capable of inducing so much suffering in other human beings? What reason could justify these acts? By exploring the first-person narrative perspectives of perpetrators, this chapter brings elements of answers to these crucial questions.

From the many interviews conducted in Rwanda and in Cambodia, the majority of the respondents indicate that the main reason is that they were simply following orders.[27] They were being obedient. Often, therefore, they feel that they were not responsible. But additional elements of their answers show how complex each situation was, and offer insight into the circumstances that led them to become perpetrators.

THE CHALLENGE OF CONDUCTING INTERVIEWS IN RWANDA AND CAMBODIA

In August and September 2021, we drove every day into different villages in Rwanda. Given the restrictions of movement due to the Covid pandemic, we only interviewed former genocide perpetrators living in the districts of Kayonza and of Bugesera. We interviewed fifty-five former genocide perpetrators, all released from prison.

The genocide perpetrators that we interviewed were all male. The first reason is that there were far fewer female perpetrators than male perpetrators.[28] The second reason is that after the genocide, while many men were put in jail, women were not generally considered to be direct perpetrators. Moreover, most of the acknowledged female perpetrators had been judged and sentenced to jail during the Gacaca courts, and they were still in jail at the time of testing.

The mean age of our respondents was 60 years old, but with a variability ranging from 41 to 79 years old. In fact, some of the respondents were minors when they participated in the genocide. Our youngest respondent told us that a group of people asked him when he was 13 years old to kill a woman they had caught, which he did. He was found guilty by the Gacaca court and spent six months in prison instead of many years because he was a child when this happened.

We faced many unexpected obstacles while interviewing. For example, on one of the days, we faced an unexpected "strike" from some of the interviewees. We arrived at the planned location but there was no one there. We had no idea what was happening, and we called Silas, another representative of Prison Fellowship Rwanda. Over two hours later, he was able to find out that the interviewees had decided to boycott the research activities. No one was able to explain why. We knew only that some kind of rumor had circulated, and no one would return. We thus packed up our material and went back to Kigali, a bit disappointed by the lost day. Amazingly, the day after, all the interviewees on strike came to be interviewed and everything went smoothly. That is an event that still puzzles me, and I really have no clue about what happened.

Individual actions and beliefs also impacted our study. Among the perpetrators interviewed, one was too drunk to consider his responses reliable. We actually tried to make him come several times to conduct the interviews, which he did. But no matter whether the interviews were conducted in the morning or in the evening, he was always drunk. We thus gave up on him. Five of our respondents also claimed that they were entirely innocent and did not conduct any crimes despite having been prosecuted by the Gacaca courts. We thus did not include them in the final analyses of the interviews, as we wanted to keep the focus on those who confirmed that they had participated actively in the genocide and agreed to answer all the questions. Those claiming innocence indeed did not answer the questions, except by saying that they were innocent.

Overall, there were three main categories of crimes for which our respondents had been convicted. The crimes included group attacks, murder,[*] and looting. Some of our respondents were actually convicted

---

[*] Many of our respondents reported "killings" instead of "murders." Killings refer to the act of killing someone and murder refers to killing someone with intent, which was the case here. However, we do not know if mentioning killings instead of murders was

for several of those crimes, and sometimes, being in a group attack also included having murdered people. As examples, some of our interviewees report the following:

> The crime I committed against the Tutsis, I was taught to go and kill the Tutsis and I went to grab a machete and slaughter them and looted their cows. (P132)

This respondent was categorized as committing murder and looting.

> I committed genocide, killed people, I reported myself and asked for forgiveness, they released me, and I did community work. How it was that time, it was back and forth, you could see a Tutsi and just hit him with a machete or a spear it would depend on what you had in your arms. I killed three people, I would also join troops that killed people, and if they hadn't killed them, I would kill them because that was my intention. (P142)

This respondent was categorized as committing murder and group attacks.

> It is Genocide. I committed murder; I went into group attacks and killed. I killed four people, but I killed two by myself and the other two I killed them with the help of others that we were together at time. (P166)

This respondent was categorized as committing murder and group attacks. We analyzed the frequencies of each reported crime among our sample: Out of 49 respondents, 19 reported that they participated in group attacks; 29 reported that they were convicted for murdering people; and 11 indicated that they were sentenced for looting or damaging the goods of others.

Overall, the perpetrators that we interviewed spent in average nine years in prison and were released around 2004. The Gacaca courts started in 2002 and lasted many years. Our participants had been judged guilty during the Gacaca courts and sentenced to prison, but because the majority had been caught and imprisoned directly after the genocide, the years they already spent in prison were taken into account.

Considering the atrocities committed, I was often surprised at the prison sentences given. Some perpetrators murdered many people yet

made on purpose, to indicate their lack of intentionality, or simply because they did not know the difference. We thus included them all in the category "murder."

only spent seven to nine years in custody. In Belgium – where I am from – such crimes involve at least twenty years of imprisonment. But Rwanda was facing several problems. First, the country had to be rebuilt and the economy had to restart. With so many men who would, in normal times, labor in fields or build houses or roads, keeping them in jail would not have been beneficial for the country. Second, the prisons were totally overcrowded. While they could host 40,000 detainees, some 120,000 men were put in jail after the genocide.[29] Upon pleading guilty, many men were released from prison and were able to go back to their lands despite the crimes they committed.

Indeed, one of the genocide victims interviewed by the author and journalist Jean Hatzfeld in the aftermath of the genocide reported that they felt that justice was stolen from them in this way.[30] Instead of being able to ensure that the person who attacked them and their family would be properly punished, they had to witness the perpetrator being freed.

Some of the interviewees spoke French, as this language was taught at school before the genocide, but we decided to conduct all the interviews in Kinyarwanda. Two research assistants from the University of Rwanda were thus trained to conduct the interviews. The interviewees were given the choice of answering the questions orally or in written form. We let them decide in order to adapt to their preferences and to ensure that they would feel more comfortable answering the questions.

Some of those who could write reported that they would feel more comfortable answering our questions on their own and not talking to someone directly. Others preferred to discuss verbally, either because they could not write or because Rwanda has a culture of oral transmission. In the case of oral interviews, we first asked the interviewees if they agreed to us recording the conversation with an audio recorder. After having obtained their consent, the entire conversation was thus recorded, then transcribed by the research assistants, and finally translated into English by an independent translator. All the interviews were anonymous in order for the respondents to feel entirely free to talk and to protect their identity.

I prepared several questions to be asked to the interviewees, but the interviewees were free to comment on other aspects if they wanted to. After indicating which crime(s) they committed during the genocide, we asked them why they did so, what their thoughts were when they committed those crimes, and what made them stop killing.

In cases where they did not mention having stopped their participation in the genocide by themselves, interviewees were also asked what internal factors, according to them, could have helped them stop. This is a critical question strangely largely ignored by previous academics. If the aim is to conduct such interviews to be able to develop prevention methods in the future, it is critical to also ask the people who have been in this "killing" state-of-mind what could have stopped them.

Conducting interviews in Cambodia was a radically different task.

When I first contacted Youk Chhang from Documentation Center Cambodia and mentioned that I was looking for victims and perpetrators of the Cambodian genocide for the research project, he seemed upset, but I could not understand why. For me, the distinction between victims and perpetrators was very clear, as mentioned in previous academic research. But he told me that in Cambodia, they are all considered as "survivors," no matter what they did during the genocide.

I had no idea how else to refer to those who were "responsible" for the death of a quarter of the Cambodian population at that time. In Rwanda, the word "survivor" is used for victims only, who actually prefer the term "survivor" instead of "victim" as it shows their strength in overcoming their trauma. I expected to be able to resolve this issue once I arrived in Cambodia, as it is always better to talk to the people from the country than reading scientific articles written by foreigners to really understand their perspective.

Once again with Guillaume, my partner, I arrived in Cambodia in January 2023. We started our journey by driving up to the city of Anlong Veng, located in the northern part of the country, close to the Thai border. This region was crucial for the research project because after the Vietnamese army took over the country and ended the genocide, a huge number of Khmer Rouge fled there and continued to resist until 1998. Anlong Veng district was the last stronghold of the Khmer Rouge and also where Pol Pot ended his life. Many of the Khmer Rouge cadres were – and still are – living in Anlong Veng.

I explained to the director of the center located in Anlong Veng and his staff that I needed to know who was a "victim" and who was "a former member of the Khmer Rouge organization." I did not dare to use the word "perpetrator," because clearly people appeared systematically upset. The distinction was important because the interviews were for "the former members of the Khmer Rouge organization" only. I thus needed to know who was who.

I faced many obstacles from the start. When interviewees were asked, they almost all reported that they were victims. Even among the research assistants helping us with the translations, they indicated that this or that person was a victim, but the director of the center told me afterwards that they were also former Khmer Rouge. It was really a much more complex exercise than expected. Even in the next centers, after explaining the distinction, the confusion persisted: I was told many times that this or that person was a former Khmer Rouge cadre, "but you know, at a very low level of responsibility, (s)he just followed orders."

I have heard this caveat so many times across Cambodia that it really started to puzzle me. Why do they systematically reduce the responsibility of the interviewees by saying that they just followed orders? I expected to hear this reasoning from the interviewees themselves, but not from others.

In Cambodia, the reduction of responsibility after following orders appears to be an accepted reason for conducting acts that should have been prohibited. The number of individuals condemned at the Extraordinary Chambers in the Courts of Cambodia (ECCC) is actually a good illustration, as only five persons in sixteen years have been condemned. They considered that only the main leaders of the Khmer Rouge had to be judged, not the others, even cadres or direct executioners, as they were just following orders.

But another key element to consider is that when the Khmer Rouge took over the country, they split families and started to give roles to everyone, whether they were children or adults, women or men. Somehow the entire population was part of the Khmer Rouge. The "real victims," as I was told by Cambodians, are dead because they did not take part in the regime. Everyone is guilty, or no one is guilty. Therefore, on the one hand, there are almost no real victims left – only members of the regime. And on the other hand, there are only victims left, as they all suffered during the regime and "just obeyed orders" to cause suffering.

Figure 1.1 depicts the number of events that the people I interviewed experienced between 1975 and 1979, either by those identified as former Khmer Rouge members or by those identified as former victims, based on what the directors of the centers told us. As one can note, these two groups experienced relatively similar suffering across all categories.

As mentioned in the Introduction, there were many roles assigned during the regime: Palm Unit, Medical Unit, Mobile Work Unit, Middle-Age Mobile Work, Women's Mobile Unit, Teacher, Military, prison

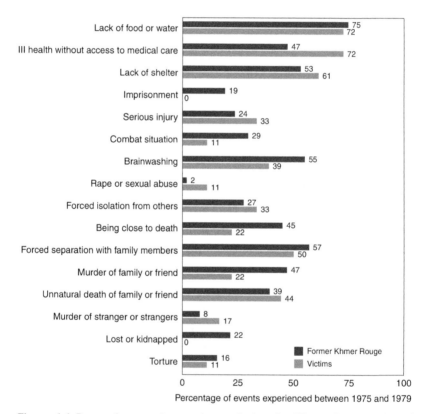

Percentage of events experienced between 1975 and 1979

Figure 1.1 Reported traumatic experiences during the Khmer Rouge regime. In Cambodia, a clear distinction between "victims" and "perpetrators" is very difficult to make. As this graph shows, both former Khmer Rouge members and victims reported similar traumatic experiences during the Khmer Rouge regime.

guards, and so on. I thus asked interviewees what their role was during the Khmer Rouge regime. I thought that knowing their role would probably help me identify those who were "responsible for injuring or killing others" and those who were simply executing their low-level roles without hurting anyone. For instance, the job of those working in the Palm Unit was to collect coconuts from the palm trees daily, and the Mobile Work Unit had to transport the rice that was collected. But I rapidly realized that knowing someone's role was not that easy when it came to determining their role as potential perpetrators. For instance, I thought that the medical unit was only taking care of people injured or ill. But I learned that some awful acts were carried out by some medical units during the Khmer Rouge regime. With the purpose of refusing anything coming from the West, the Khmer Rouge entirely rejected western medicine. People were selected to work in the Medical Unit, often without any medical qualification at all, some of them being only in their early teens.[31] It resulted in countless acts of torture and deaths. For instance, reports have indicated that they opened the bodies of people still alive and injected coconut milk into them to see if it had any positive effect on their health. Or they removed the livers of living people, without anesthesia, which resulted in immediate death. Most of them had no idea what they were doing or about traditional Cambodian medicine.

I thus decided to include in the interviews anyone who had been part of the Khmer Rouge. Regardless of whether they had killed or injured anyone, I found it very interesting to understand the perspective of everyone at that time, no matter what their position was in the Khmer Rouge chain. This is crucial to understand better how such organization and diffusion of responsibility was implemented and how it lasted for so many years.

I also asked the local staff from the centers to conduct the interviews instead of the research assistants from the university in the hopes that the interviewees might be more at ease with answering questions posed by them. Former Khmer Rouge members rarely talk about what happened, even to their own families. I talked to several people from the first generation born after the genocide, and almost all of them told me that they had no idea about the role of their parents during the regime.

Some reported that they knew their parents were soldiers at that time, but added that they never ever talked about what they did.

Overall, I did not expect much from the interviews. And my fear regarding the difficulty of them not talking during the interviews was confirmed. While in Rwanda, people openly admitted their potential crimes; in Cambodia, of the sixty interviews conducted, they all answered "No" to the question "Did you hurt someone between 1975 and 1979?"

Of course, it may be the case that I only recruited people who actually did nothing during this period. However, ten admitted working as soldiers or as prison guards transporting prisoners to the killing fields[†] between 1975 and 1979. These individuals all reported that they never hurt anyone at that time, and one declined to answer. Yet all the sixty interviewees said that they witnessed or heard about people being systematically murdered. With more than 1 million persons killed at that time and all people acknowledging witnessing or hearing about such events but no one admitting having participated in one way or another, we rapidly realized that the interviews would not be as informative as in Rwanda.

Other academics had faced similar difficulty in conducting interviews with those involved in the violence committed during the Khmer Rouge regime. Alexander Hinton, a US anthropologist, spent months in Cambodia doing research for his postdoctoral thesis. In one of his articles, he describes a conversation he had with an ex-soldier who had worked at Tuol Sleng, the infamous detention center also known as S-21, where thousands of people were tortured and died.[32] Hinton learned from other people that this ex-soldier had killed at least 400 people between

---

[†] The Killing Fields were sites where the Khmer Rouge executed and buried victims, primarily targeting perceived enemies of the state, intellectuals, professionals, religious figures, and ethnic minorities. The regime aimed to eliminate potential threats to their rule and create a homogeneous, peasant-based society. After the fall of the Khmer Rouge, forensic teams exhumed mass graves at various Killing Fields, unearthing human remains and personal belongings of the victims. They were scattered throughout Cambodia, often located near former prisons or forced labor camps. Some of the well-known sites include Cheoung Ek and Tuol Sleng, also known as S-21. The latter was a former school converted into a prison and torture center. These findings provided irrefutable evidence of the mass killings and the scale of the atrocities.

1975 and 1979. Another person, who was a former prisoner of the S-21, even reported that this man executed more than 2,000 men, women, and children. However, Hinton never succeeded in getting him to talk about such acts. The interviewee only admitted being a guard and transporting prisoners, but denied having executed anyone. After further questioning by Hinton, he barely admitted killing one or two people but added that he did that to avoid having others accuse him of being unreliable.

Beyond the difficulty of getting interviewees to talk to us, another difficulty was that the events happened almost fifty years ago, and most of our interviewees were quite old. We realized that in some interviews, the dates – and sometimes roles – were not consistent. For instance, a woman reported that in 1975 she returned to live with her husband, but that she got married in 1977. She also reported that between 1976 and 1977 she worked in a kitchen and cooked. However, she also briefly mentioned during that same interview that she was sent to join the army at that time and was the leader of a unit of ninety-seven people.

As a result, the following sections mostly focus on the answers that were obtained from the former genocide perpetrators in Rwanda. Whenever possible, however, I will integrate the stories of former Khmer Rouge members.

INTERPRETING THE INTERVIEWS

In the pages to come, I introduce the key questions asked in each interview, such as the reasons for participating in the genocide or what the respondents felt when they participated. I suggest commonalities, highlight challenges, and offer interpretation. Throughout, I offer copious examples of translated answers in the perpetrators' own words. Doing so enables us to see the complexity of genocide as a phenomenon, as it arises from the interplay of various psychological, social, political, economic, and cultural factors.

WHY DID YOU COMMIT THOSE CRIMES? In Rwanda, the huge majority of our respondents reported that they carried out their crimes because they were following the orders of the "bad government." Others reported that they were forced to commit those crimes, and others because they were influenced by the group. These three rationales represent three distinct forms of social influence that can affect people's behaviors: obedience, compliance, and social conformity.

Conformity can be defined as changing your behavior to fit with the group, even if you do not agree with the group. When they conform, individuals simply want to be accepted by the majority. The difference between obedience and compliance, however, is subtle. Obedience refers to a form of social influence in which a person gives in to direct instructions or orders from an authority figure without question, while compliance involves following the request of another person or of a group.

Examples of compliance could be a student who submits their assignment on time to avoid penalties after the teacher announces a strict deadline, or a person who donates money to a charity when approached by a persuasive fundraiser on the street. Examples of obedience would rather be soldiers following orders to engage in combat during wartime, even if they personally have moral objections, or employees follow following a company policy that they may not fully agree with, but they do so because it is mandated by upper management. Obedience is thus a more formal form of influence, as it involves obeying the orders of an official authority, while compliance refers to agreeing to follow the orders of anyone, for one reason or another. Notably, compliance can be increased by using intimidation or punishment. Compliance and obedience can be difficult to distinguish, because it depends on how the person perceives the authority and its legitimacy. Thus, a main category of "obedience" is presented below.

Group Attacks

As mentioned the introduction, in Rwanda, an armed militia, the Interahamwe, is held responsible for the 1994 genocide because its members led the killings and influenced others to join them. The word *Interahamwe* can be literally translated as "Those who attack together." Indeed, when asked about their crimes, many former Rwandan perpetrators used the word *igitero* (pl. *ibitero*) to explain how they killed, which means group attack.[33] Before coming to Rwanda, I read the work of several academics who had conducted interviews there. I knew just a few words of Kinyarwanda, but *igitero* was definitely one of them.

Our first interview was with a 61-year-old man who spent seven years in prison. He actually did not want to talk about what he did during the genocide but agreed to answer our questionnaires in written form and then to talk if we had additional questions. After he completed the questionnaires, I read his answers with one of the research assistants as he wrote in Kinyarwanda. To the question "Why did you participate in the killing acts?", I saw written in capital letters IBITERO.

I had been hoping to obtain very detailed and more precise reasons than, simply, "the group did it" – a phrase repeated in the previously published interviews I had read before my arrival. We thus talked to him as agreed, and he confirmed that there were actually no other reasons. Conducting the killing acts in a group critically influenced him and allowed him to kill even if he had never done so before. Of the 49 perpetrators that we interviewed, 19 respondents indicated that they were convicted for taking part in group attacks and 9 indicated that *igitero* was the reason for committing the killing acts.

The following examples are drawn from our interviews:

My armed group killed 7 people. Sorry, it was actually rather 7 children and their mother, making it 8 in total. (P130)

I joined group attacks to run after the Tutsis and went on patrol killing many Tutsis. (P128)

I committed a crime by joining a group attack that killed and looted. (P133)

I went on a raid and it killed someone, I played a part in that. (P154).

It is difficult to know if using the group to justify their action really reflects their understanding of their involvement or if they have developed this rationale to avoid feeling too guilty. They probably do not even know the answer themselves. As we will see in Chapter 3 and Chapter 4, the group is a powerful social construct that can drastically influence behaviors.

Obedience to (Bad) Authority

In 1992, Christopher Browning, a US historian, published a book in which he reports his analysis of the psychological profile of 125 men from the Reserve Police Battalion 101, a unit of the German Order Police (*Ordnungspolizei, Orpo*) during World War II, whose testimonies during interrogation had been recorded.[34] Many of them were middle-aged family men. They were considered too old to be useful in the German army, so they were sent to be part of the German police. In 1942, when those men arrived in Poland, their group leader, Major Wilhelm Trapp, told them to round up the Jews in the city of Józefów, to take the men to the camps and to kill the women and children.

But Trapp offered something unexpected. He told his men that any man who did not want to participate in the shooting would be excused. Trapp himself apparently did not like what they were tasked to do, but, as the orders came from the highest authority, the job had to be done.

Of the 125 men, only one, Otto-Julius Schimke, refused. Twelve more joined when they saw that Trapp's promise was real and that he protected Schimke from Captain Hoffman, the company leader, who was furious to see one of his men refusing to do the job. On July 13, 1942, that battalion executed 1,500 Jews. In total, it is estimated that the battalion was involved in the direct shooting of 38,000 persons. Taking into account those who died as a result of deportation in the death trains, the total number killed by this battalion is estimated to be 83,000. A few more men were excused duties during the executions and were given other tasks, but in total, still 80 to 90 percent of the battalion participated despite the lack of consequences if they refused such orders. And there was no element of coercion. Christopher Browning argued that obedience to authority was a critical factor in explaining why so many of those ordinary men became killers.

Expressing an absence of responsibility is one of the main reasons people use the justification that they were just following orders. They thus avoid being held responsible and accountable for their actions. The most infamous historical example is certainly the justification *"Befehl ist Befehl"* (literally "An order is an order") evoked by senior Nazi officers during the Nuremberg trials after World War II. It refers to the idea that a subordinate cannot be held responsible for a crime as he was following superior orders.[35] Senior Nazi officers claimed that they followed the leader principle (i.e., *Führerprinzip*) that governed the Nazi regime. This principle basically states that absolute or near-absolute obedience was to be given by all members of the society to the Führer.[36] The Führer's word was considered to be above the law. Since they pledged allegiance to

Hitler, Nazi officers had to follow orders. As a result, they should not be held responsible for their acts.

This claim of diminished responsibility under an obligation to obey orders has actually been observed in every genocide in the history of nations. In Rwanda, a twist to this standard response is the idea that perpetrators were following the orders of "bad" leaders.[17,37] In the interviews I conducted, 33 of the 49 interviewees reported that they conducted the genocide because the "bad" government asked them to do so. The interviewees reported justifications such as:

The reason why I did it was because of bad government that trained us to kill Tutsis. (P129)

The bad government commanded us to kill the Tutsis. It was not our intention, but the bad government convinced us. (P140)

It is bad leadership that instructed us to kill people and become animals, even though we were not animals. Yes, it is the leadership that did this, not us. (P146)

I committed the crime because of the bad government that was there at that time. It was not me as they instructed us to kill. (P148)

The crime that I committed was a massive killing that I was told to do by the leaders who were there at the time, who encouraged us to kill Tutsis saying that they are bad people. (P151)

What made me do it was the bad government that led us and encouraged us to kill our fellow countrymen. (P167)

Significantly, there was not a single overlap between the "group attack" justification and the "obedience to the bad government" justification. People reported either one or the other. This is interesting as it suggests that people may differ regarding their sensibility to different forms of social influence. As the genocide in Rwanda involved official orders from the self-proclaimed government to start the killings, and because the killings were mostly performed in groups, it actually represented a fertile ground to ensure that a majority of people would participate as well.

Respect and deference to authority are culturally important in Rwanda. Many academics and journalists have reported that deference to authority is an important factor in explaining the genocide.[38,39] Some have reported that this "entrenched culture of obedience," for instance, allowed many Hutus to kill their Tutsi wives.[40] It was therefore expected that the authority argument used by the genocide perpetrators would be widespread.

But obedience to authority, despite being an important part of the local culture, is relative and context-dependent rather than absolute. For instance, during the worldwide coffee crisis in the 1980s, prices of coffee crashed, and many farmers were tempted to shift their production to other crops. Despite being forbidden under the Rwandan Penal Code (1978), a few peasants nonetheless uprooted the coffee trees and transgressed the law.[41] Other examples involve farmers running into the banana groves to avoid local officials compelling them to attend the Gacaca courts or peasants bypassing the mandatory communal labor, known as *umuganda*[42] – a traditional Rwandan activity had been reestablished after the genocide as a way to help reconciliation.

Also during the genocide acts of disobedience were observed. Some individuals refused to participate in the massacres and even risked their own lives to rescue people. Though obedience to authority is an important factor in understanding the genocide in Rwanda, it is thus crucial to keep the agency of perpetrators in the equation, as well as the many other factors responsible for the atrocities and acts of torture, beyond "simply" killing.[43,44] Indeed, several genocide perpetrators went far beyond the received orders. In its darkest moments, the genocide in Rwanda involved numerous acts of torture perpetrated with rural tools, even against relatives.

And that is the main problem with obedience to authority. If one wants to kill without feeling too guilty, hiding behind the mantra "I just obeyed orders" is a perfect excuse. As the examples here suggest, even when respect for authority is an important part of the culture, citizens also chose to obey or disobey when it was convenient for them.

Being Forced to Participate

Ten of our 49 interviewees responded that they participated because they felt forced. Many of them actually reported that they feared consequences if they did not join in the group attacks, such as being killed themselves. Interestingly, there were some overlaps with the "group attacks" (*igitero*) in the respondents' justifications, as several of them reported that they joined in the group attacks because they considered that they had no choice or would risk their lives.

> *For the government that was in place at the time, the killings were almost law, which is why people were afraid for their lives. And I chose to do what they told me.* (P126)

> *When you refused to join them, they would take you by force since you were a young man. I joined group attacks as a way of self-defense because if one refused to join forces with them, they would beat you up, break you and you could possibly derive problems from that.* (P137)

> *At that time, when you didn't collaborate with others you were likely to be in danger so it was a way of protecting myself. They even killed my dad because they found a person hiding in our home and butchered our cow so it was a way of protecting myself.* (P147)

> *Hence, what made me agree to do it was that I left my house and was cut. I wasn't cut while home, so I would not deny it but you understand that I didn't do it on purpose; it was so my kids wouldn't be tortured that I didn't go yet I was the only one remaining at home.* (P158)

> *The reason why I went is that they took us by force. There is no other reason.* (P162)

One of the people claiming his innocence actually told us the following during the interviews:

> *During the time of genocide, we were told that the Tutsi were enemies of the country and wanted to attack Rwanda and that's why they were being killed. We were scared and that's why some people went to kill but there are some who didn't go. However, if you didn't go, you had to pay a fine. I paid an amount of twenty-one thousand Rwandan francs (21,000rwf). At the time, I was a businessman, they took my money because I refused to go.* (P157)

While some people reported that they killed because they were obeying orders or because of the influence of the group, it appears that some individuals were really afraid for their lives if they did not join. This is consistent with some reports indicating that the Interahamwe went door by door to tell the men to join the killings. Killing Tutsis was somehow an obligation at that time and refusing to join could have consequences, unless you could pay. Plenty of moderate Hutus, who did not go along with being forced to participate, also died during the genocide, even though they are less frequently mentioned in the histories.

Other Rationales

Among the other reasons mentioned for why they committed acts of violence, four respondents indicated that they participated because they wanted to loot:

> *The reason why I joined group attacks was the encouragement from the government, for the looting part; we would go because the owners would have been killed or had fled.* (P136)

> *What made me do that crime of genocide is because they had said that the Tutsi must be killed, when I saw that I was not able to kill, I went after possessions, I ran around looking for possessions.* (P143)

According to Jean Hatzfeld, many perpetrators reported that their wives, even if they did not take part in the genocide itself, motivated their husbands to continue killing when they came back home after their "working day" in order to steal and loot more. In the church of Nyamata, where 10,000 Tutsis were slaughtered, many women came to steal the *kitenge*[‡] or other personal belongings from the dead. After some families were killed, the killers' wives came inside the house and took everything that was valuable or exchangeable for money.

Only two participants said that they killed Tutsis because of their race. This is astonishing because it was the main justification given by the government to start the ethnic cleansing. Yet only two reported this reason.

> *I killed the Tutsi because of their race. The authorities said that Tutsis are bad because they killed the country's leader so they should be killed, and because I was taught in class that the Hutus should stand up for the political parties of CDR[§] who also taught us that Tutsis are bad.* (P144)

[‡] *Kitenge* is a type of brightly colored, patterned fabric that is commonly worn in Rwanda and other countries in East Africa. In Rwanda, *kitenge* is a popular material for clothing, particularly for women's dresses or skirts.

[§] The CDR (Coalition for the Defense of the Republic) was a far-right Hutu Power political party active during the period leading up to the 1994 genocide.

LISTENING TO THE PERPETRATORS OF GENOCIDE

The infrequent reporting of dehumanization or ethnic hatred is noteworthy. Based on this observation, the literature suggests that social dynamics, including authority and group conformity, played a more significant role than pure ethnic hatred.[321]

Three respondents said that they participated in the genocide because of ignorance or because they were lured by the government.

In Rwanda, the results of the interviews show that obedience to authority was the most widespread reason given to explain interviewees' participation in the genocide. Some also reported group influence or being forced to participate. However, only ten reported having felt forced to participate, which could show that elements of coercion were not necessarily used to convince people to participate in the genocide.

In Cambodia, we interviewed 60 former Khmer Rouge, but we did not obtain systematic answers to all our questions. Sometimes, respondents said it was too difficult to explain or to remember, or they preferred not to answer. In one of the questions, we asked those identified as former Khmer Rouge members, irrespective of their roles, why they participated in the regime. All of the forty respondents who answered that question explained that they just followed orders, most of the time in very succinct answers. Most of them also reported clear elements of coercion, by saying that they were risking their lives if they did not obey orders.

Of course it was so difficult living [in] hard [conditions], and it was a bitter life. There is no comparison, but we didn't know how to leave that situation. We needed to do what they told us to do. (R101)

We followed all their orders. If we did not follow them, they said we did not obey the organisation. We could be killed. (R127)

We were under them. They controlled us. (R132)

At that time, I did not hold any specific role. I was just a member of the women's unit, and I had to do anything that I was told to do. If I refused, I risked being taken away and killed. (R103)

I was ordered to do it, so I had to. (R113)

It is clear from historical reports that the regime murdered people very easily between 1975 and 1979.[45] Being considered a traitor to the ideology or not working hard enough for the regime, with or without proof, could lead to being killed, most of the time also with family members, who were considered as potential accomplices. People were living in fear of being executed at any time, an aspect that many respondents reported in much more detail than when asked to explain their participation in the regime.

> They forced us to work until death, and we did not dare to argue because we were afraid of getting killed. We did all kinds of work as they told us, and it was extremely challenging. Some people broke their arms or legs and became disabled. At that time, I was the leader of the cooperative, and sometimes they took us by car, and we did not know where they were taking us. We thought that if we died, we would die. If we were accused of betrayal, we would be killed. Fortunately, we survived. When going to sleep, we did not know if we would wake up alive because some people were called and disappeared, and it scared me. (R3)

> At that time, I worked in a mobile unit, working day and night and not getting enough food. When we were sick, they still did not let us get rest unless we were unable to get out of bed. There was no medicine in those days, we did not dare to talk to them because we were very afraid of them. Second, in 1977, they tortured us so badly, they beat us. We were punished for small problems such as taking the food to eat even if that food was grown on our land. They would kill us. (R1110)

It is a very hard task to compare the two different situations in Rwanda and Cambodia. However, in broad terms, despite very different historical, economic, and political situations, two main elements emerged from the question of why people committed the acts they did. First, it seems that obedience to authority was a critical factor in both Rwanda and Cambodia, with many people openly reporting that this is the reason why they participated, no matter what their role was during the genocide. Second, elements of coercion were also present, even though the extent to which coercion was systematically used is less clear.

In Rwanda, many did not feel forced to participate, but they nonetheless did so because they believed in the ideology of the genocide. In Cambodia, people reported that they were afraid of being tortured and killed if they did not participate. But many people also supported the ideology of the Khmer Rouge and their vision of creating a classless society. The more than

1 million deaths suggests that many people acted for the "good" of that ideology, by ensuring systematic killings of those with a different vision. Previous reports also indicated that some individuals killed others in order to be promoted at a higher rank.[46] But, as mentioned, in Cambodia, those who participated in the killings are very hard to identify and even harder to interview. While they talk openly about what happened to them or to others during that period, they almost never indicate what they may have done to others.

WHAT WERE YOUR THOUGHTS AT THE MOMENT OF THE ACT?

This is a question that was not asked in Cambodia, considering that none of the interviewees admitted hurting anyone. This question was thus only put to the former genocide perpetrators in Rwanda. I was not sure what to expect from the question at first because I had not seen past interviews asking anything similar. I wanted to have a better overview of the state-of-mind of the genocide perpetrators when they conducted the crimes they have been convicted of. Perhaps they would report that they were proud to participate in this ethnic cleansing, but perhaps they would also report very negative emotions or thoughts.

The responses were less consistent and much more variable than when the interviewees were asked why they participated in the genocide. Twelve different categories of answers were derived from the analysis, while we had only six categories when they were asked why they participated. Several respondents indicated several emotions or thoughts and were thus included in different categories.

Interestingly, 14 out of 49 reported that they were afraid when they participated in the genocide. They offered responses such as:

I would say that the emotion I had was the fear of dying. (P173)

I would be afraid, because they took us against our will. When you refused, they could even kill you. (P135)

The thought I had, I didn't plan to harass anyone or to cause conflict. Because when we refused there were consequences. My younger brother was killed and older brother too, because they refused to go in the group attacks, so as the ones left behind, we were afraid that they would take us by force. (P162)

At that time, it was sad because we did it as a way of protecting ourselves since anyone who refused to go on the hunt was called an accomplice of the Tutsi. Even finding out that you hid someone would make them kill you so that's why we engaged in the killing. (P146)

In that time of genocide, I thought that I would die. (P163)

In fact I thought that people were not supposed to die but the bad government encouraged us to go kill each other, forcibly. It used force to encourage us because if you refused to participate, you would be punished and pay a fine. That's what I can explain. (P167)

Twelve of the respondents again mentioned that their thoughts were to obey the orders received, saying things like:

We didn't have those ideas, the bad government that was in power instructed us to kill and put bad ideologies into us. (P148)

As a citizen, I wasn't thinking of anything else except following the laws set by the government of that time because they were the ones encouraging us. (P151)

Because of being ordered around and coerced by the government; we had no individual thoughts or feelings. (P153)

We were young at that time and joined others without knowing how it was planned; it was planned by the high-level leaders. (P154)

Seven respondents indicated that they had no emotions or feelings during the genocide. Their responses included reflections such as:

At that time, we didn't have emotions. We were full of heinousness and nothing good was in us. (P130)

The thoughts were to kill a Tutsi only, no emotions. (P142)

There were no emotions, you were not allowed to have emotions, and you were supposed to do what you were told. There were no emotions, it was about killing and whenever you started killing, it would become your full-time job, you wouldn't have any other occupation. (P171)

Oh well, we didn't have any conscience, we were like animals because the things we would do were very bad things that are inhumane. (P172)

Six respondents indicated that they felt like awful or cruel individuals. One, in particular, captured the tenor of these responses:

> *I felt like an awful killer. Imagine seeing someone who hasn't insulted you and slaughtering them and their cows. As you can understand I was a cruel person. In your opinion, do you think I was normal? It was insanity and greed, would you say I was a normal person then? Taking someone who used to be your neighbor, who you used to share everything with and take a machete and slaughter them, is there any inhumane act worse than that? I was heinous. I am not going to lie to you, during that time it was pure cruelty. Imagine seeing a cow and taking a machete and slaughtering it and you see the owner and slaughter them as well, and destroy their house, yet s/he hasn't stolen from you or insulted you, isn't that just more than cruelty? They were brutal killings.* (P132)

Among the participants, several emotions and thoughts were reported. Eight participants expressed that the events troubled them, while two admitted having bad intentions. Additionally, four participants held negative views about the Tutsis, and two others admitted being motivated by personal greed. Two individuals reported feeling heinous, one mentioned ignorance, and another one thought about the absence of consequences for committing the crimes.

From this section, it is clear that answers varied considerably, from not thinking at all and acting as mere machines, to considering oneself as a bad or cruel person. It may be the case that, indeed, humans vary greatly in how they feel in such situations. Whether these different feelings could be associated with the possibility of acting differently, however, remains unanswered.

WHAT (WOULD HAVE) STOPPED YOU FROM PARTICIPATING IN THE GENOCIDE? Little research has been done on how genocides end or why they end.[47] It has been argued that only external entities can stop a genocidal killing process. Of course, the first that should act is the government of the country where such events are happening. However, most of the time, the government is the entity that gave the authorization to murder another part of the population. Other nations must thus intervene to stop the process.

Past historical examples have indeed shown that genocides almost never stop by themselves, except when the targeted population had been exterminated. The Allied troops stopped the Holocaust by defeating the Nazis, the Vietnamese invasion of Cambodia ended the genocide by defeating the Khmer Rouge, the Front Patriotique Rwandais (FPR) stopped the genocide against the Tutsi in Rwanda when they took over the country, the genocide in Bosnia and Herzegovina ended in 1995 following an offensive in Croatia and intervention by NATO.

In Rwanda, we observed during the interviews that participants did not expect to be asked what could have stopped them, and they were far more hesitant about how to answer this question than the other questions we asked. Because it seems that no one had asked them this question before, it would be interesting in future research to see if their answers would be different if they could have time to prepare their answers.

Thirty-three interviewees indicated that only the intervention of the *Inkotanyi* was able to stop them. The *Inkotanyi* is the Kinyarwanda name given to the Front Patriotique Rwandais (FPR) troops and can be translated as "those who fight with the most courage." The FPR was led at that time by the president of Rwanda, Paul Kagame. On July 4, 1994, they took over Kigali and ended the genocide.

For me, what stopped the killings was the fact that Inkotanyi took over and those bad leaders that have propagated lies fled and left us in Rwanda. Basically, the genocide was stopped by Inkotanyi when they arrived in Rwanda, otherwise we would have all killed each other, we were monstrous; we would have finished killing all the Tutsis and start killing each other as well. [...]. Then Inkotanyi came and arrested me. When I got released, I had regained humanity but before I was a monster, deciding to slaughter a person? Don't you think I was monstrous? (P131)

The genocide was stopped by the FPR. Otherwise, for my part when I committed the crimes I did I thought of them as easy. (P129)

It is the Inkotanyi that came and stopped the killings. I was sent to prison. Otherwise, I might have repeated the crime and motivated my children to do the same. (P166)

There is nothing else that stopped this apart from the fact that Inkotanyi came; otherwise, due to wanting property and other things that people were hungry for, we would have killed off each other as well. (P133)

Such results actually emphasize the importance for other nations or governments of stopping an ongoing genocide. Some genocides could have been stopped earlier if international governments had decided to act faster. This is notably the case in Rwanda, as the international community required all their military to leave Rwanda when the killings started, leaving the entire population at the mercy of the killers. A woman interviewed by Jean Hatzfeld reports that at the beginning of the genocide the killers were afraid of the white men, because they had terrible and powerful weapons that could stop them. However, when the white men fled, they saw this as an incredible opportunity to continue to perpetrate the massacre without intervention.[30]

In Cambodia, the answers were all strongly consistent. Out of the 35 interviewees who answered this question, 34 reported that they would not have stopped if the Vietnamese had not taken over the country in 1979. One respondent reported that he could have stopped on his own, but did not give further details as to how. Cambodian interviewees shared some of the following thoughts:

Until they [Vietnamese soldiers] *disbanded it* [the Khmer Rouge regime], *I did not dare to leave as I was afraid.* (R112)

I believe that without Vietnam's intervention, we would not have known what happened to our country because it was very confusing. Even I, myself, did not understand the regime's motives. I did as they told and did not oppose them; otherwise, death awaited me. (R3)

I did not dare to leave it [the Khmer Rouge regime] because I was afraid. (R113)

I don't think I could have found a way to liberate Cambodia from the Khmer Rouge regime. (R129)

If it could not be stopped, we all would die and become extinct. (R135)

But in both contexts, by the time other nations or groups agreed to act and succeeded at stopping the genocide, tens of thousands of people had already been massacred. This is why it is also crucial to understand if some personal elements in the minds of the perpetrators could help them stop killing. Elements that could perhaps be emphasized in order to prevent people from joining in the killing in the first place.

Eighteen interviewees in Rwanda reported that they did stop by themselves at some point. But the reasons for stopping were quite different. Two explained that they stopped for very practical reasons. One reports, *"What enabled me to stop was that the Tutsis who were left lived far away; that stopped me from going anywhere else"* (P164) and another one reports, *"It was fatigue, you see if you go from here to there you would get tired and stop there, so it was fatigue, I would get tired"* (P171). In this regard, we could consider that they would have continued if it weren't for the distances involved.

Four of them, however, mentioned that it was God who helped them to stop or to refuse to kill others:

> *That was because of the bad government, my heart pushed me, it pushed to feel that I shouldn't do such a thing. So those who did it were used by the government, they did it. As for me God stood by me, I never abused people or shed blood.* (P134)

> *What enabled me? on my own I didn't have any strength or power. It was only God who helped me; otherwise, it seemed like the end for me.* (P158)

> *It's because of God. Because even having not killed everyone and how Inkotanyi came it was only God. I couldn't stop myself because we were driven by the laws.* (P165)

> *In life, the first thing is to trust in God even if we are running most of the time. I can say that it is God, it is not my might rather it is God's ability.* (P147)

The role of religion appears to be crucial for some, as it prevented them from committing crimes that their religion would prohibit. However, during the genocide, highly religious individuals also actively participated in the genocide. In June 2001, an unusual trial took place in Belgium. Two Hutu nuns from a convent in Sovu, Consolata Mukangango and Julienne Mukabutera, were found guilty of having handed over to the Interahamwe militia the Tutsi families who had taken refuge in the convent compound. Indeed, we can find survivors and perpetrators in Rwanda from the same religions, showing that religion does not always offer a protection from committing terrible acts.

Among those who reported stopping for personal values and reporting external influence, seven reported that they realized that what they were doing was not good. They reported things like:

Without external influence I thought about how I demolished a brother's home yet we had no dispute. I then pleaded guilty when I went to prison. I accepted to repay the house and I've finished repaying. (P143)

I thought about it as well in my heart. When I observed what we were doing to Rwandans I found it bad, I thought about that in my heart and I still do. That is why we interact and asked for forgiveness from survivors, I still seek for their forgiveness and sometimes go to lend them a hand without a problem. It was all due to the corrupt government that made us do evil crimes. (P167)

What caused me to stop, I would look at consequences associated with it, I would see my fellows dying and we were neighbors with whom we had no problems. So I decided to run away and my people died and I ended up in prison, I was under a lot of stress which led to my illness, so it showed me that what we were doing was wrong but the root cause was our leaders who sensitized us. (P172)

Three also indicated that they felt sad about what was happening. One, for example, shared:

The reason . . . what motivated me to stop doing it was, I saw how people were chased out and dying and I was sad and sorrowful . . . and I said that what we are doing has no use. After sometime things went quiet for a while, Inkotanyi liberated the country and I fled but I came back in July. I didn't stay out of the country long because I didn't feel guilty, but in the month of 12 [December], 1994, the government of reconciliation wanted to imprison those who committed crimes and then do a follow up. The government took care of us, the President of the country gave a presidential decree in 2003. In 2003 I had confessed, that's when I went home although I was convicted again later. (P131)

Among those who reported that they could not have been stopped, answers were much more difficult to obtain. Perhaps a mind blinded by hate and violence cannot be rescued. Yet five could describe feelings or emotions that could have helped them to stop – although they did not feel them at the time. Two said that they would have stopped if they had felt guilt, two indicated that compassion would have been a key emotion, and one reported love for others.

CONCLUSION

This chapter showed that by interviewing perpetrators, researchers can gain valuable insights into the psychological and social factors that contribute to participating in a genocide. Whether it was by asking what their motivations or feelings were at the time, or the way they stopped, or could have stopped, their responses help to capture the complexity of their participation.

But conducting such interviews is a sensitive and difficult process and must be carried out with caution to avoid causing further harm to survivors or perpetuating stereotypes. In addition, one should never forget that the insights obtained from these interviews only rely on what people agree to share or remember. Relying on interviews only is thus not sufficient to grasp the complexity of obedience to orders to hurt another person. Another important element is that genocides are extreme and rare events, and drawing conclusions about human behavior based solely on them may not provide a complete picture.

Experimental research helps to investigate obedience in a more general context, which can then be applied to a broader range of situations and populations. Such research allows for a controlled and systematic investigation of obedience, which is not possible in real-world scenarios like genocides. These experiments enable researchers to manipulate specific factors and measure their effects on obedience, thereby enhancing our understanding of the underlying psychological processes. However, as will be discussed in the next chapter, a gap will nonetheless always persist between what is observed in a lab context and its generalization to real-life events, hence confirming the need for an interdisciplinary perspective.

In the following chapter, we will go through the many experimental studies in psychology and neuroscience that have tried to bring elements of answers to help us understand participation is mass atrocities. And as we will see, people are also extremely obedient in experimental set-ups, even when they are asked to physically hurt another, unknown, individual.

CHAPTER 2

A Brief History of the Experimental Research on Obedience

A substantial proportion of people do what they are told to do, irrespective of the content of the act and without limitations of conscience, so long as they perceive that the command comes from a legitimate authority. ... This is, perhaps, the most fundamental lesson of our study: ordinary people, simply doing their jobs, and without any particular hostility on their part, can become agents in a terrible destructive process.

Stanley Milgram, *Obedience to Authority* [48]

If I invited you to an experiment in which I asked you, for the sake of science, to inflict shocks of increasing intensity – up to a potentially deadly shock – on another person, would you do it?

When asked what they would do, people generally agree that they would never do such a thing to hurt another person. But what experimental research on obedience shows is that there is a huge discrepancy between what people report, and what they do while in the situation. Hundreds and hundreds of participants in studies have proven that anyone could potentially obey to the point of seriously hurting someone else.

Here is an interesting question: Do we really know ourselves? Or are we just not willing to admit that we might also be obedient even if it causes pain to others?

When I present my research to a general audience, I am frequently asked: "And you, what would you have done?" Of course, I would like to answer with certainty: "I would never have obeyed an order to hurt someone in an experiment or elsewhere!" But I think the most honest answer is "I don't know."

If I consider an external and objective opinion, my mother would probably have said that I hated obeying orders and doing as I was told when I was young. I am a very calm person, respecting rules (most of the times). But when someone tells me that I should do this or this, I will probably not do it. However, is this really sufficient evidence to say that I would not have obeyed an order in a scientific study? So many people, no different from me, did obey to the point of administering a deadly shock to someone else. Why would I have acted differently? Perhaps it is wise to acknowledge that unless we are in the situation ourselves, we never know what we are capable of.

This chapter is about research into human obedience, as illustrated by historical studies and my own current research. I provide an overview of the experimental research on obedience to authority that has been conducted over the past century. The systematic study of obedience is usually traced back to 1963, when a scientist named Stanley Milgram started conducting highly controversial experiments on the topic of obedience. However, previous research conducted in the 1920s and 1940s also showed extreme obedience to a scientific authority, even though those studies are less frequently mentioned.

By tracing their experiments over time, I detail how scientists have approached the question of whether and how individuals will obey orders to cause others harm. This research cumulatively shows that humans are extremely obedient. In addition, by presenting my own research methodology, it will help us understand the *how* on a neurological level.

THE BIRTH OF OBEDIENCE RESEARCH: INSIGHTS FROM EARLY EXPERIMENTAL STUDIES

In 1924, Carney Landis published a scientific article describing different experiments for studying emotional reactions in a series of situations designed to arouse an emotional response.[49] There were several situations, such as looking at pornographic pictures, listening to popular music, reading the Bible, or looking at pictures showing skin diseases and being asked to imagine being similarly infected. Among the seventeen different situations, one is of particular interest. In this situation, twenty-one volunteers were invited to sit at a table. A flat tray and a butcher's knife were placed on that table. Then, the volunteers received a live white rat and were instructed by the experimenter to "hold the rat with your left hand and then cut off its head with the knife."

Landis reported that 15 of the 21 volunteers, which represents 71 percent of the sample, followed the instruction, although they had no specific reasons to do so. Five of the volunteers who did not decapitate the rat instead passively observed the experimenter doing so in front of them.

As a reminder, the experiment was about observing emotional reactions and not on obedience per se. Landis described that the situation caused a great variety of emotional reactions. Some of the participants cried or reported disagreement. Many of them doubted that the experimenter was serious about killing the rat. But in the end, many of them did it, and, in the author's own words, "in a rather awkward and prolonged job of decapitation." This study showed that many people were able to decapitate a live animal following the experimenter's instruction – without any form of pressure.

Twenty years later, in 1944, in an undoubtedly less gory experiment, Jerome Frank, a social psychologist, found himself unexpectedly confronted with a high level of obedience among his participants, while he actually thought that they would largely disobey. He designed several experiments in order to study what is happening when someone resists an experimenter's instructions.[50] To ensure that his participants would resist his instructions, the tasks he created were particularly disagreeable or pointless.

For instance, he asked his participants to carry a number of small blocks one at a time back and forth between two tables or to try to balance a marble on a small steel ball, which was obviously an impossible task. Critically, Frank asked his participants to perform the task for an hour and a half! Take a moment and imagine that you are doing such a task for that amount of time. You are probably telling yourself that at some point you would have stopped. Well, this is what Frank hoped as well. Yet, there was no resistance to his instructions.

Overall, he observed that almost 90 percent of his participants performed the tasks for the designated time, even though they reported that they considered quitting several times. For instance, one reported "I was frankly disgusted with it" and another one reported "It was almost entirely unpleasant because of its futility." Frank tried to explain the phenomenon of such obedience by suggesting that volunteers for an experiment make a sort of contract with the experimenter, which strongly inhibits resistance to any activity required by the experimenter. But this unexpected obedience was not further explained. He even humorously titled the first section of his paper "Preliminary experiments: Failure to obtain resistance to disagreeable or nonsensical tasks."

The studies carried out by Frank showed that, for the sake of science, people can agree to perform highly annoying tasks, even if they clearly dislike doing so.

Almost twenty years later, Stanley Milgram discovered the same thing, but in a more disturbing context.

Milgram was born and raised in the Bronx in New York City, the second of three children in a Jewish family, whose parents had emigrated from Eastern Europe. When he was a student at Harvard University, he took the classes of leading social psychologists, including Solomon Asch. Asch is famous for his experiment showing that individual behaviors can be influenced by the behaviors of the group, even if the decisions of the group are incorrect.

Asch created a study in which eight individuals, seven confederates of the experimenter and one real, naïve participant, had to report which of three lines (A, B, or C) of different length had the same length as a target line.[51] All individuals present in the room had to report aloud, one at a time, which line was similar. As part of the experimental trick, the naïve participant was always one of the last to report their answer. The correct answer was always obvious, and at the beginning all the confederates reported the correct answer to make the real participant confident. But then they deliberately started reporting an incorrect answer, which they did for 12 out of 18 trials. Participants were thus put in a situation where they had to decide either to follow their own judgment or to go along with the unanimous majority.

Asch observed that about 75 percent of the participants conformed to the group at least once by reporting the incorrect answer that the majority indicated. For instance, if the group reported that line B was similar to the target line, even though it was obvious that line C was the correct answer, participants nonetheless reported that line B was correct. In a control study without any other individuals in the room, less than 1 percent of participants gave the wrong answer. In the interviews conducted after the experiment, participants reported that they noticed that the answer was wrong, but they did not want to appear ridiculous in front of the group or thought of as peculiar.

At first glance such a result might seem a bit strange. Why would we conform to a group when we know the group is wrong? It is, however, undeniable that we all adapt our behaviors to fit with the group. We follow fashion or we decide to dress differently to adapt to the clothing style of our colleagues. We may avoid eating meat if we are surrounded by vegetarians. We follow traditions. We dance and sing at a concert, or we remain quiet in the doctor's waiting room or in a library, as the other people around us do. When you see a group of people staring at a point in the sky, you will certainly also lift your head to try to see what they are looking at. Influence of the group is well known and it is one of the reasons why, for instance, we are required to cast our ballot in the privacy of a voting booth, where we can avoid such influence.

But Milgram felt unhappy with the ecology of the procedure in the classic Asch study. The "ecology" of a task in experimental research means trying to develop a paradigm that is socially relevant and as close as possible to a real situation, despite being tested in a lab context. Milgram's Jewish heritage also led him to want to understand why so many Jews were murdered during the Holocaust. In 1961, he was following the trial of Adolf Eichmann on the television and wondered to what extent the now famous excuse "I was only following orders" would reflect a sort of reality.

When he was an assistant professor at Yale University, he designed an unprecedented experiment in which volunteers would be asked to deliver extremely painful and dangerous shocks to another person. He wondered if people would still be ready to conform when their actions could be a question of life or death for others.

THE MILGRAM'S EXPERIMENT ON OBEDIENCE

In his seminal experiment, Milgram invited two volunteers for a study, whose declared aim was to evaluate the relationship between punishment and learning.[52] Participants received $4.50 (which would be the equivalent of $35 to $45 in 2020s) and were explicitly told that they would keep the money no matter what happens.

The two volunteers were "randomly" assigned to either the role of the teacher or the learner. In reality this assignation was rigged in advance so that the real participant would always be the teacher and the other participant, who was in reality a confederate of the experimenter, would always be the learner.

The learner was taken to another room and strapped into an electric chair apparatus. The learner mentioned a cardiac weakness, but the experimenter confirmed that this was not problematic.[*] The teacher was told to administer a paired-associate learning task to the learner, consisting of reading a series of word pairs. The learner then had to recall the associated words after being told one single word with four possible associations. The teacher was instructed to administer a shock to the learner if the answer was incorrect.

There were thirty levels of different shock intensities displayed on the shock generator. Each level was clearly labelled with the voltage intensity, ranging from 15 to 450 volts. In addition, other labels ranging from *Slight shock* to *Danger: severe shock* and *XXX* were also displayed on the generator. To add pressure to the participants and enhance the reality of the procedure, the learner at first indicated that the shocks were painful. But as the shock intensity increased, the learner started to beg aloud to stop the study. At 300 volts, he even pounded on the wall of the room where he was, which could be heard by the teacher. After that, he showed no sign of being alive anymore and the task continued in an agonizing silence.

When the learner expressed reluctance to continue the task, the experimenter responded with a series of four different verbal prods: "Please

---

[*] Milgram conducted different variants of his seminal study, which will be described from place to place in this book. The "cardiac condition" of the participants is limited to some specific experiments in Milgram's studies, rather than being a common characteristic across all of them.

continue" (Prod 1), "The experiment requires that you continue" (Prod 2), "It is absolutely essential that you continue" (Prod 3), and "You have no other choice, you must go on" (Prod 4). When a participant still refused to continue the experiment after Prod 4, the experiment stopped.

Notably, before the experiment, in a preliminary study, random citizens, psychiatrists, and students were asked to estimate their own degree of obedience. Milgram presented to them the experimental procedure and asked them to report their "breaking point" – that is, when they would refuse to continue the study. All of the 110 individuals questioned on their own obedience indicated that they would never go on until the end of the experimental procedure. The majority of them reported that they would stop at around 150 volts, when they could first hear the "learner" asking to stop the procedure.

During the interviews that Milgram conducted, participants reported, for instance, that they would never hurt someone to such an extent for science, or that since they are afraid of electric shocks, they would not administer such shocks to someone else. However, as suggested by Milgram himself, asking this type of question necessarily involves a biased answer. An answer that a person may give because they do not want to be perceived as a potential torturer.

Milgram thus conducted a second study in which he asked another pool of individuals, again composed of experts on human behavior and random citizens, to estimate when an imaginary sample of a hundred of Americans, from various backgrounds, would stop. Unanimously, they all reported that no one would go on until the end of the experimental procedure, except perhaps a very few individuals suffering from a psychiatric pathology. According to the psychiatrists, almost all the subjects would stop at 150 volts, when they first hear the learner asking for the experiment to be stopped.

I conducted a similar – though less experimental – survey more recently in 2018, when my colleague the Lieutenant-Colonel Salvatore Lo Bue invited me to give a class at the Royal Military Academy of Belgium to present my studies on the obedient brain. To introduce the topic, Salvatore presented the study of Milgram to the students, who were military cadets in their first year of training. In an attempt to see if the students would provide different answers than those obtained by

Milgram in his preliminary study, he asked them if they thought they would have obeyed in this kind of study. One out of roughly thirty-five students admitted that he would have obeyed until the end.

And, indeed, Milgram's results were slightly different from these kinds of self-predictions. In his seminal study, he tested forty participants. Sixty-five percent of them administered the maximum voltage intensity in spite of the fact that they could hear the screams and pleas of the learner, who begged for the experiment to stop. Importantly, none of these participants asked to stop before 300 volts of shock intensity. These results raised important questions: Why did the participants obey? Why would ordinary people administer painful (and deadly) electric shocks to another volunteer?

Milgram tried to explain the level of obedience he obtained in his studies. He explained that when people follow the orders of an experimenter, they transfer their own agency and responsibility to the experimenter. They become "thoughtless agents of action," they enter into an "agentic state."[53] However, while some academics agreed with his theory about an agentic state when people obey orders,[54] others were concerned about its validity, as he did not conduct systematic debriefings with all his participants.[55] For instance, Milgram conducted several variants of his initial study, and the degree of obedience differed between those variants. Obedience decreases if the experimenter was giving his prods through a phone or if the learner was physically present in the same room. Some academics have mentioned that an agentic state theory would predict that a transfer of agency and responsibility from the person executing the order to the experimenter would involve similar behavior from all the participants, no matter what the experimental context was.[56] However, as we will elaborate later, this argument significantly neglects the interaction between neural processes and the environment. It is evident that no single process can offer a comprehensive explanation for an entire behavior.

A second problem for fellow academics who questioned Milgram's results is that there is little data provided to support the agentic state theory in his work. He, for instance, indicated that several of his participants reported that they thought that Yale University was responsible for the welfare of the participants. But he did not conduct systematic interviews with all his participants.

Despite the initial lack of evidence for his theory, experimental research combining explicit, implicit, electrophysiological, and neuro-imaging methods seems to indicate that Milgram was actually not entirely wrong (as we will see in Chapter 3). Of course, people can have different reasons to obey or disobey orders. But it appears that once they have agreed to comply, their brain starts processing the information differently, which leads to a reduced feeling of responsibility and agency over their own acts of obedience. However, as we will further see in subsequent chapters, agency and responsibility are not the only processes that are altered in a situation of obedience.

An interesting observation is that Milgram tested hundreds of people from various social backgrounds, with various levels of education, women and men, in the US or in Germany. He never found that one category of individuals was less likely to obey in his experiments.

OTHER STUDIES USING A MILGRAM-LIKE APPROACH

The experimental approach developed by Stanley Milgram continued to be the dominant model to study obedience in an experimental context for decades. Later, many additional experiments were conducted by other researchers, to provide additional conclusions about obedience. One of them investigated to what extent people would comply with the orders of a TV presenter to hurt another person for the sake of a television game, and another one tested to what extent people could hurt an animal for science.

When I was teaching psychology in a secondary school in Brussels before starting my PhD, I invited my students to watch the French documentary *Le jeux de la mort* ("The Death Game") broadcast by the French television channel France 2. The purpose of the documentary was to evaluate the extent to which a TV presenter would be considered as authoritative as a scientist conducting an experiment. Basically, the idea was to replicate Milgram's study in the context of a television studio with a live audience.

Jean-Léon Beauvois, Didier Courbet, and Dominique Oberlée are the French researchers who agreed to participate in the adaptation of Milgram's study in the context of a TV show. Clearly, they have guts. I am not sure I would have accepted such a challenge myself. In this adaptation, a famous female TV presenter for France Télévisions, Tania Young, was playing the role of the experimenter.

Volunteers were invited and told that they would participate in a pilot of a forthcoming TV show. Volunteers came from the Paris area and the researchers ensured they were not familiar with Milgram's research. To resemble Milgram's studies as far as possible, the experimental subject was placed in the role of a "questioner" and another subject (the experimenter's confederate) was placed in the role of the "contestant." The contestant was isolated in a sort of bubble and was strapped to a chair and connected to an apparatus that delivered electric shocks. The questioner could thus not see the contestant but could hear him.

As in the Milgram experiment, each time the contestant gave an incorrect answer, the questioner had to administer an electric shock that increased after each incorrect answer. When the questioner started to show signs of doubt or questioned the morality of the procedure, the TV presenter had five verbal prods to give in a certain order in order to incentivize the questioner to pursue the experiment. The four first prods were similar to Milgram's, but the fifth one involved the audience. At the fifth prod, the TV presenter turned towards the audience and asked them to motivate the candidate to continue, telling the participant: "You can't prevent the candidate from winning! What does the public think about that?" The audience then clapped for the candidate to continue the game, thus providing a group incentive in addition to the authority figure incentive.

Before presenting the results of the televised study to my students, I asked them if they thought they would have obeyed orders in such a TV show. Unanimously, they declared that would have never obeyed, and in their own words claimed that "those obeying are psychopaths" or that "of course not, we are not stupid or monsters."

However, the results of the TV show indicated that 81 percent of the questioners went all the way to the end of the procedure, that is, administering a 450-volt electric shock to the contestant. Either my students were not particularly inclined to obey orders, which is undoubtedly possible, or they did not want to admit that perhaps they would have also administered the lethal shock.

The researchers engaged with the TV show failed to observe any difference between male and female participants, or to observe any correlation with age. However, the researchers observed that the further participants were to the left of the political spectrum, the lower the shocks they agreed to give to the learner.[57] They also observed that the individuals who sent higher shock intensities during the experiment were also those scoring the highest on a self-report questionnaire measuring agreeableness and conscientiousness.

However, caution must be taken when interpreting such results. The questionnaires were administered eight months *after* the experiment took place. Thus inferring that something (i.e., personality traits) measured at a time X *predicts* a behavior that happened eight months *earlier* is a delicate issue. Several authors have observed that personality traits are actually very stable over years,[58] thus suggesting that the results obtained by the researchers could have been globally similar if they had measured personality traits *before* the experimental study. However, nothing prevents participants from modifying their answers to the questionnaires, consciously or not, to be perceived as nicer, an effect that we will explore further in Chapter 3. To limit this possibility, the researchers did not tell participants that they were being recontacted because of the TV show. However, participating in a Milgram-like study, in front of an audience, is likely to have left its mark on these people. They may still question their behavior even eight months later. It is thus plausible that participants who obeyed a lot during the experiment desired to be thought of favorably by any experimenters, and thus reported higher degrees of agreeableness and conscientiousness. Thus, additional studies would be necessary to elaborate a clear profile of the people who are more likely to disobey the orders of an authority, an aspect that we will approach in Chapter 7.

Nonetheless, this study famously showed that social influence – in this case by a famous TV presenter and an audience – can also lead to extreme levels of obedience.

More recently than the rat decapitation study, a team of researchers led by Laurent Bègue, a French social psychologist, investigated if people would agree to comply with orders to kill an animal for the sake of scientific research in a Milgram-like experiment.[59] The motivation of the researchers was to understand to what extent killing animals in laboratories creates moral dilemmas and distress for laboratory staff who must conduct invasive and painful experiments for scientific research.[60]

Upon arrival at the laboratory, volunteers were seated at a table with a large fish tank in front of them. Inside the tank, they could see a large goldfish moving around. The volunteers were required to incrementally administer painful chemical injections to the fish and were told that they were participating in a learning experiment to gain a better understanding of Alzheimer's disease. Volunteers were explicitly told that at a high dosage, the substance had severe consequences on vital functions and that the animal would die. Below each button, the expected probability of death of the fish was clearly written, with 100 percent for button 12.

During the task, volunteers were asked to observe the fish's behavior in a learning task and were told that the substance was going to influence the fish's performance on the task. When volunteers expressed reluctance to continue the task, a research assistant asked them to keep on pressing the buttons.

As in the classical Milgram study which relied on the use of a confederate, the fish was actually not a real fish, but a biomimetic robot. Clearly, the decapitation study of Landis with a live rat would not be authorized nowadays for obvious ethical reasons.

As the fish was fake, the study relied on a cover story. Thus, the researchers first attempted to determine which of the 152 participants appeared to trust the cover story and which did not. Several judges analyzed the videos of the volunteers, categorizing them based on their perception of whether participants trusted the cover story or not. According to the analysis of those videos, the researchers found that approximately 20 percent of participants did not believe the cover story, while about 74 percent clearly trusted it. In some videos, the judges had doubts because participants showed minimal uncertainty about the aim of the task or the credibility of the cover story (about 10 percent), but they decided to include these participants in the analysis nonetheless.

Results showed that of the remaining participants, 28 percent refused to begin the task, 44 percent administered the twelve doses (thus killing the fish), and between 1 and 6 percent stopped at the intermediate level of injections.

In a second study, the researchers tested whether thinking positively or negatively about science would influence the results. As their experimental protocol was reported to be beneficial for gaining a better understanding of Alzheimer's disease, the researchers postulated that having a positive vision of science would improve obedience in their paradigm. One group of additional volunteers were asked to promote science by writing down what they liked about science and what they thought they had in common with scientists. Another group of additional volunteers were asked to describe what they do not like about science and what differentiates them from scientists. Results showed that those who with a pro-scientific mindset were more willing to follow the research assistant's instructions to continue with the experiment.

The results thus suggest that explicit motivation to believe in science led to participants being more likely to kill a fish for the sake of the study.

As this section shows, Milgram's approach to studying obedience has remained influential because of its main findings, replicability, and wide-ranging applicability. His work has inspired numerous follow-up studies and continues to shape our understanding of the factors that contribute to obedience and resistance to authority. However, many controversies, whether methodological or ethical, have arisen regarding this experimental approach, as we will see in the next section.

FLAWS IN MILGRAM-LIKE STUDIES

Soon after the publication of Milgram's studies, criticisms burgeoned in the scientific community. Those studies created an unprecedented tidal wave of criticism, such as no other study had caused until then.

A first criticism was about the use of cover stories and to what extent participants truly believed that the whole situation was real. Imagine you are taking part in Milgram's research as the person inflicting the painful shocks on another individual. You hear that person screaming, begging for you to stop. And there, in the same room, stands the experimenter, who remains calm and distant. As if the situation was not problematic, or even stressful. At some point, it would be logical to ask yourself if this entire situation is not just a huge fake.

This point is one of the major criticisms addressed to the studies of Stanley Milgram: Perhaps the participants did not really believe that they were harming another individual.[61,62] Perhaps, deep inside, they knew that it would be impossible that such a situation was truly happening.

However, several counterarguments have been made. First, Milgram's data showed that only 16 out of 658 participants, which corresponds to 2.4 percent, reported that they were certain that the victim was not perceiving real pain.[63] The vast majority of them (i.e., 62 percent) reported that they were convinced that the victims were actually suffering during the experiment, and 22 percent reported that at some point they had doubts. An analysis of the archive of the Milgram experiments at Yale reveals that the majority of the participants reported feeling relieved when they were told that the experiment was fake and that they did not really kill the other person.[64] One participant even reported that he had been checking the obituaries for weeks to make sure that he had not caused someone's death.[65]

Second, it was clear when watching the videos recorded by Milgram that his participants exhibited visible signs of stress during the experiment, such as hand shaking or nervousness. Those signs of stress could thus be interpreted as showing that Milgram's participants actually believed that they were torturing another human being.[54]

Nonetheless, in a study replicating Milgram's paradigm but in a virtual-reality set-up, participants also showed signs of stress while hurting an obviously fake avatar.[66] In this study, the researchers replicated the experimental set-up of Milgram, but instead of administering pain to another human, participants were instructed to administer a shock to a female virtual character strapped to a chair. This procedure has the advantage of respecting ethical standards, as participants know that they are not inflicting pain on a real human being. As the situation was fake, the researchers indeed observed that obedience rates were higher than in the initial Milgram study.

However, what is even more interesting is that the researchers also evaluated their participants' self-assessment of somatic states during the experiment, such as trembling, shaking, face becoming hot, etc. They also measured electrodermal activity and heart rate to gauge their physiological responses to the experimental procedure and observed a change when they sent the shock to the avatar compared to the baseline. Such results indicate that physiological reactions to stress can be present, even when the situation is obviously fake. This is like when you watch a magic show: You know the magician is not going to cut their assistant in half for real, but it does not prevent you from experiencing stress during the show. Thus, signs of nervousness in participants in Milgram's studies cannot be taken to prove that they believe in the cover story.

It is actually very difficult to know what Milgram's participants truly thought during the task. No one was in their mind when they were pressing the buttons. However, all these contrasting interpretations of Milgram's studies actually reinforce the idea that using "cover stories" in experimental set-ups can raise major issues in interpreting the results.

Strong ethical concerns have also been raised about Milgram's studies.[62] Because of the experimental situation he created, he subjected his participants to high levels of stress, while not obtaining clear informed consent and not mentioning that they could stop at any time.[67] Apparently, Milgram also did not systematically debrief his participants at the end of the study as he indicated in his scientific publications. Some participants, including the one who checked the obituaries, had no idea that they actually did not really administer a shock to another person and only discovered that this was the case a year later, when Milgram sent a report to his participants.[65]

Another important aspect is that administering electric shocks to someone else does not reflect a behavior that one can easily find in everyday life situations, thus leaving the external validity of the task open to question. This is not a typical form of violence that an authority figure is likely to ask another person to perform in modern societies, even though cases of torture with electricity have been reported during several wars and genocides, including World War II or the Iraq War, for instance, and also on prisoners in several countries, such as Bangladesh, Peru, Syria, Turkey, or Uganda, to name but a few.[68]

Milgram's experiments were groundbreaking at the time they were conducted. They revealed the extent to which ordinary individuals could be led to obey authority figures, even if it meant inflicting harm on others, an aspect that is also observable in real-life events as we will see in the next chapter. The results were both surprising and thought-provoking, capturing the attention of both the scientific community and the public. However, the many flaws reported led other researchers, including myself, to seek alternative methods to understand how and why people can be so cruel when they obey orders.

STUDYING OBEDIENCE IN THE AFTERMATH OF MILGRAM'S STUDIES

It is difficult nowadays to find anyone who does not know about Milgram's studies given the high media coverage surrounding his work. People may not remember the name "Milgram," but just mention to them "the experiment with the electric shocks and obedience" and they will likely tell you that indeed they have heard about that study.

In the 1980s, a team of researchers from Utrecht University created a new twist to the standard approach to testing obedience.[69] They decided to investigate whether obedience would be as high as in Milgram's studies when tested in a contemporary form of mediated violence: providing very negative remarks to an applicant for a job interview.

The global procedure was relatively similar to Milgram's, with three protagonists: the experimenter, here taking the form of a research worker at the university; the participant; and a person applying for a job at the university. As in Milgram's experiment, the participant and the experimenter were seated together in the same room, and the "applicant," who was in reality an accomplice of the experimenter, was located in another room.

The test that the participant was supposed to give to the applicant was said to be critical in the selection procedure and would determine if the applicant would get the position or not. The participants were told to disturb the applicant by making negative comments about their test performance and denigrating remarks about their personality. However, it was made clear that the idea of denigrating the applicant was not in order to evaluate their suitability for the job, since the ability to work under stress was not essential for the position. Participants were told that denigration was simply to help the researcher establish a link between psychological stress and test performance. Thus, as in

Milgram's studies, participants thought that they would help science by obeying. There were fifteen negative remarks, which were highly detrimental to the applicant's performance and placed them in such a stressful condition that they failed to get the job. The remarks were not very severe at the beginning, such as "your answer to question 9 was wrong" (remark 1) or "up to now, your test score is not quite sufficient" (remark 5).[70] However, their psychological intensity increased as the experiment progressed. For instance, "this job is much too difficult for you according to the test" (remark 11) or "according to the test, it would be better for you to apply for lower functions" (remark 15). If the participant refused to carry on making the stress-inducing remarks, the experimenter, as in Milgram's studies, had four prods to motivate the participant to continue, such as "the experiment requires you to continue."

Thus, here, participants did not believe that they were torturing and killing another individual as in Milgram's studies. But they were brought to believe that they were strongly denigrating an applicant, possibly causing them psychological damage and making them fail to get a job.

Like Milgram, the authors presented the procedure to a series of random individuals and asked them if they would obey until the end. Only 9 percent reported that they would be obedient in this task. As in Milgram's studies, the "behavioral" reality was much different. In their initial study, they observed that 91 percent of the participants obeyed until remark 15, despite the fact that participants explicitly claimed that they were unhappy about causing psychological stress to the applicant.

This is higher than in Milgram's obedience studies, were "only" 65 percent obeyed until the end. Interestingly, the researchers also replicated the study with another population: personnel officers. As the job of personnel officers is to deal with applicants and as they have their own ethical code, the researchers expected them to be less obedient. This was not the case: they obeyed as much as the other participants.

Interestingly, in a variant of their study, the researchers manipulated the notion of the participants' liability. In one variant, they made participants sign a document stating that they would be legally liable for any possible damage to the applicant. The applicant during the experiment even explicitly claimed that they would take legal action against the participant if they did not quit making these cruel remarks. In this situation, the obedience rate dropped between 20 and 30 percent. However, if the experimenter told the subject that actually the psychology department, not them, was legally responsible, obedience reincreased up to 67 percent.

Using a slightly different approach than Milgram to the study of obedience, these interesting results show that people can be highly obedient as long as they are not the victims themselves. However, if there is a risk for them to become victims in some way, they suddenly become far less compliant.

However, despite bringing more ecological validity, such methods still lead to a critical, but unanswered question: How can people act in a cruel manner, be it by physically or psychologically hurting someone else, when they obey orders? None of the studies mentioned above really answers *How*. A totally different experimental approach had to be investigated, one that could more precisely be adapted to neuroscience methods.

A NOVEL EXPERIMENTAL APPROACH TO STUDYING OBEDIENCE

When my own team designed our first study on obedience, we were also working in the shadow of the Milgram experiments from the 1960s. Due to widespread awareness of his work, we thought it would be really difficult to evaluate obedience in a lab setting. At the very least, we suspected it could skew the results.

Indeed, the contours of the experimental setup pose a major challenge in light of Milgram's legacy. When people coming to an experiment think that the experimenters are going to evaluate their behaviors, especially prosocial or antisocial attitudes towards others, they may act to show their very best side and refuse to reveal that they can perform immoral acts. In addition, as most people know that Milgram draws drastic conclusions about the propensity of humans to obey destructive orders, participants could be even more tempted to resist the orders they receive. Not necessarily out of moral convictions, but simply because they do not want to be seen as mean or unkind by the experimenters.

However, being aware of Milgram's studies does not seem to be sufficient to influence obedience in a lab context. In a recent study,[71] two researchers showed hundreds of individuals videos of the experimental setup they created to study if someone would obey an order to kill a fish for science. After watching the video, participants had to indicate the number of toxic doses (between 0 and 12) they thought they would have administered if they had participated, and the number of toxic doses they thought an average participant, with the same age and gender as them, would administer. Participants were then also asked if they were familiar with the studies of Stanley Milgram.

Results indicated that people considered that they would behave more ethically than others. They reported that they would administer 2.90 toxic doses on average, and that others would inject 6.14 doses. Interestingly, those familiar with Milgram's experiments reported that others would probably inject a higher dose. But they considered that it would not influence their own obedience, which would remain low. This suggests that while Milgram's studies have been widely used in education to raise awareness about the dangers of blind and destructive obedience, it is possible that this knowledge only allows people to judge the behavior of others, rather than reflect on their own actions. Yet the many studies conducted since Milgram's with a relatively similar paradigm show that people remain highly obedient in experimental setups.

As far as I have observed, the main problem associated with knowing Milgram's studies is that participants believe that we also have hidden aims and procedures when they enter the experiment room. Milgram's studies are indeed famous for hiding information from participants and creating deception.[72] But beyond Milgram's studies, this is a general concern in psychological studies: The high use of cover stories can also impact other research, as volunteers start to develop a mistrust of what researchers tell them. Several of my participants told me that they only started believing that my explanations about the task were true when they were explicitly offered the choice to decide which role to play first and when they started receiving the shocks for real.

So, when I began to set up my own experiments on obedience, I had a lot to contend with.

It all started in 2013, when I was a visiting PhD student at University College London. I was working with Patrick Haggard, a world-leading expert on human volition and the sense of agency. I had started to develop an interest in human obedience, but this question had not been approached by neuroscientists before. I therefore had to convince someone embark on the quest with me.

But the topic was still very *touchy*, a dark cloud floating above the experimental study of obedience considering the many ethical issues associated with Milgram's studies. Ask any scientist to replicate Milgram's studies and it might give them goosebumps. But I did not want to replicate Milgram's studies or show again that people are highly obedient in a lab context, which did not need to be proved any further. Milgram and the many studies conducted afterwards with a similar methodological approach indeed already reached the same conclusions about human obedience. Rather, I wanted to understand what is happening in the brains of people when they agree to obey an order that causes pain to another individual. I wanted to understand how people can commit atrocities when they follow orders. I thus aimed to fundamentally transform the study of obedience to authority.

It took a while, but I finally convinced Patrick Haggard. He told me he was not fully motivated to approach the question at first because reproducing a Milgram-like experiment, considering the many controversies, sounded like a crazy project. If I remember correctly, it took me around a year to convince him to embark on the quest.

Reinventing Milgram's studies was a hard task. We had to develop a totally novel experimental approach that would solve the ethical and methodological issues associated with Milgram's studies, while being as ecological as possible – that is, trying to measure a real behavior where people face a moral decision. Past research conducted in the aftermath of Milgram's studies all used a method strongly inspired by his experimental design, with only small variations. Here, we had to rethink the task from scratch.

One of the biggest methodological concerns is that, to be able to record good data with magnetic resonance imaging (MRI) or with electrophysiological measures, such as electroencephalography (EEG), researchers generally need to average dozens of trials where the same event is happening in order to obtain a good signal-to-noise ratio. In Milgram's study, each trial is different from the other, as they each involve a different shock intensity and a potentially different reaction from the learner. Thus, the method is not suitable for studies seeking to understand what happens in the brain of the participants when they perform the task. Additionally, a typical stress reaction is to sweat. In an experimental situation causing high levels of stress such as in Milgram's studies, participants are likely to sweat. I challenge anyone to get a good EEG signal when the participant is sweating from the head. Sweat arte-facts, as they are called, are a nightmare for neuroscientists.

And, of course, there were other considerations. When studying whether people would choose between morally acceptable or unaccept-able actions in a given situation, it is necessary that they face a decision that actually has moral or immoral consequences. If you simply ask your participants to choose between pressing button A or B but that there are no consequences in choosing between the two, or if the consequences are not real, you do not have a real context associated with moral deci-sions. In other words, for participants, it does not make any difference whether they press button A or B.

To capture a human behavior in a more ecological way, choosing between A and B must have a moral consequence. But at the same time, ethics standards have to be respected and the methods have to be suitable for their measurements. Researchers thus have to be very invent-ive to create such an experimental approach. In our case, it took us roughly a year of reflection and discussions.

In total, two other researchers – Julia Christensen and Axel Cleeremans – joined Patrick and I to create a novel methodology. We decided that we would invite participants in pairs.[73] When we recruited them, we ensured that they did not know each other, because knowing the other person can influence behavior. One would be assigned to be the "agent" and the other would be the "victim." Halfway through the experiment, they would switch roles, so that the procedure would be fully reciprocal. We specifically wanted to avoid having our participants being in the role of the perpetrator only, as was the case in Milgram's studies, thus reducing the psychological distress associated with being a potential perpetrator. Also, contrary to Milgram's studies, our two volunteers were real participants, none of them was a confederate of ours. Indeed, we decided that we would not use deception at all, with all the procedures being entirely transparent.

We decided to use a method that would rely on the delivery of electric shocks but our procedure would be very different from Milgram's. This time, the shocks would be real, but of a constant intensity and calibrated on one's own pain threshold. Further, participants were offered a small monetary reward each time they administered the painful shock.

Our two participants sat face to face at a table, with a keyboard between them. On that keyboard, there were two buttons: one labelled "SHOCK" and the other labelled "NO SHOCK." We told our participants that when they were in the role of the agent, they were in charge of pressing the buttons. Pressing the SHOCK button would send a real, painful but calibrated, electric shock to the "victim" and would increase the agent's remuneration by £0.05. Pressing the NO SHOCK button would not deliver the electric shock and the agent would not receive the remuneration.

In one experimental condition, agents were told that they would be totally free to decide which buttons to press in the course of sixty trials. In the other experimental condition, agents were told that they would receive an order from the experimenter whether or not to administer a shock on each trial (Figure 2.1). Importantly, for the second condition, we never told our participants that they must obey our orders and the experimenter never incentivized participants to follow the orders, as in Milgram's studies.

We used the term "free-choice" to describe the experimental condition where people were free to decide and "coercion" for the condition in which the experimenter was giving orders. Note that the word "coercion" here should be considered relative, rather than absolute. A strict definition of "coercion" would refer to the use of force to persuade someone to do something that they are unwilling to do. However, true coercion should not be used as it obviously violates ethical codes. We simply used the conventional term "coercion" to refer to an experimental situation in which people obey orders from an experimenter to inflict painful stimuli on another individual.

Figure 2.1 Experimental procedure to study how obeying orders impacts the brain. An experimenter gives orders to the agent whether or not to administer painful shocks to a victim. Administering a shock leads to a small monetary reward.[73]

For delivering the electric shocks, we used a very strict protocol. We placed two electrodes on the victim's left hand. These electrodes were connected to a machine that sent electrical stimuli through the electrodes. Before starting the experiment, we calibrated the individual pain threshold of each participant in front of each other. Our participants could thus ensure that the procedure was safe but also that the shocks were real and calibrated to be painful for the other participant. Since the pain threshold differs between individuals, for each of them we had to increase the intensity of the electrical stimulation until determining when the shock was painful during the calibration phase. The selected pain threshold was then the one that we used for the entire duration of the experiment. Importantly, the intensity did not increase as in Milgram's studies. In this experiment, the mean stimulation level selected by this procedure was about 25 milliamperes (mA) for a pulse duration of 200 μs, with quite a large variability between individuals.[†]

[†] I am sometimes asked about the relationship between milliamperes (mA) reported by the machine I use for the shocks and volts (V) to compare the shock intensity to those used in Milgram's studies. Volts measure the electrical potential difference or voltage, while milliamperes measure the electrical current flow in a circuit. The machine I use

This level of pain involves a physical and visible contraction of the muscles of the hand and would feel similar to receiving a small electrical discharge if you touch an electrical outlet or experience a rapid cramp.

When I speak about my studies during scientific conferences or to the media, I can no longer count the number of times people asked me the following question: "But people know Milgram, so of course they are going to disobey your orders, aren't they?" When we designed our task, we really thought this would be the case. When people taking part in an experiment think that the experimenters are going to evaluate their behaviors, especially prosocial or antisocial attitudes towards others, they may act to show their very best side and refuse to reveal that they can conduct immoral acts. As most of the people know that Milgram drew drastic conclusions about the propensity of humans to obey destructive orders, participants could be even more tempted to resist the orders they receive. They may not necessarily act with moral conviction, but simply because they do not want to be seen as mean or unkind by the experimenters.

I have to admit that I was certain that not a single participant would obey, especially since we first targeted university students, most of whom had studied Milgram extensively. I could not have been more wrong. Almost none of my participants disobeyed my orders to administer a real painful electric shock to another volunteer.

---

is a constant current stimulator, which means it will adjust the voltage (with a maximum of 400V) to pass the requested mA of current. Ohm's Law states that the voltage (V) across a conductor is directly proportional to the current (I) flowing through it and inversely proportional to the resistance (R) of the conductor. In theory, if you receive a voltage of 400V without any amperes, you will not feel anything, but that would not represent reality. Determining the pain and dangerousness of a shock involves a complex interaction of voltage, current, skin resistance, electrode resistance, duration, and the location of the pain delivery. As Milgram's shocks were fake, we lack the information that would determine a real sensation, and I do not have the materials to calculate the resistance precisely. However, what is most important is that the feeling of pain is the same among all participants. There is considerable variability regarding pain sensitivity, and a constant pain threshold would lead to different perceptions of pain across participants, which is not what we want, as it could introduce an additional variable that might influence our results. Therefore, we select the pain threshold based on a standard protocol to ensure a similar pain perception for all our participants.

I was also sure that no one would ever administer a painful shock freely to someone for just £0.05. I remember presenting this issue in a lab meeting in London, but some colleagues were certain that people would actually do it. Again, I was totally wrong. On average across several studies conducted with this paradigm, participants freely delivered around 34 shocks out of the 60 trials to the other participant, which resulted in a remuneration of about £1.70. The variability between participants was high in this free-choice condition: some indeed sent shocks to the other participant all the time, while others did not administer a single shock. But the majority of our participants administered roughly 30 shocks.

To understand better their decisions, I thus analyzed the many reports they made during the debriefing sessions at the end of the experiment, before examining what occurred in their brains.

EXPLORING OBEDIENCE: WHY PARTICIPANTS ADMINISTER PAINFUL SHOCKS

There is a substantial debate around the definition of morality between academics,[74] and actually, my experiments made me realize how participants' different (and very personal) perception of morality can strongly influence their behavior.

Before my participants start the experiment, I always take the time to explain to them the entire experimental procedure. This is to ensure that they are fully aware of all the details of the study and can give informed consent. At some point, I thus explain to them that they will have two buttons, one associated with administering a real painful shock to someone in exchange for +£0.05 (or €0.05 or RWF50 depending on the country where the study takes place) and the other one associated with not adminstering a shock and not earning extra money. Usually, at this point in the explanation, even if people are aware of the procedure before coming to the study, their facial expression changes and they show signs of anxiety or seriousness. They either giggle as a response to their emotional discomfort or look very serious. But they all continue to listen to the explanation of the task without saying a word.

But on one day, a participant suddenly interrupted me at this phase of the explanation and asked me "But why would people press the no shock button since they will not earn additional money if they do so?" I have to admit that I did not expect this question and I had to stop myself from answering, "Well, to not inflict pain on the person in front of you!" Rather, I just answered, "It's your own decision." By contrast, the other few people who interrupted me asked why they *would* press the shock button, as €0.05 did not appear to be sufficient reward for hurting the other participant. However, this moral quandary did not seem to disturb that participant who decided to administer 60 shocks out of 60 trials to the other poor participant. Notably, that particular participant was following the psychology program at the university where Milgram's studies on destructive obedience was taught.

I usually ask my participants in a debriefing session after the experiment about the number of shocks that they decided to administer when they could freely decide and why they have sent this number of shocks. It is always very interesting to see how the notion of morality differs between people. Most of the time, when I have participants who administered a really small number of shocks, such as 3 to 5 shocks, when they could freely decide, they report that it was because they did not want to hurt the person too much as it would be immoral. Two who administered minimal shocks (0/60 shocks and 3/60 shocks) reported, for example, "I do not like to hurt others, so I did not administer shocks" and "I was very uncomfortable administering painful shocks in exchange for money. That would be immoral."

At the same time, I have a fair number of participants administering 55 to 58 out of 60 shocks to the other participant who report similarly that they decided not to send the final few shocks because it would feel immoral to hurt the other person every time. For example, one reported, "I could not send all the shocks because I don't like to hurt others" and another one indicated, "It is not cool to send all the shocks to someone even if you can." The first one sent 55 shocks out of 60 trials and the second one sent 57 shocks out of 60 trials.

Here we have similar justifications based on a moral belief across the two groupings, but highly different behaviors.

Some participants reported that they wanted to make more money, so they administered lots of shocks. They admitted openly that this was their main motivation. I even had one participant who wrote on the debriefing sheet, "Money, Money, Money," and indeed sent 53/60 shocks. Very intriguingly, some have even told me orally that if "I" had increased the amount of euros earned for each shock, they would have administered fewer shocks to the victim. It was as if for them I was bearing the responsibility for the number of shocks that they decided freely to administer. Sometimes, they also provide very detailed monetary justifications. One reported: "I have a party tonight and the beer costs 1 euro, so I sent 20 shocks."

But I also have participants reporting that they did not dare to administer many shocks because they were afraid of what it might reveal about themselves. One reported: "I felt ashamed inflicting pain in exchange for money, so I only sent 8 shocks. I was actually afraid that this experiment revealed a pleasure deep inside me to inflict pain for money." Other participants have also reported that they sent no shocks because they found it shameful to hurt someone for money. For example, one reported, "The remuneration was too weak to inflict pain on someone" or another one reported, "I was shocked by the fact that the other participant sent me shocks for such a small amount of money. That's shameful and I did not do it." Others felt incredibly sorry because they pressed the wrong button on one trial and did send a shock inadvertently: "I feel very bad. I pressed the wrong button on one trial and gave a shock by mistake" (sent 1/60 shocks) or "I am sorry I pressed the wrong button" (sent 1/60 shocks).

Other participants provided very detailed explanations. One reported, "On the first quartile, I alternated between shock and no shock, letting hazard play. It was the same for the third quartile. For the second and the fourth quartile, I considered them as resting periods, so I pressed only on the no shock button. I have also sent shocks on the last 3 trials to break the monotony" (sent 28/60 shocks). Another one reported, "I had decided to send no shock on the first trial and then to give a shock. Then, I decided to give 2 trials with shocks and one with no shock. After, I wanted to have 4 trials with shocks but then waiting 3 trials before sending shocks again. I then had to increase to 7 consecutive shocks. And so on, following the same logic" (sent 41/60 shocks). Admittedly, even after reading that sentence multiple times, I have never understood the logic behind this.

Others indicated that they knew that even if the shocks were painful, they were absolutely without risk, so they did not see the problem of administering the shocks. "I was victim first and I knew that it was not that painful, so I did not find it hard to send shocks when I was agent" (sent 31/60 shocks) or "The shocks are real, but they are really manageable as people choose their own pain threshold" (sent 29/60 shocks). Or "The victim has chosen their pain" (sent 22/60 shocks).

I make it very clear from the start that in the free-choice condition they are entirely free to decide what to do, that I do not mind about what they choose to do. This is actually true: I want participants to really feel free to act as they want. I am actually not that much interested in their behavior. Rather, I am interested in how their brain processes information when they feel free. However, a fair number of participants use science or the experiment to justify the number of shocks administered. For example, they write, "It is required for the experiment" (sent 48/60 shocks) or "Not to bias the study" (sent 31/60 shocks).

Others did it out of curiosity. One reported that they wanted to see if it would really be painful for the victim (sent 1/60 shocks) and another one reported that they wanted to see how they would feel when sending the shocks (sent 2/60 shocks). Some explicitly reported a lack of empathy for the victim: "I did not feel empathy for the victim, so I sent shocks" (sent 35/60 shocks).

I also sometimes have philosophical explanations: "Wisdom is boring. Evil is stimulating" (sent 15/48 shocks).

CAN LAB EXPERIMENTS REFLECT REAL-LIFE MASS ATROCITIES?

It is worth taking a minute before ending this chapter to consider whether the controlled settings of laboratory experiments can truly mirror the extreme and multifaceted dynamics that characterize large-scale atrocities. Stanley Milgram, in his 1974 book, drew attention to the striking parallels between his studies and the Holocaust. Notably, both studies involved ordinary individuals being placed in the role of perpetrators who, with an authority figure nearby, willingly agreed to inflict harm on innocent victims.

In 2015, a US psychologist, Allan Fenigstein, wrote an interesting article[75] on the contrast between Milgram's studies and the Nazis, and suggested that Milgram's studies alone cannot help us understand perpetrators of the Holocaust. The author argues that the extreme and sadistic cruelty displayed by the Nazis, along with their enthusiastic participation in the killing process during the Holocaust, starkly contrasts with the behavior of laboratory participants who showed remorse or moral distress when they had to send electric shocks to another person. As we will see in Chapter 3, during genocides, a revision of moral values is present, as killing against an enemy outgroup becomes the norm. Lab experiments can provide a foundation for understanding the basic cognitive and neurological processes related to obedience. However, they may lack the contextual richness and ethical challenges faced in real-world situations. In real-life atrocities, factors such as propaganda, fear, ideology, and power dynamics play significant roles in influencing individuals' behavior and decision-making.

This is a question I also pondered while designing my own studies. Naturally, there are significant differences to consider between a real-life genocide and a study involving real electric shocks. Ethically and methodologically, I cannot consider conducting experiments with electrodes in the brains of individuals engaged in wars or genocides, so I must acknowledge and address these distinctions.

From my current perspective, as we will explore in the following chapters, obeying orders does impact brain processing even in simple laboratory experiments. When combined with the many other phenomena present during genocides, such as dehumanization, intergroup prejudice, fear, and trauma, these findings might become even more pronounced. For instance, the reduction of activity in empathy-related brain regions observed when people obey orders, compared to acting freely, may be exacerbated when perpetrators feel no remorse while hurting their victims due to indoctrination by hateful propaganda. This is why, as mentioned in the Introduction, it is also essential to discuss additional elements at play during genocides. Therefore, I will briefly cover other related phenomena beyond the simple situation of obedience in the following chapters.

CONCLUSION

As this chapter shows, even in an experimental context, with or without any external pressure, the thousands of volunteers recruited to participate in experimental research (mine or that of others) show a high degree of obedience to hurt another individual. This cannot be a random effect, as it has been shown in different lab contexts, in different countries, at different epochs in time. Combined with the interviews of genocide perpetrators in the previous chapter, even though there is a world of difference between obedience in a lab context and obedience in real life, it confirms that humans can indeed (severely) harm others when they follow orders. There is a need to understand how such results are possible, and this is where neuroscience can be useful – by providing findings of what is happening in people's brains when they comply with such orders.

After several years of development, with my colleagues we had thus finally conceived a novel experimental approach that respected ethical standards and where the degree of obedience was also alarmingly high. But most importantly, this method was suitable for neuroimaging measurements, and could thus be used to answer *How* people can accept to hurt someone when they follow orders, as we will see in the following chapters.

CHAPTER 3

How Do We Take Ownership over and Responsibility for Our Own Actions?

HUMANS HAVE THE ABILITY TO RECOGNIZE THAT WHEN they perform actions, they produce effects in the external world. This ability can strongly influence our willingness to perform "good" or "bad" actions, and it is critical in our social lives.

Of course, humans are not the only animals with this mental capacity. A high number of animal studies have demonstrated that other species are able to establish causal links between their actions and outcomes as well. One of the most fascinating examples is the use of tools, which is indisputably not an exclusively human skill. The use of tools not only involves understanding the link between one's own limb and the outcome, but it also involves a higher cognitive ability to understand that an external object can be used as an extension of one's own limbs in order to achieve a goal.

The use of tools has been widely observed. For instance, chimpanzees use wooden sticks to fish for ants or termites in their nests. A study published in 2007 further showed that chimpanzees can also create weapons to hunt for small mammals, beyond the simple use of their teeth and hands.[76] The use of tools in nonhuman species is not only driven by food – it also helps them to master their natural habitat. In 2005, a team of researchers witnessed a female gorilla named Leah using a meter-long stick in order to evaluate the depth of a pool of water she wanted to cross in a forest in northern Congo. She then entered the water and used the stick to help her progress into the pool.[77]

Indeed, humans are clearly not the only animals able to understand causality between their actions and outcomes or that they can modify their environment through the use of objects. Animals in our own homes prove this time and time again as well.

When I defended my PhD thesis in December 2015, my friend Juliane gave me a small box, which was actually supposed to be a sort of piggy bank. You have to put a coin on the top of the box and then press a button. The lid then opens and the small figure of a cat emerges and swipes the coin into the box with its paw. The cat actually meows as it pokes its head out of the box. The sound of the meow alerted my own cat, Euclid, who approached to inspect the box. Admittedly, the meowing sounded really realistic. Euclid was intrigued, so I decided to show him that by pressing the button, the cat would appear and meow.

This was a huge mistake. Not only did Euclid very rapidly learn the principle of causality between the button press and the cat popping out of the box, he enjoyed doing it so much that he became crazed, continually pressing that button – *40 to 50 times a day.*

Of course, my scientific spirit decided to test the limit of this principle of causality. I presented the box from different angles, resulting in the button being located on different sides. But it did not disturb Euclid. He just continued to find and press that button. Sometimes, he would wake me up in the middle of the night with it. Eventually, I had to take drastic measures and take the box away from him. The situation had become critical. By observation, my other cat Newton learned to use the button as well.

The situation was clearly no longer tolerable, and yet my curiosity remained. After all, I had just defended a PhD thesis on a closely related topic. So I wondered, was Euclid experiencing a feeling that "he" was the one doing the action?

In humans, the ability to perform actions is accompanied by a feeling of authorship, a feeling that "I" am the one who did it. This is what academics have called the sense of agency. The sense of agency is an incredible facet of human ability, probably one that has allowed us to achieve critical steps in our development across human history. More than any other animals, humans have transformed and built their environment. Agriculture, house building, tool development, weapon creation, means of transport – all the technological advancements that we have achieved are the product of our mental capacity to change the world around us and to take credit for our accomplishments.

This neurobiological capacity to experience a sense of agency has marked our modern world.[78] Henri-Louis Bergson, a French philosopher, famously used the concept of *Homo faber*, that is, "Man the Maker," to refer to the idea that humans were able to control their fate as they learned to create and develop tools. And indeed, without this capacity, for better or for worse, we would not be at the top of the food chain.

Yet even if we have a sense of agency over our actions, we do not experience agency over every single action we perform. If we did, our attention system would probably be overloaded with too much information. We would not be able to focus on other tasks. In fact, most of the actions that we perform on a daily basis are automatic; we are not even conscious we complete them. To prepare my hot chocolate every day, for example, I take the (dark) chocolate from the cupboard, I put it in the special machine that makes delicious hot chocolate with milk, which I take from the fridge and add in the required quantity. Then I press the button and *voilà*. This activity is so automatic that I do not have to think about it. I can even complete multiple other tasks while doing it, like talking to my relatives, listening to podcasts, or watching a movie.

My brain only needs a very small amount of cognitive resources to make my hot chocolate, and I do not need to experience agency when making it. I just have to think of the pleasure it will bring me, especially while cozied up under a good blanket. Nonetheless, I can consciously experience authorship over my actions. And if someone interrupts me and asks me what I am doing, I would be able to describe precisely what actions I am taking.

Now it's your turn. Take a moment. Just five seconds. Think about all the actions that you are doing right now with your hands and fingers. It could be preparing yourself to turn a page with your fingers, drinking a cup of tea, or scratching your nose. You were possibly doing these actions without even consciously thinking about it. But now that I am asking you to describe what you are doing, you can retrace the origins of these actions to yourself. You are experiencing authorship.

Agency will also be consciously processed when, for example, you engage in a novel activity. For instance, I really dislike coffee and I am terrible at making it for my guests because I almost never do it. So when someone asks for it, I have to think carefully about all the steps: What machine should I use, the Italian coffee machine or the supermarket one with the filters? How much ground coffee should I put in? How much water should I add? Which button starts the machine? What would be the final outcome? There are too many steps and actions to consider that are clearly not automatic. I am thus more likely to experience agency over my actions because I have to think carefully about all my movements and their coordination.

Driving is another great example. When you are an experienced driver, you drive your car without having to deeply think about which pedals to push, when to change speed, or how to place your hands on the steering wheel. But remember how cognitively exhausting it was when you first drove? All the actions that you had to consciously process at the same time? The coordination of your movements to safely drive the car? Well, now that driving your car is automatic and you have mastered all the motor steps, you do not have to consciously think about the authorship you have over your actions. But when something fails in your chain of actions, thus breaking the flow between your initial intention and the final outcome, you experience agency. If, for any reason, you lose control of the car, you will suddenly realize that you are the one driving it.

Thus, this is another critical aspect of the sense of agency: When something fails, authorship over the failure will pop into your mind and make you realize that *you* are the author of the failed action.

THE SENSE OF AGENCY AND THE HUMAN BRAIN

As healthy adults, we all have the capacity to recognize our actions as our own, even if we do not experience authorship as such all the time. However, some psychiatric or neurological diseases are associated with a disturbance in the sense of agency. In these cases, patients have difficulty recognizing their actions as their own.

Schizophrenia is one of the most well-known psychiatric diseases associated with a reduced feeling of agency over one's own actions, even if the motor system is intact. It means that for schizophrenia patients, the production of the movement is perfectly functional, but intentionality over the movement is disturbed. A researcher working with schizophrenia patients reported in a scientific publication[79] the case of a 29-year-old typist, who describes her experience:

> when I reach my hand for the comb it is my hand and arm which move, and my fingers pick up the pen, but I don't control them . . . I sit there watching them move, and they are quite independent, what they do is nothing to do with me . . . I am just a puppet who is manipulated by cosmic strings. When the strings are pulled my body moves and I cannot prevent it.

As in this case, schizophrenia patients sometimes experience their actions as not their own. Rather, they are imposed by an external agent. And when humans do not experience agency, they are not likely to experience responsibility for their actions. This is why schizophrenia patients may not be recognized as responsible for their actions in court.

Another example of a psychiatric condition in which the sufferer does not experience agency is the anarchic hand syndrome. This is a neurological disorder that causes a movement of the hand without the will of the patient. Patients generally report a dissociation between their own will and the movement of their hand, as if the hand had moved by "its own will."[80] These patients report that the movement of their hand was not under the control of their intentions, and that they cannot suppress or cancel the movement. They can, however, perfectly recognize that the moving hand is their own, suggesting that their sense of body *ownership* is not altered. They do accept that the movement has been made by their own hands, but they do not accept that the "I" is the source of this action.[81]

The principle here is similar for patients with Tourette syndrome. These patients have motor and vocal tics that are not under their control. For instance, they may involuntarily produce grimaces, jump, shake their head, or even vocalize insults. These tics lead them to experience a reduced sense of agency over their tic movements. A recent study even found a correlation between the severity of the motor symptoms and the sense of agency: the more severe the symptoms, the more reduced the sense of agency.[82] This study further showed that activity in brain regions associated with the sense of agency is reduced compared to a group of healthy controls. Patients with Tourette syndrome may thus have difficulties when it comes to experiencing agency over and responsibility for the consequences of their own actions.

In a healthy human brain, performing a voluntary action requires different levels in the transmission of information. It starts from regions of the brain that are involved in the generation of intentions and ends in the muscles controlling the movement. Brain regions associated with intentions mostly involve the prefrontal cortex. The prefrontal cortex is part of the frontal lobe and is localized near the motor regions. Over the course of evolution, this structure has grown in size particularly in humans compared to other species. Recent studies suggest that the prefrontal cortex represents about 30 percent of the total cortex, making it the largest ratio across all animal species.[83] The prefrontal cortex allows us to plan an action, make decisions, or control social behaviors, such as avoiding hurting someone else.

After the creation of the intention comes the creation of the motor plan that will be used to realize the action. The motor plan involves an interaction between the premotor cortex and sensory information from the parietal areas, the basal ganglia, and the sensory cortices.[84] The parietal cortex is particularly known for computing information from the environment, as well as the actual position of the body in space. Sensory cortices receive sensorial inputs from your eyes, ears, and even skin. All this information is computed and used to finalize the preparation of the motor plan in the premotor cortex.

Once the motor plan is realized, the information is sent to the primary motor cortex (M1), which executes the command by transmitting the information to the spinal cord and then to the muscles[85] (see Figure 3.1).

The brain circuit associated with the production of voluntary actions and the sense of agency has been illuminated by several neuroimaging studies as well as by lesion studies. In neuroscience, lesion studies have frequently been used to understand the implication of a specific brain region in a specific cognitive process. If a neuroscientist finds a patient with a lesion in a specific part of the brain, they can observe how this lesion affects the patient's cognition. For instance, if a patient comes to the hospital for a brain scan and this highlights an injury in a brain region thought to be associated with language comprehension, a neuropsychologist will conduct relevant tests. Let's say this patient shows a lower score in language

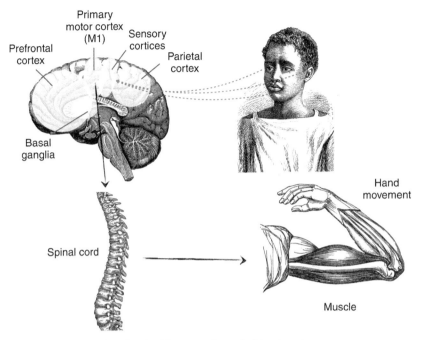

Figure 3.1 Brain regions involved in computing a decision to act

comprehension compared to noninjured individuals of the same age and educational level, but their other cognitive processes are still intact. An accumulation of evidence would allow researchers to infer that this particular brain region is associated with language comprehension.

Regarding the sense of agency, lesion studies have shown that an injury in the prefrontal cortex or in the parietal lobes alters the sense of agency and the perception of being in control over one's own actions. A team of researchers in 2004[86] observed that patients with brain damage in the parietal cortex have difficulties consciously monitoring their actions. In 2009,[87] the same team further used brain stimulation techniques in order to stimulate the parietal cortex. They confirmed their hypothesis. Indeed, brain stimulation is an incredible technique in neuroscience, as it allows researchers to interfere with the electrical activity of the targeted brain regions. We can see how the stimulation influences the cognitive processes of interest without having to wait to find a patient with a brain lesion in that particular area. Brain stimulation in fact helps reproduce, or simulate, lesions in the brain so we can study their effects on cognition and behavior.

Using brain stimulation, the team of researchers introduced above found that altering electrical activity in the parietal lobe led to a deficit in recognizing the action as one's own. Similarly, bypassing both the prefrontal and the parietal cortices by directly stimulating M1 made a movement happen in test subjects without triggering a corresponding feeling of agency. In other words, a person with altered electricity in the parietal lobe will not recognize a triggered movement as their own. They may thus experience a reduced feeling of responsibility for the consequences of the movement.

As this section shows, the sense of agency, despite being a subjective experience, is also a neural process that any healthy individuals experience over their actions. As we will see in the next section, the sense of agency is tightly linked to the feeling of responsibility and can help explain why people choose to act in a "good" or a "bad" way.

TAKING RESPONSIBILITY FOR ONE'S OWN ACTIONS

While almost all human actions have some external consequences, actions made in a social context are particularly important because their effects impact not only the agent themself but also other people. All human societies require and endorse individual responsibility: People are seen as being aware of their actions and their consequences on the world and on others. They should thus be able to choose right over wrong actions and behave responsibly.

In Roman law, an individual is held responsible for a crime not only when they acted (*actus reus*), but also when they had the conscious intention to act (*mens rea*). In order for an *actus reus* to be committed, there has to have been an act that involves a bodily movement, realized with or without the use of an external object. During a trial, the first step is thus to understand if the accused really committed the act based on the evidence. Evidence can be various, such as the presence of someone witnessing the scene, or fingerprints on the murder weapon. Evidence helps to determine with more or less certainty *actus reus*. If evidence is sufficient to demonstrate that the accused committed the act, it means they are causally responsible for the crime.

The second step consists in determining whether or not the act was intentional. Did the accused *mean* to hurt the victim? Or did they do it by accident or because they were under a delusional state at the moment of the act? The intentionality, or willingness, associated with the crime refers to *mens rea*. If experts agree that *mens rea* was missing during the act, responsibility can be called into question. For instance, it is widely assumed that schizotypal or psychotic patients are not responsible for their acts because they did not generate a conscious projection about their actual action. But one has still to prove or disprove that the accused was under such a state at the moment of the act – a task that falls mainly to psychiatric experts.

Determining the presence or absence of *actus reus* and *mens rea* can be a difficult mission, and many variables can complicate the task of judge and jury in establishing criminal responsibility. There is an example I particularly like to illustrate this complexity, which is known as the "Armadillo case." In April 2015, a man in the US shot an armadillo for reasons unknown. However, instead of stopping in the animal, the bullet ricocheted off the armadillo's armor, went through the back door of his mother-in-law's mobile home, continued through the chair she was sitting on, and hit her in the back.[88] *Actus reus* was clearly present, as the man indeed took the gun and pressed the trigger. But what about *mens rea*? In this absurd situation, did the man feel responsible for having hurt his mother-in-law? Should he have been able to predict that an armadillo's armor is sufficiently robust to deviate a bullet to such an extreme degree? Such can be the complexity of determining criminal responsibility.

Beyond legal responsibility determined by the justice system, however, is one's own perception of being a responsible agent, which can strongly influence choosing between right and wrong actions. That said, it is easier to find examples of humans minimizing their responsibility than examples of accepting responsibility for negative events.

Psychologists have for a long time recognized and quantified the tendency of humans to reduce their responsibility for the consequences of their actions, especially when the consequences of those actions are bad. One of the most common tendencies is known as the self-serving bias: Individuals have the tendency to take credit for positive events or outcomes, but blame others or outside factors for negative outcomes. This phenomenon can be observed in relation to severe and less severe events. If you successfully passed an exam, you may believe that it is because you studied hard. However, if you failed the exam, you are more likely to blame the teacher who did not explain the subject correctly or the neighbors who made too much noise the night before.

Self-serving is a cognitive bias that allows you to protect your self-esteem. When you attribute positive events to yourself, you boost your self-confidence. When you blame others for failures, you absolve yourself from personal responsibility, thus protecting your self-esteem.

Social desirability is another bias. Relatively close to the self-serving bias, it reflects how you wish to be perceived by society. It refers to the tendency of individuals to show favorable images of themselves and to act in a way that is thought to be appropriate during social interactions. For instance, if you are a heavy smoker, but you meet someone who dislikes cigarettes and who asks you if you smoke, you may be tempted to hide the fact that you smoke, or reduce your consumption by saying "Yeah, but just one or two cigarettes per week." However, you might tell the truth to another person smoking as well. Or if I asked if you use illicit substances, you might say, "Yes, but only when I am at a party with my friends" instead of revealing that you consume the substance more frequently. Being afraid of others' negative judgment leads to a tendency to reduce one's own culpability and responsibility for our behavior.

The self-serving bias and the social desirability bias complicate the task of psychologists evaluating human attitudes and behavior. When asked questions about their involvement in something, individuals may bias their answers, consciously or unconsciously, to fool themselves or people around them. This is particularly true for questionnaires, as participants can more easily guess what is being evaluated by researchers. I remember, for example, a narcissistic inmate that we tested in prison. He wanted us to guess how many degrees he had and how many languages he could speak. He repeatedly told us how smart he was and asked us to check on the Internet about who he was and what he did. And believe me, he perpetrated truly horrific acts against children. During the experiment, he answered a series of questionnaires, including one regularly used to measure narcissistic traits. Strangely, he scored low on almost every item. He told us at the end of the experiment that he wanted to be perceived as a good person by anyone reading his answers, even though he knew the data were processed anonymously.

Researchers using questionnaires thus have to be very careful to control for the self-serving bias and the social desirability bias, especially when the research project involves individual responsibility and moral decisions. By contrast, biases are easier to circumvent when using implicit or more objective measures and methods, such as neuroimaging.

So here is my question to you: Do you usually take responsibility for your actions?

You may be tempted to answer "Yes, of course," but please do not. The idea that you are not affected by cognitive biases is also a form of self-serving bias. If you think more carefully about it and try to find some examples, are you sure that you are not fooling yourself? Are you sure that you are totally unaffected by cognitive biases?

The notion of what is wrong can of course differ greatly between individuals in part because humans have different and competing values regarding what is moral or not and how one attributes responsibility for one's own acts. It is also clear that the tendency to minimize responsibility varies a lot between individuals and may also be driven by contextual factors. Personal factors also influence this tendency, such as age, culture, clinical diagnosis, and more. But the tendency to minimize our own responsibility for negative actions is observable widely across populations.

You may not have this tendency in all contexts, and some individuals have it more than others. But it is worth trying, instead, to take responsibility in your own life and for your actions. As we will see in the next section, the negation of responsibility is one of the critical factors enabling people to commit atrocities on the grounds that they were simply "obeying orders."

DIFFUSION OF RESPONSIBILITY BETWEEN INDIVIDUALS

A well-known psychological phenomenon associated with a reduction in feeling responsible is the so-called bystander effect.

In 1968, two researchers in social psychology, Bibb Latané and John Darley, created a study to investigate how the presence of others influences an individual's response to an emergency situation.[89] Their desire to understand how diffusion of responsibility influences human behavior was actually influenced by the high media coverage surrounding the case of Kitty Genovese.

On March 13, 1964, in Queens, New York City, Kitty Genovese was brutally attacked and murdered outside her apartment complex during the late evening hours. The attack was prolonged, lasting for over thirty minutes, and occurred in three separate phases. What made this case so shocking was that despite the numerous witnesses (37, as reported by the *New York Times*[90]) who were aware of the ongoing assault, no one intervened or called for help.

This story, which has been reported by many media, taught in many social psychology classes, and has even been the central story of many novels, was actually wrongly reported, with exaggerated or incorrect elements.[91] However, it has been clearly established in scientific experiments, such as that of Darley and Latané, that the presence of others reduces the likelihood that people will help in an emergency situation because it reduces their own implication and responsibility.

In Darley and Latané's study, participants were placed in separate rooms and told they would be taking part in a discussion through an intercom system. Unbeknownst to them, there were other participants in neighboring rooms who were actually confederates of the researchers. Suddenly, while engaged in the discussion, participants started hearing what sounded like another participant experiencing a seizure or medical emergency through the intercom. That person even reported that he could perhaps be dying.

The researchers observed that the level of intervention and time it took to report the emergency differed considerably depending on whether participants were alone in the task or if they were with other people. When participants were alone with the victim, 85 percent reported the emergency situation in an average of 52 seconds. However, if a third person was present, the percentage of reported emergencies dropped to 62 percent, taking an average of 93 seconds to make the report. With four other persons present, that percentage dropped again, with only 31 percent of participants reporting the emergency, and an average time of 166 seconds. In other words, for the latter group, 31 percent of the participants took almost 3 minutes to report the emergency.

Such effects, tested in many different experimental situations, have been largely replicated by different teams of researchers around the world, thus showing how robust this effect is.[92]

Diffusing responsibility between individuals is also a well-known mechanism to enable people to kill on command and to attenuate the psychological distress that may accompany their acts. For instance, to kill a condemned person, all members of a firing squad are instructed to fire simultaneously in order to obscure who fired the lethal shot and diminish the psychological consequences associated with killing another human being. Psychological distress is thus reduced for all members of the firing squad.

On a grander scale, diffusing responsibility between individuals engaging in group actions also allows the perpetration of massive exterminations such as those observed during genocides. As we have seen in Chapter 1, many former genocide perpetrators said that they took part in group attacks because of the group momentum.

A team of researchers tried to understand whether this diffusion of responsibility is a post-hoc experience which is likely to be influenced by the self-serving bias, or whether it has a direct effect on how our brains process the outcomes of our actions.[93] In their task, participants watched as a marble rolled down a bar, and they had to perform a keypress to stop it and prevent it from crashing. In one experimental condition, participants were performing the task alone, while in another experimental condition, another person was present. The experiment had a trick. Stopping the marble from crashing was costly: participants could lose points that gave extra remuneration after the task was completed. But not stopping it could also lead to a loss of points. Thus, the outcome was almost always negative for the participants. The reason for this setup was that researchers were interested in the phenomenon of diffusion of responsibility when acting has negative consequences. In the brain, there is a specific marker to process the negative consequences of our actions. It is called Feedback-Related Negativity (FRN). The FRN is a negative deflection in the brain's electrical activity that can be observed with electroencephalography. Its amplitude is typically measured, with a higher amplitude being associated with a higher neural processing of errors or negative feedback. In the present study, the author measured the amplitude of the FRN when participants received negative feedback (i.e., losing points) when they played alone or together with another player. The researchers also asked participants about their sense of agency during the experiment.

The first result is that participants reported a lower agency when another player was present compared to when they were alone. This is very interesting because participants were always the authors of their actions in the two experimental conditions. Yet their subjective experience of having control over the outcomes of their own actions was reduced by the mere presence of another person. When looking at the amplitude of the FRN, the researchers observed that it was also reduced, suggesting a lower processing by the brain, when they were together with another player compared to when they were acting alone. Again, the outcomes were exactly the same in the Alone and in the Together condition, so the FRN should not have differed in principle. Yet the social context clearly influenced its amplitude.

In other words, this study suggests that the mere presence of another potential agent was sufficient to reduce the sense of agency of the participants, as well as the neural processing of the outcomes of their actions.

Notably, in the case of obedience to authority, responsibility is not really *diffused* between individuals, but rather *displaced* – for example, from an executioner to a leader, or the opposite.[94] However, even if academics have created a conceptual distinction between a hierarchical situation and a group situation, the common factor is that responsibility is attenuated for all parties involved, thus potentially leading to malevolent acts.

Pol Pot, the leader of the Khmer Rouge, demonstrated how far obedience could go in human societies.[95] The Khmer Rouge regime, similar to that of the Nazis, perfectly understood that displacing responsibility between individuals at different levels of the chain creates a more efficient system to exterminate another group – the majority complies with those orders. During the Khmer Rouge regime, many cadres indeed reported a constrained agency over their acts given the highly hierarchical structure of the regime.[96] In the central extermination center S-21, a table of ten security regulations was displayed. Examples of these regulations include: "Do nothing, sit still, and wait for my orders. If there is no order, keep quiet. When I ask you to do something, you must do it right away without protesting"; or "If you disobey any point of my regulations, you will get either ten or five electric shocks." In this way, the Khmer Rouge regime created an army of fully obedient soldiers who have frequently been referred to as "killing machines" or "robotic obedient individuals."

More recently, a video showed heavily armed Russian soldiers shooting two unarmed Ukrainian civilians in the back and looting their business. One of those soldiers, a 21-year-old man, was caught and tried for war crimes. In front of the judges, he claimed that he just followed orders and succumbed to group pressure.[97]

Committing shocking acts on the grounds of obedience is not only a behavior observable during genocides and wars of aggression. There are countless examples in everyday civilian life in which people did appalling acts on the grounds of obedience. For instance, the boss of a company may urge you to remove from the application list candidates that are from a minority group. Since your boss is the one asking you to commit the act of discrimination, you might comply and subsequently experience a diminished sense of personal responsibility while doing so.[98]

In this book, genocides are a prime illustration of human behavior because they are an extreme example of what blind obedience can lead to. Genocides are, in fact, frequently referred to as crimes of obedience, with many of them having a majority of perpetrators complying with orders to kill as the commonality. Genocides thus represent an extreme form of violence with a massive extermination of human beings on the grounds of obedience.

Orchestrating a genocide nonetheless requires a revision of moral values, as perpetrators will commit acts that are prohibited in regular circumstances. In Rwanda, many of the genocide perpetrators never killed anyone before starting to kill their neighbors. Morality has thus to be neutralized in order to allow the cruelest acts to be committed.

The concept of moral neutralization refers to the many ways that perpetrators find to justify their acts and to avoid a dissonance between what they did and their morality. The more excuses you find to reduce your own implication in an event, the more likely you are to convince people to commit atrocious acts. As we have seen in Chapter 1, expressing an absence of responsibility is one of the main reasons for people to justify that they were just following orders, thus avoiding being held responsible and accountable for their actions.

In the case of genocide, the notion of what is wrong can differ drastically from regular peacetime. In peacetime, killing an individual is forbidden and leads to a prison sentence. During a war, the military are allowed to kill the enemy on the battlefield. During a genocide, however, even citizens can be called on by self-proclaimed officials to exterminate another group of individuals. More than seventy of the perpetrators interviewed by Kjell Anderson, a jurist and social scientist specialized in human rights, reported that the Rwandan government obliged them to kill Tutsis or they would be killed.[17] But the fact that the government authorized the act of killing led to people experiencing a reduced feeling of responsibility while doing it.

Having freedom to commit awful acts while not feeling fully responsible is an open door to a wide range of evil acts.

THE NEURAL ROOTS OF DIMINISHED AGENCY
AND RESPONSIBILITY IN OBEDIENCE SITUATIONS

We have seen that people claim diminished responsibility and agency when they obey orders. But does it reflect only a reconstructive process to preserve one's self-esteem and to avoid punishment? Or is our brain actually wired to experience less agency and responsibility when following orders?

When individuals claim reduced responsibility because they were "only obeying orders," this defense is often viewed with skepticism, because the defendant has a clear motive of avoiding punishment. However, scientific methods have not previously been used to investigate the *experience* of receiving orders and how it influences how the brain processes information. The subjective experience of acting under orders, and the effect of compliance on our cognition, are crucial aspects to understanding *how* and *why* people can be coerced.

During my PhD, I wished to understand whether obeying orders really alters the basic experiences of agency and responsibility and the underlying neuronal processes, or whether people merely *claim* a lack of responsibility for the outcomes of their actions. As cautioned in the Introduction to this book, the aim of studying the *experience* of agency in obedience with a neuroscience approach certainly did not aim to legitimate Nuremberg-type defenses. Based on Roman law, a reduced *mens rea* during an action would indeed be considered as a mitigating circumstance for attributing less accountability for an event. But every situation of obedience can be different, and the main difficulty is to understand each of them. On the one hand, there are situations with clear elements of coercion or immediate threats that might reduce the decisional processes of the person. This could entirely fall within the category where "obeying orders" becomes a more valid explanation and can be perceived as a mitigating circumstance. But some others might obey an order to hurt another person because they have a financial interest: receiving a monetary reward in case of contract killers, for instance, or looting, as seen during the genocide against the Tutsi in Rwanda. Their intrinsic motivation is thus drastically different than the first case, even though the result is the same. There are then also other cases when people follow the orders of an authority, for instance, because they are truly convinced that exterminating other people is the right thing to do following propaganda. For those individuals, obeying orders might be a deliberate decision. Even a good one, as they may feel less responsible for their actions while still conducting actions congruent with their own ideology. This is why I want to underline that experiencing a reduced sense of agency and responsibility at the neural level when obeying orders must not necessarily be taken as a reason for reducing accountability in the eyes of law. Every situation must be carefully examined, and the reasons for obeying orders must be understood.

Before presenting the results of the studies conducted, however, we must digress briefly to explain how the sense of agency is measured in cognitive neuroscience. Accessing the inner mental life of individuals can be challenging, since explicitly asking people questions about their implication in a moral context can be biased by a series of effects, including the self-serving bias and the social desirability bias discussed above. In the studies that we conducted, my colleagues and I could have simply asked our participants: Do you feel that you are the author of the action you just performed? But this question would have been unreliable for two reasons. First, cognitive biases can influence participants' answers. Second, the critical point of obedience situations is that agents are always the authors of their actions. There is absolutely no doubt about who performed the action. Thus, this question would be pointless.

So, we decided to use implicit methods in addition to neuroimaging and electrophysiology to access and measure the sense of agency and the feeling of responsibility under obedience.

Implicit methods refer to methods that allow us to investigate our targeted cognitive process without participants receiving any contextual clues about what we are investigating, thus limiting the influence of biases. In the sense-of-agency literature, the most common implicit method is based on time perception. Numerous studies have shown that when you perform voluntary actions, you have the impression that time elapses faster between your actions and their outcomes compared to when you perform involuntary or passive actions.

Let's take an example to illustrate this notion. When you are at work, if you are busy and active, time will appear to pass faster than if you are passively waiting for time to pass until you finish your working day. But every physicist will agree that time elapses at exactly the same speed in the two situations. Only your subjective perception of time will differ. This is an oversimplistic example, but the same principle has been used by neuroscientists to measure the sense of agency. In the most commonly used experimental approach, trial participants are told to press a button whenever they want. Pressing a button whenever one wants allows them to generate a sense of volition and intentionality over the action. After a few hundred milliseconds of pressing the button, participants hear a tone that is the consequence of their action. Their task is to report how many milliseconds elapsed between pressing the button and the tone.[99]

Participants usually have to perform such a task in two different conditions. In one condition, already explained, they press a button whenever they want, thus involving intentionality over the action. In another condition, the button press is made involuntarily, without any intentionality. Getting participants to produce an involuntary button press can, for instance, be done by the use of brain stimulation techniques. If an electrical stimulation is sent over the part of the motor cortex controlling the participant's finger movement, an involuntary button press will result. Again, participants have to report how many milliseconds elapsed between the involuntary button press and the tone.

Interestingly, while action–outcome intervals are physically exactly the same in both cases, it has been systematically reported in the literature that when people perform voluntary button presses, they report shorter time intervals compared to a situation in which the movement is involuntarily performed. Studies using such techniques thus show that volition influences time perception by making it seem to elapse faster.

The relationship between time perception and the sense of agency can appear indirect and odd at first sight. However, the scientific literature has indicated that the link between agency and time is mediated by the involvement of striatal dopaminergic activity. Striatal dopaminergic activity refers to the level of dopamine – a neurotransmitter that is involved in many important functions in the brain, including motivation, pleasure, and attention – released in the striatum. Striatal dopaminergic activity is also crucial for time perception[100] and drives information from basal ganglia to frontal motor areas,[101] both key brain regions in generating a sense of agency.

Notably, these studies rely on indirect evidence, since no study has reliably investigated the neurobiological basis of the experience of agency (yet). Nonetheless, several studies have shown that the dopaminergic system appears not to work normally in schizophrenia patients.[102] Further, most of the antipsychotic medications for schizophrenia patients are dopaminergic.[103] This additional evidence appears to support the involvement of dopaminergic activity in the sense of agency, thus supporting the relationship between time perception and the sense of agency.

With this understanding of how the sense of agency is measured through implicit methods and the brain circuits associated with the sense of agency, let's go back to the main question of this chapter: What are the neural roots of diminished agency and responsibility in obedience situations?

To answer this question, my colleagues and I adapted the paradigm explained in Chapter 2 in order to measure the sense of agency under coercion with implicit methods, using the task of interval estimates described above. On each trial, participants had to press either the SHOCK key or the NO SHOCK key. As a reminder, when they were pressing the SHOCK key, they delivered a real but calibrated painful electric shock to the other participant and earned +€0.05 in addition to their baseline remuneration. To measure the sense of agency, a tone was displayed after each keypress, no matter whether a shock was delivered or not, and participants had to report the time that elapsed between the keypress and the tone in milliseconds. Critically, they had to do it in both a free-choice condition, in which they could freely decide whether or not to deliver a shock during the course of sixty trials, and in a coerced condition, in which the experimenter ordered them to press a certain key.[73]

We observed that obeying orders led to the interval between action and tone being perceived as longer than when the action was freely chosen. Participants indeed reported that more milliseconds elapsed between their action and the resulting tone in the coerced condition when compared to the free-choice condition. This result implies that participants felt less agency over the outcomes of their actions when they were told what to do, compared to when they decided for themselves. And with this approach, participants could not make the link between a task of interval estimates and the assessment of their sense of agency, thus limiting the possibility that this effect is driven by social desirability.

This result really surprised us at first because, in both cases – that is, whether people can freely decide or are instructed – they are *always* the author of their actions. There is no doubt regarding who pressed the key, and we did not use brain stimulation techniques that could have made them press the key. Participants simply received an order to deliver or not deliver a shock to the "victim"; they just had to execute the motor action associated with the order. Importantly, this result has been replicated many times, including by other research teams and with different forms of pain.[104,73]

Interestingly, when asked explicitly about their feeling of responsibility, our volunteers reported that they did feel more responsible in the free-choice compared to the coerced condition. Considering that experiencing agency is a condition for experiencing responsibility, our results suggest that people who obey orders could actually feel less responsible for the outcomes of their action: They may not be simply *claiming* that they feel less responsible. People appear to experience a sort of distance from the outcome of their actions when they are obeying instructions. To reiterate, however, it is important to distinguish between how our minds generate our subjective feelings of responsibility, and the objective facts of responsibility. *Feeling* less responsible does not necessarily imply that you *aren't* responsible and should not be held responsible by society. As mentioned before, the circumstances for agreeing to follow orders may differ considerably from one situation to another, and sometimes agreeing to follow an order is a decision in itself. In the end, society has to deal with the objective facts of what an individual does.

We then sought to understand how obeying orders influences the brain circuits associated with the sense of agency and the feeling of responsibility.[105] We thus adapted our paradigm to an MRI scanner environment and ran our first study at the Wellcome Trust for Neuroimaging in London. Now, if you have ever gone to a hospital to get an MRI scan, you may remember that you are isolated in a narrow and noisy cylinder. If you are claustrophobic, it may have even been one of your worst life experiences. Because of the narrowness and the noisiness of MRI scanners, it is difficult to preserve social interactions. The person being scanned is totally isolated. Thus, social neuroscientists have to use their ingenuity to preserve social interactions and study social behaviors when they do MRI scanning.

In our case, using an MRI to understand the brain circuits associated with a reduction of agency under coercion meant that our agents were isolated from the experimenter, but also from the "victim." To prevent the loss of social contact, we used two means. First, agents received instructions from the experimenter through headphones. In addition to being very narrow, MRI scanners are extremely noisy. Even if I had been sitting next to the participants in the scanner room, they would not have heard me at all. Second, we used a real-time camera to record the victim's hand receiving the shocks and display it inside the MRI scanner. Agents could thus visualize the outcomes of their actions on the victim even while isolated in the scanner.

Again, we used an implicit measure of the sense of agency – based on the perceived interval between an action and its outcome – to measure the degree to which the sense of agency is affected by obedience to orders. And once again, results indicated that the reduction of agency and responsibility in obedience situations may actually be strongly rooted in our biology. We observed that the sense of agency and the feeling of responsibility were associated with activity in the medial frontal gyrus, which is located in the frontal lobe in a region associated with voluntary action selection.[106] More specifically, we observed that people who had the most reduced feeling of agency when obeying orders also had the most reduced activity in this brain region. A similar effect was found using explicit responsibility ratings: The more participants reported that they experienced feeling responsible for their actions in the coerced condition, the more activity was observable in the medial frontal gyrus.

These findings suggest that volitional processes during action planning and execution may help to preserve a strong sense of agency under coercion.

THE IMPACT OF HIGHLY HIERARCHICAL SOCIAL STRUCTURES

All the research I have described thus far has been obtained from civilians, who are not frequently confronted with situations of strict compliance to rules. Of course, even as civilians, we all have to face compliance to some rules. It could be from our boss, from the police, from our parents. But in some social structures, such as the armed forces, there is a strict hierarchical organization where people are required to follow orders. For example, the professional role of military personnel implies compliance to hierarchical authority, based on the mandate society has given to that authority.

A critical question is thus to understand how working in such an environment influences our sense of agency when performing free-choice acts and obedience acts. Focusing on the military and hierarchical environments can provide a nuanced understanding of the complex interplay between authority, obedience, and the sense of agency. It allows researchers to explore the psychological and sociocultural factors that shape individuals' decision-making in situations where authority figures hold significant power and influence. It could be surmised that working in an environment that involves daily compliance would have a detrimental effect on one's own sense of agency, since obedience has been found to have a detrimental effect on agency.

This is the hypothesis we wanted to test in our research with the military.

I have to admit that it did not even cross my mind to conduct my studies on the military until I met the Lieutenant-Colonel Salvatore Lo Bue in a conference. As already underlined, in neuroscience, researchers focus mostly on students from the universities, or on patients with cerebral damage. And when you are taught over your entire academic path about studies only focusing on these samples, it can be difficult to think outside the box and open your mind to other options. Including the military in my research is highly relevant, but it probably would have taken me a few more years to realize its relevance and value.

But I was lucky enough to meet Salvatore at the Belgian Association for Psychological Science in 2016. I was presenting a poster on the results of my study on how coercion influences the sense of agency. Salvatore, in addition to being a military officer, also held a PhD in psychology. He was appointed as a psychology professor at the Royal Military Academy in Belgium, and he remained interested in research activities. In fact, he was at this conference to try to find opportunities for collaboration. We discussed my results, and the scientific match was obvious. Something I have learned over the years is that it is always easier when you find someone interested in what you do. The doors will open far more easily after that.

I thus started to consider conducting projects in a military environment. Admittedly, this is a very intriguing world for a civilian to enter. Such an organized structure, such organized people, so many rules. I remember once I was eating with a colleague while we were on a military base between two testing sessions. It was wintertime and really cold outside, so I came with my jacket. When I sat down, I put the jacket on the back of my chair and started eating. Two military personnel approached me and requested

that I remove the jacket. I spontaneously asked why, since I like to understand the reasons for obeying rules. But that is not something you do in the
military. They just told me it was the rule and that I had to do it, so I just put
my jacket on the chair next to mine, which was okay. I never understood
what the point was with the jacket on the back of the chair, but, in any case,
I realized the potential to conduct research projects on this population the
moment I entered the environment.

Indeed, the military is a highly hierarchical institution, composed of
dozens of military ranks, each associated with specific responsibilities.
Very roughly, you have those acting to execute an order, and you have
those giving orders. Of course, this distinction is really too simplistic
because you still have several ranks that determine your function and
ability to make decisions. Broadly speaking, in the military, orders are
generally embedded in a very long chain of command, with higher-
ranked officers transmitting orders to lower-rank officers who are themselves sending the orders to those executing them.

How would working in such an environment influence one's sense of
agency?

Together with my colleagues, we conducted a first study to compare
civilians to junior cadets from the academy.[107] Junior cadets are individuals who are in their first year at the military academy and are seeking to
become officers. We replicated our paradigm for research testing, but we
also wanted to evaluate if the identity of the person giving the orders
would influence the results. In the military, receiving orders from
a civilian or from a ranked officer makes a huge difference. Half of our
sample was thus tested by Salvatore and the other half was tested by my
colleague and friend, Pedro. I was present as well, but simply presented as
a research assistant.

We observed that for both groups, agency was low when they were
obeying orders. But critically, for junior cadets, their sense of agency was
also low when they were free to decide which button to press. These
results were intriguing because they suggest that being in a highly hierarchical environment and drilled to follow orders makes you process
your free decisions as if they had been ordered. Critically, this effect
was present no matter who the experimenter was. That is, the effect was
not stronger for the ranked officers than for the civilian experimenter.

This result replicated something that we had actually already observed in another study:[108] The identity of the experimenter giving orders does not influence the sense of agency. It does not mean that in a war situation obedience would be similar if orders are issued by a civilian or by a ranked officer, of course. Our experiment was not comparable to any war situation. But the study does suggest that obedience effects do not depend on the particular social status of the person giving orders. Rather they reflect a more general difference between coercion and autonomy contexts. In other words, once an individual has agreed to comply with the orders of another person, the effect that obedience has on the sense of agency is the same.

The year after, we decided to conduct an extra study, this time recruiting different categories of military members. We recruited three groups of military personnel: privates, junior cadets, and senior cadets. In comparison with junior cadets, seniors have received on average five years of officer training and have reached the rank of lieutenant. They have thus worked for longer within the military than junior cadets and have been trained to be accountable for their own actions (including giving orders to others). Privates correspond to troop soldiers and are mostly at the level of receiving orders to execute. They have a lower rank within the military system and, in comparison to cadets, accountability is less emphasized during their training and career, although they work for a similar number of years in this type of organization.

The idea was that by comparing those groups, we would be able to understand how prolonged experience in the social environment of a military organization influences the sense of agency when people obey orders and how the different notions of responsibility enshrined in the training of officers and of ordinary soldiers might influence the sense of agency.

The results were interesting. We observed, yet again, that for junior cadets there was no difference in agency between deciding freely and obeying orders. We observed that this was also the case for the privates: They had a low sense of agency when they could freely decide, thus showing that working for a prolonged period in a military environment is negative for the sense of agency. But the most interesting results were for senior cadets – those military officers trained to be accountable for their actions and the actions of their troops. We observed that these military officers had a high sense of agency when they could freely decide, even while working in a military environment.

If we can observe that military officers have a higher sense of agency due to their training associated with greater accountability and responsibility, can we imagine transposing such training to civilian life? Could such training involve a greater responsibility over one's own actions for civilians as well? This is certainly something I would like to see implemented in the future.

CONCLUSION

Healthy humans have a biological disposition to experience a feeling of authorship and responsibility. However, as this chapter shows, obeying orders impacts the sense of agency at the brain level, which demonstrates the power of obedience situations. Such findings can also explain why perpetrators of genocide claim no responsibility when they obey orders. On the one hand, there is an attempt to reduce individual accountability to avoid prosecution. But on the other hand, choosing to obey orders has a negative influence on a person's sense of agency and responsibility, which may prevent them from taking the full measure of their decisions.

CHAPTER 4

Moral Emotions under Obedience

YOU HAVE PROBABLY WATCHED THE FAMOUS 1942 DISNEY movie, *Bambi* – one of the most-watched films of all time. Even without reading further, you may already have a clue as to which scene I am about to discuss. You are perhaps already apprehending the feelings you may start to experience, and I apologize in advance for awaking the negative emotions associated with this scene. But for those who may not have seen the film, I have to relate it.

At around the thirty-sixth minute, we see Bambi and his mother. They are starving, enduring a harsh winter. While searching for food, they suddenly find a small area of grass to graze. But suddenly, Bambi's mother straightens. She has heard hunters. Sensing the danger, she tells Bambi to run back into the forest as fast as he can in order to hide. She runs after him, urging him to continue while gunshots are heard in the distance.

Suddenly, the gunshots are louder, and you no longer hear Bambi's mother urging her son to hide. Bambi safely enters the deep forest and starts enjoying the fact that they can now be safe. But Bambi's mother does not arrive. He leaves the forest to look for her, desperately calling her in hope of an answer. But after several minutes of searching, Bambi meets the Great Prince of the forest, who tells him that he would no longer see his mother.

At that precise moment, in a scene considered one of the most significant moments in cinematic history, you may have cried. You likely felt all of Bambi's distressing emotions. Why? Because you have *empathy*.

You can probably think of dozens of examples right now of moments in your life where you felt the pain and distress of another human being.

When we witness another person experiencing pain, be it emotional or physical, we have an empathic reaction. And this is thought to be what makes us averse to harming others. Empathy can be broadly described as the capacity to feel and understand the emotions of others. It has been extensively studied by a vast range of disciplines and can have various definitions. This chapter takes a neuroscientific approach to illuminate how empathy occurs in the brain, how this neurological capacity can influence our decisions to act in a prosocial way towards others, and how our inner capacity for empathy is influenced by obeying orders.

OUR BRAINS ARE WIRED TO FEEL EMPATHY

Empathy is an incredible capacity for shaping and coloring our social interactions, as it allows us to understand how others feel. Understanding the feelings of others is of course also shaped by both environmental factors – such as our culture, education or life experiences – and context-ual factors. But first and foremost, our capacity to empathize with others is wired deep inside our brains. Empathy is primarily an inner capacity that all humans possess.

Theoretical developments have suggested that empathy is composed of three different subprocesses, which are supported by distinct neural systems. They include *experience sharing*, which allows us to understand and imagine what others feel by processing their emotions and pain within our own neural system; *mentalizing*, which corresponds to our capacity to understand the internal states of others and their thoughts; and *empathic concern*, which refers to our feelings of compassion and care towards others.

Empathy can be triggered by the emotional states of others, but also by the psychological and physical pain that they can experience. Here, we will mostly focus on *empathy for physical pain*. We will try to understand why, when someone inflicts physical pain on another person after obey-ing an order, they do not appear to experience much empathy for the pain they caused. In fact, they can sometimes even go beyond the act of killing on command by brutalizing and torturing the human targets.

If you hurt yourself by cutting your finger with a knife while cooking, your brain will process that painful sensation. Anatomically, the nociceptors in your fingers will send the pain message to the spinal cord, up to the brainstem and the thalamus, and then to brain regions that involve the secondary somatosensory cortex, insular regions, and the anterior cingulate cortex, as well as motor-related brain regions such as the supplementary motor area and the cerebellum.[109] This neural pathway, or pain network, is what makes you feel the pain.

Notably, our ability to feel pain protects us from harm and is critical for our survival. Patients suffering from congenital insensitivity, for instance, which is a medical condition that suppresses the ability to feel pain, have a higher rate of early mortality compared to others.

In 2004, a team of researchers led by Tania Singer published a study in the prestigious *Science Magazine*, which revolutionized the field of social neuroscience.[110] The authors' idea was to understand to what extent this pain network is also activated when individuals witness someone else suffering from the same pain. They invited sixteen couples to take part in the study. The female partner was placed in the MRI scanner and her partner was sitting nearby. With a system of mirrors, the female partner could see both herself and her partner receiving painful stimulations from within the MRI scanner. The painful device consisted in electrodes placed on their hands and connected to a machine that was sending electrical stimulations. The intensity of the stimulations was determined prior to the scanning session in order to ensure that the selected threshold was at the pain level. In different trials, the female partner could see either herself or her partner receiving either a high stimulation (pain) or a low stimulation (no pain).

Similar to previous studies, the authors observed that when female partners were seeing and experiencing their own pain, it activated the pain network. Interestingly, when they were seeing the pain of their partner, it activated a part of that pain network as well, especially the anterior cingulate cortex and in the anterior insula, brain regions that are part of the limbic system (Figure 4.1).

The limbic system, commonly referred to as the emotional brain, is a deep, subcortical, brain structure. It has been mostly associated with emotions and affective states and behaviors.*[111] The results show that

---

* Affect, emotions, and mood are interconnected but distinct psychological constructs. Affect is a comprehensive term that encompasses various feelings, including emotions

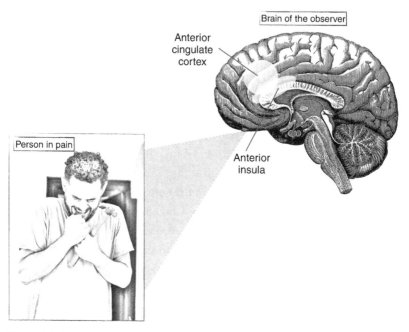

Figure 4.1 Brain regions involved in our understanding of others' pain. When we witness someone in pain, it triggers activity in the anterior insula and anterior cingulate cortex, which helps us understand the pain of others.

witnessing the pain of others does not trigger the entire pain matrix, but just a part of it specifically located in the limbic system, which is important. This indicates that witnessing someone else in pain does not, in fact, trigger a sensory pain feeling, but rather an emotional and affective feeling towards that pain. In other words, you will not physically feel the pain of others, but you will affectively process it and understand it.

The results obtained by Tania Singer and her colleagues have now been replicated many times, even on people who are not engaged in a romantic relationship. Empathy is thus frequently defined in neuroscience as our capacity to feel what others feel as it triggers a similar brain

and moods. Emotions are intense, brief feelings directed at a specific stimulus, while moods are less intense and more enduring mental states that may not be tied to a specific trigger. For example, if someone experiences a negative event, an emotion may develop into a mood, with a persistent and general sense of sadness without specific triggers.

response. Our brains are wired to process the pain of others by making us imagine and understand what others experience. Neuroscientists have associated empathy and its interindividual variation with how strongly participants activate brain regions involved in their own actions, emotions, and sensations while viewing those of others.[112]

But what is the mechanism behind such shared activation? Why do the anterior cingulate cortex and the anterior insula activate when one both experiences pain and observes someone else experiencing the same pain? To answer this question, we have to turn to mirror neurons and animal studies.

The storyline behind the discovery of the mirror neurons is actually very nicely related by one of my former mentors Christian Keysers in his book *The Empathic Brain*.[113] Christian worked at the University of Parma in Italy with the team who discovered the presence of mirror neurons in the brain, notably with Giacomo Rizzolatti. The interesting part of the story, beyond the fact that the discovery of mirror neurons has revolutionized the field of neuroscience, is how this discovery was actually made. Sometimes, the greatest revolutions come from random events, and this is the case here.

Rizzolatti and his team were recording the electrical activity from neurons in the premotor cortex of macaque monkeys in order to study the implication of these neurons in the planning and initiation of movements.[114] The electrodes were placed within several individual neurons and connected to a device that produced noise each time the neuron was fired. With this device, the researchers could tell when the neuron was activated, as they could hear the noise on the machine. But one day, the researchers did not turn off the equipment and went for lunch.

One of the researchers came back and started eating an ice cream in front of the monkey, which still had the activated device on its brain. To his surprise, the machine started to produce the noise that is produced when the neurons are firing. Yet the monkey was not moving. It was just passively watching the researcher eating his ice cream.

This neural response obviously puzzled the research team, so they decided to do some extra tests. They realized that when the monkey was the one making a movement to bring food to its own mouth, the machine was producing the expected noise. But the noise was also present when the monkey was observing the research team bringing food to *their* mouths. It also worked with other small experiments such as grasping objects or watching the experimenter grasping an object. In other words, even if the monkey is not moving, those neurons in the premotor cortex are *mirroring* the observed actions. This is how *mirror neurons* were discovered, the term "mirror" coming from the fact that those neurons mirror the information that is brought to them.

While this discovery was truly groundbreaking and eventually revolutionized neuroscience (as well as other fields), the researchers took years to realize what they had discovered. The study was initially published in a small neuroscience journal and was barely cited by other researchers. Nowadays, however, after some decades of additional research, neuroscientists have been able to discover that those mirror neurons are not only present in the motor cortex, but also in other parts of the brain, such as the anterior cingulate cortex and the anterior insula, thus also explaining why those regions allow us to process the emotions and the pain of others. Due to the presence of mirror neurons, the anterior cingulate cortex and the anterior insula mirror what another person feels, thus allowing us to understand their emotional and physical states.

A common example is yawning. If a person next to you is yawning, you will probably yawn yourself. In some cases, it also works if you watch a movie character yawning, you see your pet dog or cat yawning, or if you hear someone yawning. Just by seeing yawning being written, you could eventually yawn right now. This is not just an impression. Yawning is actually contagious, and there is a scientific explanation behind this phenomenon. In 2013, a team of researchers from Zurich put eleven volunteers in MRI scanners and showed them videos of other humans yawning, laughing, or with neutral expressions.[115] As the researchers expected, when the volunteers saw a video of someone yawning, they yawned themselves in more than 50 percent of the cases. When they were experiencing the contagious yawning, brain activity was present in the inferior frontal gyrus, a brain region known to have mirror neurons. Interestingly, this brain activity was not present when volunteers were seeing other videos with neutral expressions. But when you see someone yawning, mirror neurons present the action of yawning in your own brain, which can as a result influence your behavior and make you yawn.

Proving the existence of mirror neurons in the human brain is complex, as it requires invasive techniques. Single neuron procedures – such as the one Rizzolatti used on the macaque monkeys – are very invasive as they require opening the scalp to access the brain and position the electrodes on specific individual neurons. While this procedure is authorized to be performed on animals under some very strict regulations, those techniques are ethically not authorized on humans. The unique opportunity we have for doing single-neuron recording in the human brain is on patients who are going to have brain surgery, when their brain is going to be open anyway, such as in the case of a cingulotomy procedure. And this is actually what a team of researchers did in 2010.[116] They recorded the activity from a thousand cells in the medial frontal cortex and in the temporal cortices while patients were executing or observing hand-grasping actions. They observed that while some cells reacted only to action execution, some were active both during action execution and action observation, thus suggesting evidence for the presence of mirror neurons in humans as well.

Evidence suggesting that there are also mirror neurons in the anterior cingulate cortex and anterior insula, key brain regions for empathy, have not been fully proven in humans yet because these are deeper brain regions and difficult to access. Evidence from the presence of mirror neurons in the anterior cingulate cortex and insula thus come from animal studies. Yet using animals to study empathy has also provided an opportunity to understand if nonhuman species have empathy and how this process has grown over the course of evolution.

We tend to believe that us humans are the only species able to feel moral sentiments and feel empathy for others. Animals have generally been considered as "soulless" entities, unable to process the pain of others. This idea has clearly been challenged by recent neuroscientific studies, however, which have shown that plenty of other species have an empathic reaction to the pain of other members of the same species. Actually, many prosocial behaviors associated with empathy, such as avoiding hurting others for food, are also present in different animal species.

In a recent study, a research team from the Netherlands Institute for Neurosciences in Amsterdam trained several rats to press one out of two levers,[117] both associated with the same food reward. After some training, the rats could successfully distinguish between the two levers, developing of natural preference for one of them. Once the rats had developed their preference for one lever, the researchers slightly changed their device, so that one of the levers was associated with an unpleasant electric shock delivered to another rat. This modification made the rats decrease their preference for the lever delivering shocks to others, in favor of the one that was not associated with discomfort in the other rat. This was true for cage mates but also for total stranger pairs of animals. These results thus show that rats, like humans, are averse to causing harm to others.

In addition to the literature showing that in humans the anterior cingulate cortex is critical to perceiving the pain of others, several rodent studies offered evidence that this region contains mirror neurons. The same researchers administered a local analgesic in the anterior cingulate cortex of the rats, thus reducing the activity in this brain region, and made them perform the same task. Under the local analgesic, rats stopped avoiding hurting other rats: to get the candy, they pressed the lever that was associated with the shocks, even if the other lever also provided food without causing pain in others. The rats could, however, still switch levers in another task, suggesting that the anterior cingulate cortex is specifically involved in the emotional social component of pain.

Other studies have proved similarly suggestive. When mice witness other mice receiving several electric shocks on their feet, they develop a freezing behavior that mirrors the receiver's reaction. This effect is amplified when the mice receiving the foot shocks are socially related to them, such as mating partners or siblings. In a study conducted in 2010,[118] when a team of researchers deactivated the anterior cingulate cortex, this freezing behavior was impaired. In another study conducted in 2020,[119] a team of researchers trained six rhesus monkeys to indicate if they preferred to keep juice for themselves, give it to another monkey, or do neither. Overall, all six monkeys showed a preference for keeping the juice for themselves first, but then they all selected giving it to the other monkey rather than doing neither. They thus showed a preference for prosocial actions over neutral actions. However, three of those monkeys underwent surgery, with the researchers creating artificial lesions in their anterior cingulate cortex. The three others did not undergo surgery and were kept as controls. Results showed that while the two groups of monkeys displayed similar prosocial preferences before the surgery, prosocial preferences for the other monkeys tended to be reduced after the surgery compared to the control group. Further, the researchers tested whether or not the monkeys could develop novel prosocial preferences after the created lesion, as they did before the surgery. The researchers observed that the monkeys that underwent surgery could not develop new prosocial preferences while the control group could.

Studying empathy in nonhuman species helps us understand how this neural capacity evolved over the course of evolution. Rodents, for instance, diverged on the evolution tree around 90 million years ago,[120] thus showing how old our aversion to hurting others is.

But the question remains: How does empathy motivate prosocial behavior?

The term *prosocial behavior* refers to any actions that aim to alleviate another organism's suffering and to improve its welfare.[121] Empathy plays a critical role in promoting prosocial behavior and reducing others' distress. If you are walking in the street and suddenly see a person sitting on a bench crying, if you can't prevent yourself from imagining their pain, you are more likely to go and sit next to that person and see if you can be of any help. Seeing and understanding the distress of others can indeed motivate helping behavior.[122] If your actions cause pain to someone else, the more you experience this pain yourself, the less likely you are going to cause extra pain to that person.

Even though empathy plays a critical role in promoting prosocial behavior, their relationship is of course not absolute. It would be too easy to make the world a better place to live if empathy alone as a neural process had to be targeted. Not all forms of prosocial behavior are elicited by empathy. Sharing and cooperating are good examples here, as these behaviors can be triggered without feeling empathy for the other persons involved.[123] Other cognitive processes also explain prosociality, such as the sense of agency, the feeling of being responsible for one's own action, compassion, the ability to understand others, emotion processing, emotion regulation, and how rewarding it is to help others. For instance, people may engage in acts that violate their self-interest in order to benefit others, even though such actions may seem counterintuitive for our own survival or wellbeing. When you give up your seat to an elderly person on the bus, you accept that you will continue the bus journey in a less comfortable position, standing on your feet. When you give money to charity, you accept that you are donating your own money with which you could have bought things for yourself. When you hold the elevator for another person to come in, you accept that you are losing time.

Despite the fact that these decisions may affect your welfare, most of the people engaging in prosocial acts actually feel very good. You likely smile after performing an altruistic or prosocial act. You probably feel a deep satisfaction after helping someone. Numerous studies conducted in psychology and neuroscience have actually shown that prosocial actions are rewarding. For instance, people tend to report a higher sense of wellbeing after engaging in prosocial actions such as donating to charity[124] or after spending money on others rather than on oneself.[125] Neuroscience research has shown that when people make charitable donations, it activates brain regions in the mesolimbic system associated with reward processing.[126] The mesolimbic system involves the ventral tegmental area, a deep midbrain structure that contains only roughly 5,000 neurons. Five thousand neurons are almost nothing if you consider that the human brain has billions of neurons. However, those neurons in the ventral tegmental area have long connections – the maximum recorded so far is 74 cm – and pass into different brain regions, including the limbic system. They are thus involved in highly diverse brain functions. It turns out that these neurons are also involved in the transmission of dopamine, a neurotransmitter involved in several brain functions, such as reward processing, learning, addiction, or gambling. When you are eating delicious food[127] or when you have won money,[128] it produces activation in the dopaminergic midbrain that causes you to consider such events rewarding.

When you choose prosocial acts, it activates similar brain regions, suggesting that you are processing these events as positively rewarding.

But it may be important to underline that sometimes empathy, as an emotional response to others' suffering, can lead to biased and irrational decision-making. Paul Bloom, a prominent psychologist, wrote a book entitled *Against Empathy: The Case for Rational Compassion.*[129] He highlights that empathy can be narrow and favor people we love and care about while inducing negative attitudes towards people that we do not consider as part of our own group. Bloom proposes that instead of relying solely on empathy, rational compassion, which involves more objective and thoughtful consideration of the broader consequences, should be promoted for making ethical and just decisions. A section dedicated to the human tendency to categorize each other into groups will be addressed later in this chapter, as it is a fundamental component that is frequently observed and justified in many conflicts, wars, and genocides.

INCREASED AGGRESSION, REDUCED EMPATHY, AND EMPATHY REGULATION

Understanding the link, as we now do, between empathy and prosocial behaviors, what can we glean about reduced empathy? Specifically, this section explores whether increased aggression when obeying orders can be explained by a reduced empathy. How do we explain that in Rwanda, for example, many citizens who had never killed anyone before started to massacre, mutilate, and torture their neighbors? Our inner capacity to feel empathy for the pain we cause should prevent these unnecessary and perverse atrocities.

In my quest to understand how obeying orders affects behavior, I naturally started to investigate whether our capacity to feel empathy is blurred or diminished when we follow orders.

I developed this line of research between 2017 and 2019, when I was a postdoctoral researcher under the supervision of Christian Keysers and Valeria Gazzola at the Netherlands Institute for Neurosciences in Amsterdam. We decided to replicate the paradigm described in Chapter 1 inside an MRI scanner,[130] but this time, we wanted to focus on empathy as a neural process of interest. Again, we had an agent and a victim, the agent being located inside the MRI scanner and the victim outside the scanner. We used the system of real-time video recording to display, in real time, the hand of the victim receiving the painful shocks on the screen of the agent inside the scanner.

To measure empathy for pain, a critical aspect is that participants have to see the pain being delivered. If they close their eyes, or if they do not see clearly the painful event, you are less likely to see activity in brain regions associated with pain processing. The procedure with the shocks is thus particularly relevant here. When the electrical stimulation is delivered, as the electrodes are placed on the muscles of the victim's left hand, it produces a visible muscular contraction for each shock received. This visible element is what triggers the neural empathic response in the brain of the observer. In a free-choice condition, agents could freely decide to deliver a shock to the victim to earn +€0.05. In the other condition, the agents received orders from the experimenter to deliver the shock or not. Again, due to the high level of noise produced by the MRI scanner, agents received the orders through headphones, but I was present in the room to reinforce the impression that I was actually commanding and giving real-time orders. However, I had to hide from the participants' view to avoid creating extra activity in the occipital cortex if participants were watching me. The occipital cortex, located at the back of the brain, is indeed primarily responsible for processing visual stimuli, translating incoming light signals from the eyes into coherent visual images.

For the behavioral results, we observed that our participants administered fewer shocks when they could choose, compared to when they followed my orders, which had a fixed number of shocks being ordered (i.e., 30). However, nothing prevented them from disobeying those orders, even if they were not explicitly told so.

Critically for our research question, neuroimaging results showed that empathy-related regions were less active when obeying orders compared to acting freely. We indeed observed that brain activity, notably in the anterior cingulate cortex and the anterior insula, was reduced when our participants obeyed orders compared to when they freely decided.

These results confirm that obeying orders impacts our capacity to empathize with others. And after this seminal study, we actually replicated the effects several times, even with other methods such as electroencephalography,[131] which measures brain activity in real time. This finding is particularly interesting because our participants knew that the pain intensity of the shocks was exactly the same across the two experimental conditions. They tested the machine before starting the experiment and they were explicitly told that the threshold would never change during the experiment. The electric shock, which was exactly the same between the two situations, was nonetheless processed as less painful when an individual obeys an order. These results highlight how obeying an order relaxes our aversion to harming others, despite still being the author of the action that led to the pain.

It is also possible that such reduced empathy when people follow orders explains why genocide perpetrators often brutalize their victims before killing them in a manner that exceeds the orders received. By not feeling empathy for their target, they might be more inclined to vent their rage. But future research should be conducted to confirm or refute this hypothesis.

I remember a discussion that I had with one volunteer after the experiment. He told me he knew of Stanley Milgram's experiments and that, before coming to the experiment, he was planning not to deliver any shocks to the "victim" participant and not to obey my orders. Yet, while he did not administer shocks to the victim when he could freely decide, he did obey all my orders to send the shocks. When we discussed this, he told me that he was actually very surprised by his obedient behavior and how simple it was to just follow orders. He added that disobeying would have been more demanding on him and that administering shocks when receiving orders was just an easier option – and one for which he did not feel fully responsible. He told us that this experiment really disturbed him because he did not think he was capable of obeying such orders.

He is actually not the only participant to express this kind of response. We had numerous people who came to participate and who were actually planning to resist orders. Yet none of them did, and they all told us how "easy" or "simple" it was to just follow orders, even if those orders involved administering real pain to someone else. It is not as if you can't feel empathy in coercive situations. It is just easier not to feel it. As we will see in the next section, empathy is a capacity that we can also control and regulate.

Of course, in this experimental setup, pain is real but tolerable as based on one's own pain threshold. We thus cannot directly relate the fact of delivering a painful shock to someone else to mass atrocities that are conducted on the grounds of obedience. Yet, if in an experimental scenario with controlled pain we can observe that simply obeying orders impacts our capacity to feel the pain of others compared to acting freely, it is likely that in the context of a genocide or any obedience-based acts, this effect is amplified.

So, the question remains: To what extent can people control their empathy?

As we have seen, empathy is deeply ingrained in our brain with the presence of mirror neurons and is shared by numerous other species. You have thus no reason not to experience empathy when you witness another person suffering. Yet experiencing empathy for others can be influenced by your willingness to feel others' mental states and pain: Empathy can indeed be a motivated choice.

One of the classic examples associated with a lack of empathy for others and increased aggression is psychopathic individuals. Media and popular culture have systematically portrayed individuals with psychopathic traits as having no empathy for others. Using neuroscientific terms, it means that those individuals do not possess the neurological capacity to feel the pain of others, which makes them more likely to inflict pain on others. Several studies have indeed shown that psychopathic individuals have a reduced neural processing of the pain of others. In a study conducted in 2013 led by Jean Decety,[132] the researchers used an MRI scanner to examine brain activity in 121 incarcerated males classified as high, medium, or low psychopaths. The inmates were presented visual stimuli showing hands and feet in painful or nonpainful situations. For instance, they were shown a toe being caught under a heavy object or a finger being pinched in a door. There were two experimental conditions, one in which the inmates had to imagine that those situations were happening to themselves and one in which they had to imagine that those situations were happening to someone else. Results showed that when imagining the pain happening to themselves, psychopathic individuals had a typical activity in pain-related brain regions, such as the anterior insula and the anterior cingulate cortex. However, when they had to imagine that the pain was happening to someone else, activity in the brain regions associated with taking the pain of another into perspective was reduced compared to controls.

This reduced empathic activity in individuals diagnosed with psychopathy appears not to be linked with a structural inability to feel the pain of others, but rather as an inhibition of a neural process which is actually intact. In another study conducted in 2013 on inmates diagnosed with psychopathic traits as well as on healthy controls, the researchers asked their volunteers to observe videos displaying painful stimulations on other human beings.[112] During the task, they recorded their brain activity in an MRI scanner. In the observation phase, the researchers confirmed previous studies, as their results indicated less activation in brain regions associated with empathy in the psychopathic group compared to the healthy control group. Interestingly, in a second phase, the researchers asked their volunteers to try to empathize with the pain observed in the videos instead of passively watching the videos. Thus, volunteers had to really try to feel the pain of others. With this experimental manipulation, results were totally different. The researchers observed that when asked to empathize, activity in brain regions associated with empathy for pain was similar for psychopathic individuals and healthy controls.

These results thus challenge the classic view regarding psychopathic individuals as people having no capacity to feel empathy. Rather, they can inhibit their empathy more easily and more automatically than experiencing it. Such results can actually open some novel ideas regarding the treatment of psychopathy: Rather than trying to create a formula for empathy, therapists could try to make this existing capacity more automatic. But, as the authors of this study suggest, if people do not want and are not motivated to change, as is frequent in psychopathic individuals,[133] the task appears to be a real challenge.

Interestingly, it seems that everyone should be able to regulate empathy for the pain of others. In 2022, we conducted two studies where we asked our participants to simply watch pictures showing either painful or nonpainful stimulations on the screen.[134] We recorded their brain activity with an electroencephalogram and, as expected, we observed that their brain processed painful and nonpainful stimuli differently. Yet our participants were also asked to perform two additional exercises. In another condition, we asked them to try to increase their empathy, to try to really feel more the pain of the person in the picture.

In another condition, we asked them to decrease their empathy, to try to consider the same painful stimulations as less painful. Results were really interesting because we observed that people could successfully modulate their neural response to the pain of the person presented on the picture. In the increased condition, their neural response to painful stimuli was indeed higher compared to the neutral condition. In the decrease condition, their neural response to the same painful stimuli was not lower than in the neutral condition.

In some cases, especially with repetitive exposure to the pain of others, it is important to be able to regulate empathy, by attenuating it. For instance, healthcare professionals are more likely to experience burnout and compassion fatigue, which are detrimental for their wellbeing, if they do not learn to manage their empathy for their patients' suffering. Not managing their empathy for their patients can also impact their capacity for helping and taking care of them. While they should be able to regulate their emotional empathy, to avoid *feeling* the pain of others, they should nonetheless preserve their capacity to *understand* the pain of others, a capacity named cognitive empathy.

To illustrate the difference between emotional empathy and cognitive empathy, a nice example is a conversation that I had with the president of a Brussels-based association, DoucheFlux, which helps homeless individuals by providing showers and the possibility to clean their clothing. When asked if it was easy to find people doing volunteer work for his association, he told me that they actually receive a fair number of requests, but they do not accept everyone and actually conduct interviews with potential volunteers. He told me that he was able in an instant to distinguish between people who would be good at helping homeless individuals and those who would not. He said that sometimes, on the very first day, volunteers invite homeless people to sleep at their place. They are so willing to help that they do not even consider that it is not the most efficient way of going about it. They are focusing on a single individual for whom they could not help but feel a deep emotional empathy, but they ignore all the others. He told me that he prefers people who can understand the pain and difficulties of others but act in a more pragmatic way to help instead of taking emotional decisions.

He added that people with a higher capacity to regulate their emotions were actually far better as volunteers.

In other words, having an emotional response prevents us from providing help efficiently – it is better to have a cognitive response. This is why medical doctors learn to manage their cognitive empathy over their emotional empathy. If they had to feel all the emotions of their patients and their families, they would be totally overloaded and would not be able to make correct decisions. This is also why therapists and medical doctors are discouraged from providing care for their own family members. It is indeed more difficult to regulate our empathy and emotions with our relatives than with strangers.

Cognitive and emotional empathy actually rely on different brain regions. Emotional empathy is more often associated with activity in the limbic system, notably with the anterior cingulate cortex and the insula, whereas cognitive empathy involves brain regions associated with the understanding of the state of mind of others, specifically the right temporo-parietal junction and the dorsomedial prefrontal cortex. As already mentioned in Chapter 3, the prefrontal cortex is a critical area for taking decisions and controlling one's own behavior. In the case of empathy, the prefrontal cortex regulates the activity of regions associated with emotions and pain processing. This allows us to avoid being submerged by emotions and to act in a more pragmatic way.

Knowledge about the role of the prefrontal cortex for regulating emotions is actually starting to be used in clinical practice. Real-time neurofeedback is a relatively recent method, which relies on neuroimaging methods such as electroencephalography to provide people with real-time access to activity in specific parts of their brains. An EEG is placed on their head and they can view a neurofeedback bar displayed on a screen, which indicates in real time the intensity of the activity in the targeted brain region. By providing feedback regarding the intensity of the activity in the prefrontal cortex when they process emotional pictures, neurofeedback can actually help people to regulate the intensity of the negative emotions perceived. This technique is particularly relevant for individuals suffering from depression, who tend to be overwhelmed by negative emotions, and for individuals with post-traumatic stress disorder, who cannot control the occurrence of traumatic memories, as we will see in Chapter 6.

Being able to regulate cognitive and emotional empathy is also a capacity that researchers have to manage when they work with populations that experience intense suffering – first and foremost for their own wellbeing, but also to be able to stay neutral when acquiring their data. In the scientific projects I conducted with my research team, notably those in prisons or with victims of the genocide in Rwanda, managing emotional empathy was critical to avoid being overloaded by emotions and be able to continue the projects.

I remember that day when I saw our local research assistant in Rwanda suddenly leaving the building where we were conducting a study with victims of the genocide. I went outside and she was crying and could barely tell me what happened. She was helping one of our volunteers, an old man who could not read and write, to fill in the questionnaires. When asked what he experienced during the genocide, the old man started crying. In the Rwandan culture, men avoid expressing and showing their emotions, even if their grief or sadness is intense. Showing their emotions could make them appear weak or not trustworthy to their counterparts. Even though she was able to manage her emotional empathy when female victims cried, she told me that seeing an old man crying was too much for her considering that men are not supposed to show their emotions. She had to take a rest with the testing and was unable to continue the questionnaires with that man.

Even though empathy is partly a motivated choice, and we have the ability to regulate it to some extent, our capacity to feel empathy for the suffering of others is from the beginning unfortunately not equal towards all human beings. There are many individuals for whom we have a natural, and potentially unconscious, reduction of empathy. This is notably the case when we see suffering individuals that we do not recognize as part of our own group.

In the next section, I will delve into the process of categorization and its neural underpinnings. Additionally, I will explore a crucial aspect linked to many mass atrocities: the phenomenon of dehumanization, which emerges from categorization. Understanding these elements is essential for gaining a comprehensive grasp of mass atrocities and their underlying mechanisms.

"US" VERSUS "THEM" – A PATHWAY TO DEHUMANIZATION
AND MASS ATROCITIES

Human beings are a very social species, with the huge majority of us evolving daily in more or less large groups. Those groups can range from our direct relatives, to our friends, to our colleagues at work, to other supporters of our favorite football team, or to individuals sharing a similar culture or similar religious or political beliefs. Living in groups helped us to progress throughout history, as it clearly has a lot of advantages. We are part of those groups because we need to have a feeling of belonging, a feeling that we are not alone and are protected by others. You can receive help from your group, be supported, develop cooperative tasks, share resources.

Being isolated and excluded from a group is not part of our deeper nature and can lead to depression, aggression, and death-related thoughts. Research in neuroscience has shown that social exclusion actually shares similarities with experiencing physical pain. In 2003, Naomi Eisenberger, a US professor of psychology, and her team sought to investigate how experiencing social rejection from a group actually "hurts."[135] They invited volunteers to play a virtual ball-tossing game with two other players. In reality, the game was actually controlled by the computer: There were no other players. Across different experimental conditions, volunteers were simply observing the two other players throwing the ball to each other, or they were included in the game, or they were being excluded by the two other players, who stopped throwing the ball to the volunteers and continued to play only between themselves. This latter experimental condition created a feeling of social exclusion for volunteers.

During the entire session, volunteers were lying in an MRI scanner in order for researchers to obtain a precise map of the brain regions active during social exclusion. The researchers found that volunteers who were left out of the social game displayed higher neural activity in two specific areas of the brain that we have seen before and which are linked to painful experiences, that is, the anterior cingulate cortex and the anterior insula. The researchers further observed that brain activity in the anterior cingulate cortex correlated with the level of distress that volunteers reported after the experiment when they felt excluded. Social pain is thus relatively similar to physical pain, hence the popular expression to describe experiences of social separation: that getting rejected "hurts."

From an evolutionary perspective, the neural mechanisms associated with the perception of physical pain, which are critical for our survival as they allow us to avoid potentially hurtful situations, were present a long time before human beings evolved as a social species. As social inclusion became critical for survival in groups over the course of evolution, the main current theory in the scientific community is that to punish individuals not participating in the group, social exclusion has built upon already-existing brain networks associated with physical pain.[136]

Our biology thus motivates us to be part of groups, thus underlying our natural tendency to create groups, which we may belong to. However, the human's propensity to self-segregate also sometimes leads to creating negative biases towards other groups in order to protect our own group. These prejudicial attitudes towards outgroups can take many forms, ranging from negative thinking, antisocial attitudes, reduced prosociality, social exclusion, hate speech or, in its more extreme forms, wars and genocides.

An interesting study in social psychology showed how far this tendency to create negative biases towards outgroups can go. Henri Tajfel, a social psychologist, explored the factors that create prejudice towards outgroups by putting people randomly in different groups. Thus there were no specific factors that supported the creation of a specific group, such as shared ideologies, friendship, or anything else. Tajfel observed that people started to view their own group as better than the other, even without having met the members of the other group before.[137]

Neuroscience research has enabled us to highlight the time course of social categorization. In a study conducted in 2003,[138] the researchers used electroencephalography to study with a millisecond precision when our brain starts to process differences between individuals. The authors showed that when presented with pictures of individuals of African descent or of European descent those of European descent had a higher neural response only 120 milliseconds after seeing the picture of an individual of African descent compared to pictures of another individual of European descent. This response is specific of a higher attention, probably in response to the skin color. The process of distinguishing differences between "us" and "them" thus occurs very rapidly in our brains.

A wide range of studies in neuroscience has also shown that prejudice towards outgroups is deeply ingrained in our biology.[139] A typical negative outgroup attitude is expressed in the use of stereotypes. Stereotypes represent the fixed attributes that are linked to a particular group regarding their culture, society or physical appearance, which most often are false. For instance, blond girls are unintelligent, or punks enjoy taking drugs. Usually, those stereotypes are negative because we tend to hold unfounded negative biases towards outgroups. In the brain, stereotypes rely on structures such as the anterior temporal lobe,[139,140] that is associated with semantic memory – a specific form of memory which refers to general world knowledge that we have accumulated throughout our lives – as well as the regions that are involved in impression formation, such as the medial prefrontal cortex.[141]

In the literature on empathy, it has largely been observed that when the individual experiencing pain is perceived as an outgroup member, whether based on ethnic, cultural, religious, or political differences, the neural empathic response is attenuated for the observer. In a study conducted in 2009,[142] the researchers recruited Caucasian and Chinese[†] volunteers. They showed them pictures of faces of Caucasian and Chinese individuals who were being pricked by a needle. The MRI results showed that the anterior cingulate cortex was more active when both Caucasian and Chinese volunteers watched the pain of their own ingroup, compared to their respective outgroup. In another study conducted in 2010,[122] the researchers observed activity in the anterior cingulate cortex and the anterior insula was reduced when volunteers were watching pictures of supporters of a rival football team in pain compared to fans of their own team. In my own research conducted in

---

[†] This distinction has been reported as such by the authors in their paper, even though it contrasts a large group of individuals from many different countries to a group of individuals from a single Asian country. In addition, the term "Caucasian" is heavily racially connoted, whereas "of European descent" is more appropriate from an anthropological perspective.

Rwanda,[143] we observed that empathy was systematically reduced between former genocide perpetrators and survivors while it was intact for their own ingroup. We also observed that children of former perpetrators or children of survivors exhibit the same reduction of empathy for the other group as their parents. This shows that outgroup biases can also be present in the next generation, which may partially explain the perpetuation of conflicts.[144]

Importantly, it is not that empathy cannot be felt at all for outgroup individuals. For instance, several studies have shown that people who believe that empathy is a socially desirable characteristic also act more empathically, even towards outgroup members.[145,146] Other studies have shown that when living in an outgroup country, this natural tendency to reduce empathy for the outgroup is reduced.[147] A previous fMRI study showed that cultural variation in preference for social hierarchy modulates the neural response underlying intergroup empathy, with a higher preference for social hierarchy being associated with a higher intergroup empathy bias.[148]

Those studies suggest that it is not that we cannot feel empathy for outgroup members. Rather, we are not *motivated* to feel empathy for them. This is similar to obedience, where it is easier to simply not feel the pain we cause to others, because we can easily displace our responsibility onto the authority.

Notably, our natural tendency to feel threatened by other groups and the willingness to protect our own group have been widely exploited by extreme right-wing parties. Their political campaigns have been largely based on triggering negative emotions, such as fear or anger, towards outgroup minorities. They know that we are naturally inclined to develop negative biases towards other groups. For instance, they may say that migrants will steal our jobs or impose their culture and religion. They target our evolutive processes that lead us to protect our own group. The imperative for all of us is to check the facts rather than be guided by our instinctive biology. If we do not, extremists will have succeeded in dividing human societies even more and there are already more than enough group conflicts with their disastrous consequences in this world.

What genocidal regimes all have in common is that they have succeeded in exacerbating differences between "us" and "them" through
their propaganda. They use ethnicity, religion, nationality, or political
ideology to accentuate categories and to split societies. Germans and
Jews. Hutus and Tutsis. Turks and Armenians. Bosnian Serbs and
Bosnian Muslims. The "civilized" and the "savages." This is a common
characteristic of all genocides: Individuals are not considered as individuals with their own characteristics, but as members of their group alone.
After a successful categorization, genocidal regimes then implement
another critical step to reach their objective: removing the humanity of
the other group.

Not a single genocide could have started just because suddenly an
authority figure ordered the extermination of other human beings
because of their political ideology, their ethnicity or their religious
beliefs. It is likely that neither the gas chambers used during the Nazi
genocide, nor the mass killings with machetes in Rwanda could have
happened without a process of dehumanization of the targets. Without
indoctrination leading people to believe that "they are better off without
the others."

During wars and genocides, a very commonly used method used by
perpetrators is to distort the perception of the target humans by making
them appear as subhuman or even nonhuman. In other words, by
removing their humanity. In Rwanda, the radio station Radio
Télévision Libre des Milles Collines, allied with leaders of the government, started to describe the Tutsis as *inyenzi*, which means cock-
roaches, and as *inzoka*, which means snakes. By referring to the Tutsis
as animals that are most of the time considered as pests that must be
killed, the promoters of the genocide removed their targets' humanity.
A month later, vast numbers of Tutsis, whether they were elderly,
adolescents, or babies, were hunted down, tortured, and killed without
mercy. Using the radio was actually a well-thought-out means to ensure
that a maximum number of people would hear those messages.
Listening to radio is a daily activity in Rwanda, an activity with family
members after a working day.

During the Holocaust, the Nazis reported that Jews were like rats. It is
wrong to kill a person, but acceptable to exterminate a rat. When

arrested, Jews in the death camps were identified by number rather than by name. *Untermenschen* (subhumans) is a word which has been used by the Nazis to describe inferior, non-Aryan people, such as Jews, Roma, and Slavs. In a propaganda brochure printed roughly 4 million times in the German language and translated into different languages, you can read the following:[149]

> Just as the night rises against the day, the light and dark are in eternal conflict. So too, is the subhuman the greatest enemy of the dominant species on earth, mankind. The subhuman is a biological creature, crafted by nature, which has hands, legs, eyes and mouth, even the semblance of a brain. Nevertheless, this terrible creature is only a partial human being.
>
> Although it has features similar to a human, the subhuman is lower on the spiritual and psychological scale than any animal. Inside of this creature lie wild and unrestrained passions: an incessant need to destroy, filled with the most primitive desires, chaos and coldhearted villainy.
>
> A subhuman and nothing more!
>
> Not all of those who appear human are in fact so. Woe to him who forgets it!
>
> Mulattoes and Finn-Asian barbarians, Gypsies and black skin savages all make up this modern underworld of subhumans that is always headed by the appearance of the eternal Jew.

During the Cambodian genocide, over one and a half million people died, which represented roughly 20–25 percent of the Cambodian population. However, during the genocide committed by the Khmer Rouge in Cambodia, the differences were less clear between the "perpetrators" and their "victims" because the genocide was mostly perpetrated by ethnic Khmers against ethnic Khmers. Indeed, when I started to get interested in the Cambodian genocide, I had a hard time understanding why the Khmer Rouge mass murdered their own population without clear and rigid distinctions between individuals, as was the case in other genocides. More than for any other genocides I read about, I could not get the question out of my head "But how have they been able to convince so many people to perpetrate a genocide against other Cambodians?" Other genocides used pre-existing differences between people, such as

religion or etchnicity, exacerbated by past conflicts, tensions, and inse-
curities. Considering how easy it is to accentuate prejudicial attitudes
towards other groups, building upon pre-existing group differences and
group tensions makes it easier to understand how a society can be
divided, eventually leading to a genocide.

This is not the case in Cambodia. Sometimes, the Cambodian genocide is referred to as an "autogenocide" because of the lack of a clear
distinction between the perpetrators and their victims. However, this
designation is not quite accurate as it denies the fact that other minorities were exterminated by the Khmer Rouge, including Vietnamese,
Chinese, Muslim Chams, Christians, and Buddhists. In 1975, Pol Pot and
his army captured Phnom Penh, the capital city of Cambodia, and
forcibly evacuated its inhabitants to the countryside. The Khmer
Rouge believed that urban people were part of the bourgeoisie and
represented a threat to the agrarian revolution, which they sought to
establish. People living in cities were forced to move to the countryside
to work as farmers. Anyone considered an intellectual – teachers, lawyers, doctors, and clergy – were targeted by the regime and re-educated
or killed outright.

The Khmer Rouge created the differences by representing opponents
as "hidden enemies burrowing from within," "diseased elements," or
"feudal-capitalist/landowning class" threatening the society and its
productivity.[32] They created differences between people based on their
ideology and started to use words such as "clean up,""crush," or "kill."
Those people were a source that threatened the novel ideology of their
regime and needed to be eliminated.

Colonialism is another disastrous example of how dehumanization
has been used as a method to justify the mistreatment of the individuals
who were already inhabiting the colonized land. In order to justify
colonialism and slavery, in order to ensure that people would not find
it wrong to inflict such mistreatment on the colonized population and
even agree with it, the most efficient way is to remove humanity from
them. By calling them "uncivilized" or "savage" or "wild," it was easier to
justify slavery so that the companies could make a profit, to justify
converting them to another religion considered more civilized, to
take their lands, to justify exploitation and abuse.

As this section shows, categorization is a powerful process that can drastically impact empathy for the pain of the outgroup members. Combined with a process of dehumanization, it becomes easier for a government or an authority figure to justify violence or mistreatment, as the targeted people are seen as less than fully human and therefore not deserving of the same rights and protections as others. As we will see in the next section, dehumanization also impacts behavior and specific brain processes.

DEHUMANIZATION IMPACTS HUMAN BEHAVIOR

Removing the humanity of the targets in order to allow more violent misconduct is perfectly illustrated in the TV show *Black Mirror*. The episode "Men Against Fire" is set in a dystopian future, in which soldiers are implanted with a device called MASS that enhances their combat abilities and perception. However, the true purpose of MASS is to dehumanize the enemy, whom they believe are monstrous, inhuman creatures called "roaches." In reality, the roaches are innocent civilians, and the MASS technology alters the soldiers' perception to dehumanize them, making it easier for the soldiers to commit atrocities without guilt or remorse. While this story is only fiction, it highlights the power of dehumanization to influence behavior,[‡] an effect that has also been captured by researchers in their lab.

Two weeks after Hurricane Katrina struck the southern part of the United States, a team of researchers investigated how humanization of the hurricane's victims would be associated with helping behaviors.[150] They recruited White American and African American participants and asked them to make inferences about the emotional state of either a White American victim or an African American victim and to report their willingness to help such victims. The method of emotion attribution, which requires participants to infer what the emotional state of others might be, has been frequently used in psychological research on

---

[‡] This episode, in line with the central themes of the *Black Mirror* series, also highlights the ethical implications of technology that can manipulate perception to justify violence against others.

(de)humanization. Emotions are usually characterized as of two kinds: primary emotions and secondary emotions. Primary emotions encompass, for instance, anger, joy, and sadness, while secondary emotions encompass much more complex states-of-mind, such as pride, guilt, nostalgia, satisfaction or regret.[151] Usually, we tend to attribute only primary emotions to dehumanized humans, as we would do for animals, denying that those humans can also experience much more complex emotions.[152]

In the study on the victims of Hurricane Katrina, the researchers observed that the less people attributed secondary emotions to out-group victims of Hurricane Katrina, thus implying denying their humanity, the less willing they were to help them. It thus seems that humans are less likely to help other humans when they do not grant them humanity.

In another study conducted in 2008,[153] a team of researchers investigated the extent to which Dutch people felt guilty regarding the involvement of the Dutch UN soldiers in the fatal events that happened in Srebrenica in 1995. This event happened during the ethnic cleansing and mass killing in Bosnia, where about 8,000 Bosnian Muslims were killed by Bosnian Serbs in a genocidal process. Dutch soldiers were acting as United Nations peacekeepers and they should have known that the 300 Muslims who sought refuge in their camp would be tortured and murdered by the Bosnian Serb troops if they turned away. The soldiers were insufficiently supplied and ill-equipped and failed to stop the Bosnian Serb troops entering the camp and killing the 300 men. In their study, the researchers observed that the more their Dutch participants dehumanized Muslims, the less they felt guilty when they read about the negative role of Dutch soldiers in the massacre of Srebrenica.

But dehumanization can also lead to more dramatic behaviors than the likelihood of helping or feeling guilty. Many academics have argued that dehumanization is a critical psychological process that underlies people's willingness to torture individuals who are considered as out-group members. Remember the horrifying images of torture of prisoners at the Abu Ghraib prison in Iraq. During the Iraq War, members of the US army violated many human rights against the detainees of the Abu

Ghraib prison, including rape, sexual and physical abuse, tortures, and sodomy. Pictures depicting those crimes released in the press sent shock waves around the world especially among defenders of human rights. You could indeed see images of a detainee with human excreta smeared on his body and face, or two military soldiers posing behind a human pyramid composed of naked detainees, or even a female military officer watching and laughing at naked detainees forced to masturbate in front of her. How could human beings make a mockery of the mistreatments they were inflicting on other human beings?

In 2013, a team of researchers sought to put together pieces of the puzzle and it appeared that dehumanization plays a key role in such acts.[154] They recruited Christian participants and showed them images of the Abu Ghraib torture scenes. The participants were asked to indicate the likelihood they would have behaved like the soldiers. The results were compelling: Participants who reported a lower degree of humanity to Muslims were also those who reported a higher proclivity to torture the detainees. If Muslims were in addition presented as a potential threat, the relationship between dehumanization and a proclivity to torture was even stronger. Of course, it does not mean that everyone is capable of such atrocities simply because they are facing a dehumanized human being. A lot of additional factors have to be considered, but such results explain that dehumanization underpins the willingness to torture outgroup members.

In 1975, another team of researchers invited several volunteers recruited by groups of three.[155] The experimenter and his assistant told them that another group, that arrived earlier, was also present in another room. The experimenter explained that the study was about punishment on the quality of collective decision-making, and he offered participants the possibility to behave punitively, with (fake) electric shocks of different intensity, towards the other group. In one experimental condition, the other group was humanized by being presented as perceptive and understanding, but in another condition, the other group was dehumanized and presented as an animalistic, rotten bunch. In a control condition, no references were given to the other group. The authors observed that people were more punitive towards a group that had been dehumanized, compared to the neutral and humanized groups. This study shows the power of humanization to counteract punitiveness. The process of dehumanization is actually highly efficient because it impacts our neural ability to feel the pain of others and to take their perspective. By dehumanizing their targets, promoters of wars and genocides separate them from other human beings, by making them appear as part of a subhuman group. As we have a natural tendency to feel a reduced empathy for outgroup members, it is thus not surprising to observe that a critical way to allow genocide to happen is to emphasize group differences and to resort to a process of dehumanization.

Neuroscientists have started to investigate how exactly dehumanization occurs within the brain. The medial prefrontal cortex, mentioned before regarding its importance for the creation of stereotypes, has been established as critical for social cognition. Several studies have indeed showed its implication for many different social tasks. In a study conducted in 2006,[156] the researchers scanned the brains of their volunteers in an MRI scanner while they were observing pictures of extremely dehumanized individuals, such as drug addicts or homeless people, as well as nondehumanized individuals. The researchers observed brain activations of the medial prefrontal cortex when participants watched the pictures of all individuals, except those that were dehumanized. It thus suggests that there is no automatic activation of the brain networks involved in social cognition when witnessing dehumanized individuals. More critically, the researchers observed that viewing pictures of dehumanized individuals actually triggered brain activity in brain regions such as the insula and the amygdala. The amygdala is a deep brain structure that is also part of the limbic system. Several studies have confirmed its role in processing fear and have confirmed the role of the insula in generating disgust. The results thus show that dehumanized individuals generate no social cognition, but in addition trigger emotions such as fear and disgust.

There is also a study that I discovered a couple of years ago, which I think is worth mentioning.[157] The researchers wondered if the attribution of humanness would be sufficient to elicit a neural response to the pain of nonhuman entities. Concretely, the researchers showed their participants pictures of vegetables, such as pumpkins, broccoli or eggplant, being hurt by the needle of a syringe allegedly penetrating the vegetable or being stroked by a nonpainful Q-tip touching its skin. In one experimental condition, the vegetables were given human names (Carlo, Laura, ...) and in another, they were given adjectives associated with their taste (sweet, tasty, ...). The authors measured the neural response to the pain of the vegetables using electroencephalography. Interestingly, the authors observed that vegetables with a name triggered an empathic reaction in the participants' brains when they saw the vegetables being hurt, which was not the case when they visualized vegetables with an adjective. Of course, these results by no means imply that simply giving a name to a dehumanized human would produce similar results and would be sufficient to alter dehumanization processes. But it is interesting to observe that we are able to feel empathy for nonhuman entities which are humanized. Such a finding would definitely deserve a replication in the future and should be extended to humans as well.

Dehumanizing targets, instilling fear of another group, and granting governmental authority for mass murders are some crucial mechanisms that unveil the underpinnings of genocide. A pressing societal question, therefore, is understanding how to halt an ongoing dehumanization process. External entities, like governments or NGOs, have a pivotal role as they can shut down radio programs or any media used to propagate hate messages targeting specific groups. However, these actions must be carefully done to avoid unwanted interference from other countries while still fighting against hate speech, which can be a tricky and often difficult task. Also, it is hard because we need to deal with the deeper social and political issues that lead to people being treated as less than human. This means we have to do more than just stop the bad messages. It involves education, promoting understanding and empathy among diverse groups, and fostering environments where inclusive dialogue can thrive. Despite these challenges, the urgent need to prevent the horrors of genocide makes striving to understand and interrupt the process of dehumanization a critical global imperative.

OBEYING ORDERS IMPACTS THE NEURAL BASES ASSOCIATED WITH THE FEELING OF GUILT

Guilt is a powerful emotion which usually arises when social norms are violated.[158] It is considered to be a prosocial and moral emotion, as it motivates transgressors or perpetrators to make amends, to restore damaged social relationships, and to perform good deeds. If you feel guilty about an action, you are less likely to repeat the same action in the future.

In 2014,[159] a team of researchers conducted a longitudinal study in which they interviewed hundreds of inmates shortly after their incarceration regarding their feelings of guilt over what led them to jail. Approximately one year after their release, the researchers contacted the former inmates again, this time asking them whether they had been rearrested for a serious crime or whether they had committed a crime but had not been caught. Results of this study showed that the more the inmate reported feeling guilty after the first incarceration, the less likely they were to commit a crime. Feeling guilty for an event usually prevents one from performing the same act again.

Feeling guilty is different from being considered guilty by the law. For instance, a perpetrator may have committed a serious crime and been found guilty, without feeling any guilt. Ted Bundy, an American serial killer who kidnapped, raped, and killed at least thirty women and girls in the 1970s, stated in 1981 that "Guilt doesn't solve anything, really. It hurts you ... I guess I am in the enviable position of not having to deal with guilt."[160] These statements are frequent in antisocial personalities, who usually feel no remorse or guilt over what they did.

In other cases, however, one may feel guilty for something when one hasn't done anything wrong and is not responsible. If you invited a friend for your birthday dinner but they had a serious accident on the way, you may experience guilt even if you were not responsible for the accident.

Ted Bundy was somehow right when he stated that feeling guilty hurts. It can lead to anxiety, depressive tendencies, and even self-punishment. This is why people usually tend to choose actions that are considered as morally right, at least from their own perspective, in order to avoid feeling guilt and its negative psychological effects. Self-punishment for removing guilt is largely documented throughout history. For instance, many religious traditions have pain rituals when a transgression has occurred.

Researchers in psychology have also been able to capture self-punishment after guilt in experimental setups. In 2011, a team of researchers invited sixty-two volunteers to participate in a study.[161] Some of the volunteers were asked to write for 10 to 15 minutes about a time when they rejected or socially excluded another person. The other volunteers, which were the control group, were asked to write about an interaction they had had the day before with another person. When asked to judge how they felt regarding this event, as expected, volunteers who had to recall an act of ostracism judged themselves more negatively than the control group. After writing the essay, volunteers were told that they would participate in a different study on physical acuity. They were presented with a bucket of freezing cold water with a temperature of about 1°C and were instructed by the experimenter to immerse their nondominant hand into the bucket for as long as they could. Participants then finished the experiment by completing a questionnaire assessing their feeling of guilt regarding the event they had to write about.

The results were quite compelling. The researchers observed that volunteers who wrote about an act of ostracism held their hand in the icy water for a longer time than those who wrote about a neutral inter-action, as if they were punishing themselves through the act of physical pain. Interestingly, the researchers also observed that volunteers who went through the icy water test reported that they felt less guilty after-wards, compared to other volunteers who had to hold their hand in a bucket of warm water (38°C). This study suggested that people tend to use physical pain as a means to "cleanse their soul" to reduce their feeling of guilt about an event.

In another study, researchers randomly assigned volunteers to three different groups, where they were asked to recall a time when they felt guilty, or a time when they felt sad, or simply when they went to the grocery store.[162] The volunteers were then told that they would receive six mild electrical shocks, which were calibrated to be detected but not painful. However, volunteers were also told that they could choose to raise the voltage for each successive shock. Results were also quite com-pelling. The volunteers who had recalled feeling sad or going grocery shopping before the experiment did not raise the shock level past the unpleasant threshold. However, volunteers who had recalled feeling guilty raised the level of shock up to a mildly painful threshold.

Wanting to avoid feeling guilty prevents many people from conducting immoral acts. However, some people use a different strategy, consciously or not. In the case of dramatic events, another strategy consists in minimizing guilt, if no acts of "repair," such as increasing prosociality or self-punishment, are planned to be conducted. Minimizing guilt can be achieved by finding external justification for one's own actions. During genocides, perpetrators tend to reduce their feeling of guilt, consciously or not, by blaming external sources, such as their government or the group.

So, we wondered, does obeying immoral orders impact the perception of guilt?

In all the studies I have conducted on the obedient brain so far, participants systematically reported that they felt less sorry for the victim and less bad for delivering the shocks when they obeyed orders compared to when they acted freely and delivered the same shocks. It is as if their guilt suddenly flew away, simply because they obeyed orders, while they conducted exactly the same acts when they were able to freely decide. Interestingly, this finding is consistent with a large investigation that was conducted in Rwanda during the Gacaca courts, which showed that people rightly accused of having perpetrated the genocide expressed only moderate levels of personal guilt.[163] Other qualitative research also showed that child molesters tend to play down their crimes even after conviction.[164]

However, it is difficult to know if perpetrators minimize moral guilt to find justification to their actions *a posteriori* or if it reflects a process that had already happened when they conducted their crimes. Narratives from perpetrators have to be examined critically and carefully as plenty of social bias, combined with a desire to reduce the prison sentence, can influence what they say. It is indeed the case in many judicial systems that expressing guilt or remorse can reduce the prison sentence or lead to an earlier release from prison. In Rwanda for instance, perpetrators expressing guilt can be released earlier from their prison sentences. Subjective assessment of guilt in such contexts is thus highly complex.

Since we observed that our participants reported being less sorry and feeling less bad for the shocks they delivered when they obeyed orders compared to choosing freely, we considered that it would be interesting to see if obeying orders would reduce activity in guilt-related brain regions compared to acting freely. There has been an extensive literature in neuroscience seeking to reveal brain regions associated with the feeling of guilt. Results indicate that experiencing guilt elicits activations in different brain regions associated with our capacity to understand the thoughts and emotions of others, such as the temporo-parietal regions, the dorsolateral prefrontal cortex,[165] and the precuneus,[166] and with brain regions in the limbic systems associated with the processing of negative emotions, such as the anterior insula and the anterior cingulate cortex. These results would suggest that perpetrators' guilt may originate from their understanding and emotional processing of their victims' suffering.

We thus again used a brain approach in order to understand if obeying orders would reduce brain activity in regions associated with the feeling of guilt and this is exactly what we observed. When they obeyed the order to deliver shocks to the "victim" compared to freely choosing, activity in guilt-related brain regions was reduced, which could suggest that indeed people feel less guilty when they obey orders to hurt someone.

CONCLUSION

Moral emotions are critical as they directly influence our moral behaviors.[167] As we have seen in the present chapter, moral emotions such as empathy for the pain of others and guilt are attenuated when someone obeys orders compared to choosing freely. Combined with a reduced sense of agency and responsibility under obedience, such results highlight the power of hierarchical situations and can explain why atrocities can be conducted on the grounds of obedience to authority, as our natural aversion to hurt others is altered.

But in hierarchical situations, there is not only the person obeying orders. There is also the one giving orders. In the following chapter, I will present several studies that showed that even though one might hope that at least those giving orders feel responsibility and empathy for the victim, brain results suggest that this may not necessarily be the case.

CHAPTER 5

Just Giving Orders? In the Brains of Those Who Command

Power tends to corrupt and absolute power corrupts absolutely.
Great men are almost always bad men . . .

Lord Acton (1887[168])

Most human societies rely on leaders in various fields – political, religious, or professional – in order to function effectively.[169]

From an evolutionary perspective, humans have developed to function in social groups, and systems led by a single person may have provided a significant advantage for survival and reproduction in our history. From our earliest days as a species, our ancestors relied on leaders to make crucial decisions regarding resource allocation, defense against predators or rival clans, and resolutions for group conflicts.[170] A strong leader could help the group coordinate and act cohesively, thus improving the chance of survival.

The positive impact of leaders for our survival may explain why humans have a natural inclination towards hierarchies and leaders. Scientific studies have shown, for example, that people tend to follow those who are perceived as strong, competent, and confident. This phenomenon could be due to a variety of factors, including the need for protection and security, the desire for social cohesion, and the advantages of effective decision-making.[171]

Humans are not the only species with complex hierarchical structures and leaders, however. Nonhuman animal studies have shown that the same holds true for many species. Many wild animals live in cooperative groups ruled by a single leader, similar to what is observed in human societies. Some authors have argued that as long as there is social activity between members of the same species – whenever there are collective activities or a social structure – a leader will naturally emerge.[172] In other words, our need to have leaders and follow them may be as deeply biologically ingrained for humans as it is for any other species on earth.

In human societies, leaders sometimes impose themselves on a population by force, sometimes they are democratically elected, sometimes they inherit their position, and sometimes they make their way into power through other means. There are indeed numerous pathways to power. And interestingly, the pathways to power in nonhuman species are as various as in human societies. Take, for example, the structure of honeybee colonies. A honeybee colony generally consists of three kinds of adult bees: the workers (i.e., sexually undeveloped female bees), the drones (i.e., male bees), and the queen. Honeybee colonies need this social structure to survive, and each bee has a specific role. The queen bee is usually the only sexually developed female, and her main purpose in the colony is to reproduce with the drones.

Because of her role, the queen bee has a physiognomy that is different from the other bees, with a longer body, a larger thorax, and longer wings. She receives more food from the workers than the other bees to ensure she can fulfil her role. If a queen bee is lost, killed, or too old and removed, she is immediately replaced by "emergency queens" selected from among the worker bees. After the selection, the potential candidates for queen bee are left alone and battle it out until only one survives. The queen gains access to this position after a difficult fight, but notably, the initial decision to be selected as a potential candidate is out of her control.

Hyenas represent a different model of leadership. Like in some human societies where the leader's position can be inherited, spotted hyenas live in matriarchal clans where the leadership position is passed from mother to child. They live in big clans of about eighty individuals, which are ruled by a succession of alpha females.[173] Alpha females and their cubs have access to more food and resources, and receive greater social support for their kin, thus ensuring better reproduction. When the matriarch passes away, her youngest female cub will take over as the new matriarch, which maintains social rank within the clan.[174]

Some species of animals don't rely on a single leader at all. There are species that use, for example, something more like a voting system for a more democratic mode of decision-making and function among their groups. Meerkats and African wild dogs are two such species. They emit vocalizations prior to a collective movement towards another location, and it is only once a sufficient number of individuals have vocalized – thus confirming the decision – that the group departs.[175,176] In other species, the vote happens not through vocalization, but is rather based on body orientation. The most famous example reported in the literature is the African buffalo.[177] During rest periods, African buffalos use their body orientation to indicate their preference for the direction of travel. When the herd starts moving after the resting period, the average orientation indicated by group members decides the final direction.

Other groups are more dominance-based. Chimpanzees live in complex social groups with a clear hierarchical structure. Alpha males, who have the highest status within a group, do not benefit from a birth privilege. Rather, they have to compete for dominance and often use aggression to maintain their power and related advantages, such as access to food and fertile females. Other males may have to create coalitions to challenge the alpha male.[178]

These examples show the diversity and complexity of hierarchical structures in nonhuman species and actually reveal how similar they are to even some modern human societies. However, what seems to be more specific to human societies is that leaders may strongly abuse their power. Abuse of power frequently leads to corruption, oppression, marginalization of certain groups, and sometimes even mass atrocities.

Giving power to leaders involves assuming that they will act for the good of the society. People expect their leaders to take responsibility for their directives, especially when their decisions have severe consequences for others. However, leaders may sometimes act in ways that are not for the collective good. For example, some leaders may prioritize their own interests over the interests of the society they lead, which can lead to decisions that benefit them personally. Other leaders may feel pressure from powerful interest groups or lobbyists who seek to influence their decisions in a way that benefits them. Some leaders may also have a limited perspective on the issues they must deal with, which can lead to decisions that do not fully take into account the long-term implications for citizens.

In these cases, leaders can use a self-regulatory mechanism called moral disengagement to commit transgressions while maintaining

a clear conscience.[179,180] Moral disengagement involves reframing
one's actions so that they appear less harmful, diminishing the
perception of distress caused to others, or minimizing one's own
responsibility. For instance, during a war, leaders sometimes use
moral disengagement to justify civilian loss, arguing that it is
a necessary evil for a greater good, or portraying the enemy populace as complicit with or supportive of enemy combatants. During
the Iraq War that began in 2003, there were instances of civilian
infrastructure being targeted. While these actions were often
explained as targeting essential nodes in Saddam Hussein's regime
to weaken the regime and liberate the Iraqi people from oppression,
some attacks resulted in widespread civilian suffering and loss of
life.[322]

Is this process of moral disengagement an attempt to reduce
accountability in the case of an indictment when their decisions
lead to harm? Or does being in the position of leader impact how
the brain processes the act of giving orders and their consequences,
thus impacting one's own perception of responsibility? In a war or
a genocide, the responsibility for the tragic events does not rest
solely on the perpetrators who carried out the violence, but also on
those who gave the orders to commit these acts. In an attempt to
find out where any feelings of responsibility lie, a chapter had thus
to be dedicated to those sharing equal, most of the time even higher,
accountability for such tragedies.

Studying the brain activity of leaders when they give orders can provide valuable insights into their decision-making processes and help us
better understand how they make decisions that affect society. By understanding the neural processes that underlie effective decision-making, we
may be able to develop interventions that help leaders make better
decisions. Further, recognizing that leaders may not always fully process
their responsibility, it becomes pertinent for those executing orders to
acknowledge that their responsibility is not entirely deferred to leaders,
and that they, too, must exercise judgment and uphold moral and ethical
standards in their actions. While previous chapters focused on those
obeying orders, the present chapter, using a similar methodological
framework, will thus focus on those *giving* orders.

ON THE COMPLEXITY OF HIERARCHICAL CHAINS

On an evening in 2013, I found myself watching a famous Belgian television show – *Devoir d'enquête* ("Duty to investigate") – about criminal investigations. The journalists in the episode I was watching were presenting the case of a kindergarten teacher who hired two contract killers to murder her partner in order to get the money from his life insurance.

Even though the case was interesting, it was not the story in itself that captured my attention, but rather the verdict pronounced by the court. In their defense, the two contract killers pleaded that they should be judged less responsible because they acted without intent. They were just following orders. At the end of the trial, the verdict was pronounced: The two contract killers received prison sentences of 18 years each, while the kindergarten teacher received a prison sentence of 23 years.

After watching the documentary, I began to wonder: Is it easier for those executing orders to take responsibility for their actions, since they are the ones acting, or is it easier for those giving orders to take responsibility, because they bear the accountability for ordering the actions in the first place? In this specific criminal case, the law punished those who carried out orders less severely than the one who gave the orders. But does this reflect what the defendants themselves felt? Who did they think bore the ultimate responsibility for what happened?

Hierarchical situations are a complex example for determining individual responsibility. In typical hierarchical situations, a superior communicates a plan, and a subordinate executes it. Thus, the superior bears responsibility for the decision but is distanced from the outcomes, while the subordinate experiences authorship over the action but may not experience responsibility for its outcomes.[181]

If those obeying orders do not appear to experience the feeling of responsibility that they should, as we have seen in the previous chapters, an important element of responsibility could lie with those who *give* orders. Does the person giving orders feel responsibility, or experience a feeling of guilt, or a sense of agency in relation to the outcomes of their orders? Do they experience empathy for the victims of their orders? Or, in hierarchical situations, does the subjective perception of responsibility simply evaporate?

These are critical questions, because if no one experiences responsibility for what is happening, what can prevent actors in hierarchical systems from committing atrocious acts of obedience like genocide?

In the case of the kindergarten teacher and the contract killers, the hierarchical chain was relatively simple: At the top, there was a person giving an order; directly below were the two contract killers who acted on the order. As in this case, there are many contexts in which hierarchical chains are pretty simple. Imagine that your boss asks you to sign documents certifying the conformity of a product you know to be defective. Or your boss asks you to fire someone on their behalf. This is a simple hierarchical chain for executing immoral or uncomfortable actions, with no intermediaries between the one giving the order and the one receiving the order.

But in many organizations, orders are embedded in a much longer chain of command in which orders received from a superior are relayed through one or more commanders to a variety of actors. This is the case, for example, in the military, where different levels are involved in planning and executing an operation. A military officer can order an attack on a specific location based on recommendations received from intelligence personnel. Another officer may decide, following the recommendations from additional intelligence personnel and lawyers, who the exact targets of the attack should be. Yet another officer might be in charge of transmitting the orders to the person or group asked to execute the attack itself.

In these kinds of situations, commanders are also intermediaries – an aspect of their position in hierarchical structures which can influence their individual feeling of responsibility over the potential consequences. Numerous historical examples, including the Nazis or the Khmer Rouge, have shown the power of fractionating operations across different individuals to facilitate atrocious acts of mass annihilation. Such examples may support the idea that it may not be that easy for some leaders to acknowledge responsibility.

HOW OFTEN DO LEADERS TAKE RESPONSIBILITY FOR ATROCITIES CONDUCTED UNDER THEIR COMMAND?

In Cambodia, only five individuals were ever brought to justice by the Extraordinary Chambers in the Courts of Cambodia (ECCC) for the decimation of a quarter of the Cambodian population. It took a decade after the genocide for the ECCC to be created and established, and more than a decade to prosecute the five individuals brought before the court.[182] Notably, Pol Pot, the main leader of the Khmer Rouge regime, was not included in these cases, as he died in 1998 before he could be brought to trial for the atrocities committed under his rule.

In the end, and about $400 million later, only three of the five people were convicted for the atrocities of the Khmer Rouge regime. One of the indicted died in March 2013 while the case against him was still ongoing, and another was found to be suffering from Alzheimer's disease and died in August 2015. Meanwhile, the tribunal faced numerous challenges and criticisms, including accusations of corruption and political interference, which contributed to the slow progress of its cases.

International prosecutors at the ECCC had wanted to pursue cases against several other Khmer Rouge officials, but the Cambodian judges in the ECCC blocked the procedure.[183] Today, no other person involved in the acts of torture or killing has to fear official prosecution. Yet those five individuals, as well as Pol Pot, did not act alone. Why, then, have the trials ended? It may again be a question of leadership and responsibility. The former prime minister of Cambodia, Hun Sen,* who was himself a former Khmer Rouge military officer, indicated that continuing the prosecutions beyond the top leaders would only reopen the wounds of the Cambodian society, which he argued was not desired.[184]

The very low number of people officially convicted for all the atrocities committed during the Khmer Rouge regime makes Cambodia a rather unique example regarding the attribution of responsibility. Expectations from the victims and an entire country were high regarding who would be seen as accountable for this tragic episode in their history. Yet only individuals considered as top leaders went to trial. They bore all the charges on their shoulders alone.

So, did these leaders acknowledge this level of responsibility for the atrocities committed?

---

* When the interviews reported in Chapter 1 took place, the prime minister of Cambodia was still Hun Sen, who held office between 1985 and 1993, and then from 1998 to 2023. In August 2023, after being reelected, he transferred power to his son, Hun Manet.

In 1997, a US journalist, Nate Thayer, obtained a rare interview with Pol Pot and asked him if he felt responsible for what happened during the Khmer Rouge regime. The journalist also asked him if he knew about all the acts of torture and death that were happening under his regime – for example, the 16,000 men, women, and children who died in Tuol Sleng, the infamous detention center S-21, where people were interrogated and tortured until they admitted crimes that they did not even commit.

Pol Pot answered with the following: "Please understand, with my high level of work, I only made decisions concerning the very important people. I did not supervise the base, the lower ranks. . . . So, as far as my conscience and my mission were concerned, there was no problem. "[185] Pol Pot died peacefully in his sleep nine months later due to heart failure, never having acknowledged responsibility for the atrocities conducted when he was the General Secretary of the Communist Party of Kampuchea (CPK).

More recently, on November 16, 2018, Khieu Samphan, one of the main Khmer Rouge leaders, was sentenced to life imprisonment after four years of trials for a bevy of crimes against humanity: genocide and grave breaches of the Geneva Convention of 1949, including wilful killing, torture, or inhumane treatment; wilfully causing great suffering or serious injury to body or health; wilfully depriving a prisoner of war or civilian the rights of fair and regular trial; unlawful deportation or unlawful confinement of a civilian. He appealed the decision, however, because he denied responsibility for the crimes he was accused of. During his first trial, he claimed:

> It is easy to say that I should have known everything, I should have understood everything and thus I could have intervened or rectified the situation at the time . . . Do you really think that that was what I wanted to happen to my people? The reality was that I did not have any power. [186]

On September 22, 2022, the ECCC confirmed its initial decision without the possibility of further appeal. The prosecution presented clear evidence that contradicted Khieu Samphan's claims, including documents and witness testimony that showed that he was a key member of the Khmer Rouge leadership and played a significant role in the decision-making process. He may have denied responsibility, but the court unequivocally disagreed.

Nuon Chea, also known as Brother Number 2, was the party's chief ideologist and Pol Pot's right-hand man. He was accused in his indictment of having planned and directed the purges during the Khmer Rouger regime. During the ECCC trial, Nuon Chea was charged with crimes against humanity, grave breaches of the Geneva Convention, genocide (of the Cham and Vietnamese), homicide, torture, and religious persecution. However, Nuon Chea also denied the majority of his involvement in the Khmer Rouge regime's atrocities: "I was president of the National Assembly and had nothing to do with the operation of the government. Sometimes I didn't know what they were doing because I was in the assembly."[187] Yet, as the pieces of evidence accumulated, Nuon Chea started to express remorse. Unlike Khieu Samphan, he acknowledged a sense of responsibility: "As a leader, I must take responsibility for the damage, the danger to my nation. . . . I feel remorseful for the crimes that were committed intentionally or unintentionally, whether I had known about it or not known about it." He nonetheless added that he was not aware of the heinous acts committed by the other leaders, which had caused the tragedy for the nation and people.[188]

Kang Kek Iew (sometimes spelled Kaing Guek Eav), alias Duch, was the head of the *Santebal* ("Keeper of peace"), the secret police of the Khmer Rouge in charge of running prison camps and internal security. He was also the prison director of the S-21 detention center. He was charged with crimes against humanity and grave breaches of the Geneva Convention. In addition to unknown individuals, Duch also executed many of his relatives, friends, professors, and superiors. Duch, unlike the other Khmer Rouge leaders, did not dismiss his crimes at first. He acknowledged responsibility and apologized. On March 31, 2009, during his trial, he spoke up and told the court:

Whenever I recall the past, I am deeply pained, and I am racked with remorse. I am appalled whenever I recall the activities which I was ordered to carry out, and the orders I gave to others that affected the lives of many innocent people, including women and children. Though I acted out of respect for Angkar's orders, I am still responsible for the crimes. . . . At present, I have the deepest sorrow and regret, and I feel ashamed and uneasy. As a perpetrator, I know that I am personally guilty before the entire Cambodian people and nation, before the families of all the victims who lost their lives at S-21 and before my own family, some of whom also lost their lives.

On March 30, 2011, he added "I still maintain my position to ask for forgiveness for the soul of the victims of 12,273 people who lost their lives at S-21, and for the families of those victims to accept my apology and grant forgiveness."[†]

Intriguingly, however, despite his acknowledgement of his responsibility, Duch asked the court to find him not guilty and to be released. It was a request that shocked the judges and the victims.[189] It begs the question: can a man express guilt and ask for forgiveness, while at the same time requesting that he should not be found guilty in the eyes of law? Notably, during the trial, he laughed many times. A psychological analysis of Duch reported that he had no empathy, although Duch claimed that he was able to feel what others feel. Perhaps this analysis explains his ability to simultaneously accept responsibility while asking to be found not guilty in the eyes of the law. It is difficult to know.

As this section shows, it is not guaranteed – and it is in fact unusual – for those giving orders to take responsibility for actions committed under their leadership. Despite the testimonies from dozens of individuals and years of accumulation of pieces of evidence against them, the leaders of the CPK judged during the ECCC, as well as Pot Pot himself, mostly tried to deny their association with the crimes. Was this denial an attempt to avoid prosecution? Did it reflect a reality in their brains? Would the fact that they alone were being asked by the ECCC to bear accountability for an entire genocide increase their desire to deny responsibility?

These are extremely complex questions, not least because what they themselves report can be biased or not fully accurate, as discussed in Chapter 1. Perhaps experimental research can help us understand how these leaders' positions influence moral behaviors and related brain mechanisms.

[†] The full apology statements can be read in Khmer, English, or French on the website of the Extraordinary Chambers in the Court of Cambodia / Case 001.

MORAL DECISION-MAKING IN LEADERSHIP

In the scientific literature, previous work conducted in lab studies has investigated to what extent being in the role of the person either *giving* or *transmitting* orders changed moral behaviors towards victims, compared to being the direct agent executing the action.

Experimental research has shown that being in an intermediary position increases obedience to orders to hurt someone in comparison with being the author of that action or being the person giving the orders. As mentioned in Chapter 2, Milgram conducted many variants of his seminal study on obedience. In Experiment 18, participants were no longer being asked to press the shock buttons. They simply pulled a switch that enabled another (fake) participant to deliver the shock. They thus had an intermediary position and let another person press the buttons. In this situation, 37 out of 40 participants, which corresponds to 92.5 percent, continued to pull the switch up until the fatal shock was delivered.[48] Compared to his seminal study in which participants were those pressing the shock buttons themselves – where 65 percent continued up to the fatal shock – Experiment 18 suggests that being in an intermediary position increases the likelihood of obeying orders to hurt another person.

In a study replicating Milgram's experimental setup, two researchers, Wesley Kilham and Leon Mann, directly compared the position of intermediary and of agent executing orders to analyze the degree of obedience in a Milgram-like paradigm in the two roles.[190] In their study, they had a real participant and two confederates in addition to the experimenter. In an experimental condition, the real participants were in the role of the transmitter and had to ask someone to deliver the electric shocks. In another experimental condition, participants were themselves in the role of the person delivering the electric shocks. Results clearly indicated that being in the intermediary position increased the likelihood of participating in destructive obedience: Overall, when participants were in the role of the transmitter, they were more obedient compared to when they were executing the action.

In other words, when people are in an intermediary position, it appears that they are even more obedient and can be linked to more harm delivery than when they are the agents. At the psychological level, it is quite comfortable being in an intermediary position: You do not bear responsibility for the initial command, and you do not bear the responsibility of carrying out the act. As Adolf Eichmann claimed during his trial in Israel in 1961: "In actual fact I was merely a little cog in the machinery that carried out the directives of the German Reich."[12]

In a study published in 2022 with my colleagues from the Netherlands Institute for Neuroscience, Christian Keysers, Valeria Gazzola, and Kalliopi Ioumpa, we compared the number of shocks participants decided to deliver to a victim when they were in the role of the person giving orders (hereafter referred to as the commander) versus in the role of the intermediary who was transmitting orders.[191] Participants took over the two roles in two different experimental conditions in order to allow comparisons. We observed that when participants were in the role of an intermediary, they pressed the shock button more frequently than when they were in the role of the commander. Such results might suggest that being distanced from both the orders and the action leading to pain in others increases antisocial conduct.

I also conducted two studies in 2018 comparing how being in the role of the agent versus the role of the person giving orders would influence antisocial behavior.[108] We had three real participants, one being in the role of the commander, one in the role of the agent executing orders, and one in the role of the victim. Their roles were switched during the experiment, so that each participant was associated with all the three different roles. In a first study, we observed that participants administered more painful electric shocks to the victims when they played the role of commander than when they played the role of agent. Such a result would suggest that indirect agency – that is, when you are not the person pressing buttons – can increase antisocial behavior.

However, interestingly, in a second study where we changed the experimental protocol slightly, results were reversed, with participants inflicting more electric shocks on the victims when they played the role of agents than when they played the role of commanders. In the first study, commanders had to give their orders out loud, thus being heard by all the persons present in the experimental room. However, in the second study, the orders were given through a button press. Only the agents executing the orders could see the orders displayed on their screen and decide to follow them or not. Thus, in the second study, victims did not know whether the decision to harm was actually taken by the agent or by the commander, because they could not see the screen displaying orders. This lack of information may have allowed agents to diffuse their sense of responsibility even more to the commanders, since the victim could not know whether the agent was "only obeying orders" or was acting voluntarily.

In other words, agents could "hide" their own decision behind the commanders' instruction, unknown to the victim. This form of diffusion of responsibility might be described as "informational": People may feel less responsibility when they know that the social context makes it difficult to recover the decision they made. Being able to hide a misdeed in the eyes of society may motivate individuals to engage in more such antisocial behavior.

I also systematically asked the participants to estimate how responsible they felt in each role – commander or agent – and to describe in a few words how they felt during the testing. Participants systematically reported that they felt more responsible when they were in the role of the commander compared to when they were in the role of the agent executing orders. In addition, their debriefings also suggested that they felt more responsibility, even though some participants reported an equal feeling of responsibility between being commanders and agents, and others had no opinions on the question.

The participants' reports are illustrative (all translated from French):

I felt responsible when I was in the role of the commander, but not when I was in the role of the agent.

When I was commander, I asked the agents to send more shocks compared to when I was agent. I liked being in the position where another person does not think about your orders.

When I was in the role of the commander, I felt: authority, power, responsibility, free will, choice. When I was in the role of the agent, I felt: compliance, obedience.

As commander, I felt a feeling of powerfulness because I was the one who could decide.

As commanders, you feel more distanced from the victim. We are less impacted by what is happening.

I felt more responsible as a commander. But isn't it normal for commanders to feel 100% responsible for what is happening?

As commander, I took more time to decide between sending a shock or not to the victim compared to when I was in the position of the agent. I sent less shocks to the victim when I was commander compared to when I was agent. As agent, I felt as if I was a simple robot. But as a commander, I had more pity for the victim.

I felt guilty giving orders that implied [delivering] a shock to another person, because it is as if I was less responsible myself by asking someone else to execute my orders.

I had less remorse when I was obeying orders compared to when I was giving orders myself.

At this point in the experiment, I thought, "so far, so good!" Many people seemed to claim more responsibility when they gave orders. However, caution must always be taken when interpreting explicit claims. People can indeed easily claim responsibility in this experimental context, as they did not have to fear any prosecution for the shocks delivered. In real-life examples, leaders or commanders are legally accountable for their directives, which can influence their willingness to defend themselves in the case of an official prosecution. Furthermore, our participants may also have answered in a way that they thought was expected of them, in order to please the experimenter or to appear responsible as a human being.

As this section shows, participants overall claim that they feel more responsible as commanders compared to being in the position of an agent executing orders. Usually, more responsibility comes with a decreased level of antisocial conduct. However, the number of shocks participants delivered, or their level of obedience, indicated that being in a commander's or intermediary's position can have a negative influence on moral behavior, as they overall perform more antisocial actions when they give or transmit orders rather than when they are agents. To solve these rather controversial results, neuroscience, and the use of implicit methods, can be used.

IN THE BRAINS OF COMMANDERS AND INTERMEDIARIES

As a neuroscientist, the experiments I ran in 2018 made me wonder to what extent the subjective experiences of participants reflected how their brains were processing the information. I thus decided to look more closely at what the brain would reveal about being in the position of giving orders.

The scientific literature shows that being in a situation of power has an influence on different affective and cognitive mechanisms. In two different studies, a team of researchers decided to investigate the extent to which being in a high or a low power position would influence how the brain responds to the pain of others, as well as their sense of agency. They invited participants into the lab and asked them either to recall a situation in which they had had power over another individual (i.e., high social power condition) or a situation in which someone had power over them (i.e., low social power condition). Such procedures are called "memory retrieval" in the scientific literature, and they involve asking participants to remember and relate a certain state-of-mind or a life event for several minutes while the researchers observe its influence on the targeted processes or behaviors.

In their study targeting the sense of agency,[192] participants were asked to perform voluntary actions after the memory retrieval procedure and then to estimate the delay between their action and an auditory outcome. As a reminder from Chapter 3, this implicit method is based on time perception and has been associated with the experience of agency: Shorter estimated time intervals are associated with a higher sense of agency. The researchers in this experiment observed that when participants had to recall a situation of high power, it did not influence their sense of agency compared to a neutral condition. Thus, being in a high-power position does not appear to boost the sense of agency. However, when participants were remembering a situation associated with low social power, their sense of agency was reduced. This result could suggest that those executing orders have a reduced experience of agency compared to those having power.

In these researchers' second study, they targeted the brain's response to others' pain.[193] After the memory retrieval procedure, participants were invited to sit in front of a computer where they witnessed hands with tools capable of causing painful physical harm and hands with tools not capable of inflicting pain or causing painful physical harm. Participants' brain activity was recorded with an electroencephalogram in order to measure the neural reaction to pain in the two experimental conditions. The researchers observed that participants had a higher neural response to the pain seen in the pictures when they had just recalled a situation of high social power. Interestingly, they had a lower neural response when they had just recalled a situation of low social power. In other words, their results indicated that having high social power seems to increase the brain's response to others' pain compared to having low social power.

However, a strong limitation in these studies is that even though participants were asked to remember real-life events, they were not per se in a high or in a low social power situation during the experiment. They were imagining what it feels like to be in a high or in a low social power condition, but they had no actual power at all during the task. And as Stanley Milgram's studies have taught us,[48] there is a huge difference between *imagining* being in a situation and really *being* in a situation.

In 2018 we decided to first study the sense of agency of those giving orders. We wanted to understand if the sense of agency would be different between commanders and agents executing orders, when their actions or orders have real-life consequences for a third person.[108] In one experimental condition, the participants played the role of the agent; in another experimental condition, they played the role of the commander. As in previous studies, they could decide to deliver – or order to deliver – a mildly painful shock to a victim in exchange for €0.05. We used the implicit measurement of the sense of agency based on time perception. With this implicit measurement, we wanted to avoid having social biases influence our results, which is more frequently the case for explicit reports. As seen in previous chapters, implicit measurements prevent participants from guessing what the experimenters are measuring, and thus limit the possible influence of social desirability on their results.

As our participants reported explicitly feeling more responsible when they were in the role of the commander compared to when they were in the role of the agent executing orders, we would have expected to see a higher sense of agency in the commander role. However, this is not what we observed with the implicit measurement. When they were commanders and decided which order to give, participants' sense of agency was reduced compared to when they were agents deciding freely. We actually observed that the commanders' sense of agency was as low as when they were agents executing the commander's order. Complementing previous research on those obeying orders, the results indicated that, in a hierarchical chain, everyone has a reduced sense of agency. Neither the person carrying out the orders nor the one giving them had an increased sense of agency.

Notably, we observed that commanders with the most reduced sense of agency when they gave commands were also those scoring the highest on a scale measuring psychopathic traits. This means that psychopathic traits appear to increase the risk that people will fail to feel agency – and thus responsibility – when they give a command. This is a particularly worrying suggestion, given that previous work has highlighted a high prevalence of psychopathic traits in leaders in business and other spheres.[194,195] Of course, no one has tried to replicate this result, so caution must be taken when drawing conclusions. Still, we also observed in another study that commanders with the most reduced sense of agency and the most reduced feeling of responsibility when giving orders were also those who most frequently ordered the delivery of painful shocks to the victim.[191] When taken together, these results show that when one does not experience agency or responsibility for one's orders, it can lead to more harmful behavior towards others.

Next was focusing on the empathetic experience of commanders when their orders cause pain to a victim. We conducted a study with fMRI in order to understand how a person giving orders to an agent to hurt a victim would impact their capacity to resonate with the pain of others.[191] We had two experimental conditions, one in which our participants could freely choose which orders to give to the agent and one in which they received an order from the experimenter that they had to transmit. Participants were thus either in the role of commander or in the role of transmitter.

Our results showed that when participants are in the role of the commander or in the role of the intermediary, there is activation in the anterior cingulate cortex and the anterior insula, thus supporting the idea that witnessing a shock being delivered to the victim triggers an empathic reaction in their brain. However, this activation was not as high as we might have hoped. When we compared the activations in empathy-related brain regions of commanders giving orders to the same activations in transmitters and to the same activations in agents executing orders – thus reflecting a typical hierarchical situation – the activations were equally low in the three roles. Further, the activations in guilt-related brain regions were also equally low for commanders giving orders, for transmitters, and for agents executing orders. Such results suggest that moral emotions are commonly or often impacted in hierarchical situations, affecting many individuals within the chain.

In addition to the numerous episodes throughout history that have shown the power of fractioning operations to implement mass atrocities, experimental research shows how such power occurs. Hierarchical chains can create conditions where individuals in the chain of command may be more likely to engage in moral transgressions or other unethical behavior, as agency and moral emotions are split across two or more individuals.

Is not feeling moral emotions and agency in hierarchical situations an inevitable process? Hopefully not. First, the results that are presented are group results. It means that even if the majority of individuals had a reduced agency and reduced processing of moral emotions when they obey or give orders, it was not the case for the whole sample of participants. Some appear to be less affected by coercive contexts than others. Second, as we have seen in Chapter 4, humans have the capacity to modulate their empathy, even though empathy is a biological process. Successful interventions could thus be implemented to train people to resist the detrimental effect of situations where power is divided between several individuals. Proposed training could, for instance, first start by teaching people about what empathy is and why it is important. They could be encouraged in perspective-taking, to help them to see situations from another person's point of view. This can be done by asking them to imagine themselves in another person's shoes and think about how they might feel or react in that situation, even if the situation involves putting responsibility on someone else's shoulders. But, of course, it requires people to be willing to engage in such processes.

COMMANDING THE MACHINE: NEW CHALLENGES
FOR HIERARCHICAL CHAINS?

We are entering a new era. Hierarchical chains, previously only involving human beings, now also include new technologies at different levels of the chain. The use of robots, artificial intelligence (AI), and drones is changing the landscape of human responsibility in complex and far-reaching ways. And as these technologies continue to evolve and become more integrated into society, be it civilian or military, it will be important in the future to develop new frameworks for understanding and assigning responsibility.

Even if people executing orders may have a reduced empathy for the pain of their victims, as we have seen in Chapter 4, they can nonetheless have a small portion of empathy that can help them not perpetrate atrocities by potentially disobeying orders. But robots or drones are clearly not designed or manufactured to feel empathy or responsibility, or to disobey orders. Does the use of these novel technologies eradicate empathy and responsibility from the chains of command? Or does it, conversely, help those giving orders regain some sense of responsibility and empathy over the consequences of their actions, as they can't displace their responsibility onto another human?

In a small investigation, we asked 200 respondents to watch several videos of five potential agents: two humans (male and female), one humanoid robot, one robotic arm, and a basic motor. We asked them if they thought that these different agents were responsible for their actions, and, if they found themselves in the role of giving orders to these different agents, would they feel responsible for the consequences?

Results indicated that humanoid robots were judged as less responsible entities than humans but were considered as being nonetheless more responsible than nonhumanoid robots. Such results suggest that human features on a robot can increase the perception of this entity's responsibility. Results also indicated that respondents would feel more responsible if they had to give orders to a robot, be it humanoid or not, than to a human. This is consistent with the prediction made based on the phenomenon of diffusion of responsibility: Acting with another entity considered to have their own responsibility diminishes one's own feeling of responsibility.[196] Humanoid robots, despite their human-like attributes, are judged less responsible, thus increasing the perception of responsibility of the human asking them to accomplish tasks.

Indeed, the scientific literature has started to approach this question of agency and responsibility when co-acting or giving orders to robots, using implicit and neuroimaging measurements. In a study published in 2020,[197] a team of researchers investigated the extent to which interacting with a robot reduces the sense of agency compared to when one is interacting with another human being. The authors used a task where participants had to stop the inflation of a balloon before it reached a pin and burst, which would result in a loss of points. They could stop the balloon inflation at any time, but the later they stopped it, the more points they could earn, even though it also involved a higher risk of bursting. Across different experiments, participants were performing the task alone, or in the company of a small robot, or alone but with a non-agentic air-pump, or with another human and a robot. The results showed that when participants were performing the task with a robot or with a human, their sense of agency was reduced compared to when acting alone, suggesting a diffusion of responsibility phenomenon. However, when they were acting with an air pump, their sense of agency was not reduced. Such results suggest that when interacting with a robot which could create the illusion of intentionality (in contrast to the mechanistic air pump), participants' sense of agency was reduced, similarly to when they are interacting with another person.

In that study, however, the relationship between the nonhuman entities and the human participants was egalitarian, as both had an equal role to play in the action to stop the inflation of the balloon. On the other hand, in a hierarchical relationship or situation, responsibility is often more clearly defined and may be concentrated at the top of the hierarchy. In both situations, responsibility is present, but the nature of that responsibility can differ depending on the roles and expectations of the parties involved.

In a study conducted in 2022, we investigated whether giving orders to a robot compared to a human would influence empathy and the sense of agency of the commanders.[191] We observed that the sense of agency in commanders did not differ when they gave orders to a robot or to a human. However, they explicitly claimed more responsibility in the robot condition. This may reflect that explicit claims and implicit measurements are sensitive to different sources of influence.

Further and quite interestingly, while we had observed that giving orders to another human being reduced empathy for the pain of the victim, results tended to suggest that giving orders to a robot restored some of the reactions to the pain in commanders, as measured with electroencephalography. Such a result may raise hope because if empathy is reduced by those at the forefront executing orders, introducing nonhuman entities in the chains of command may perhaps enhance responsibility and empathy at higher levels in the hierarchy.

The diffusion of responsibility from humans to robots is an important area of study because it has the potential to significantly impact human behavior in various contexts. If humans are able to diffuse their responsibility onto robots, this could affect their decision-making processes. They may become more willing to take risks or make decisions they would not otherwise make, knowing that they can shift the responsibility to a machine. Studying the diffusion of responsibility from humans to robots can help us better understand the potential impact of robots on society and how to design and regulate them to maximize their benefits while minimizing their risks.

CHAPTER 6

Desolation Is Everywhere

AFTER A GENOCIDE, A WAR, OR ANY DRAMATIC CONFLICT, only desolation remains.

There are of course the countable consequences: the number of deaths, the number of wounded individuals, the number of refugees, the number of war prisoners, the number of orphans seeking a foster family, the number of destroyed infrastructures, the estimated cost for the economy of the country. The estimation of the consequences of conflicts is usually based on such objectifiable numbers. On Wikipedia, for example, you can immediately see the number of deaths associated with different conflicts. But there is almost nothing about the less visible consequences of wars and genocides; the psychological and emotional consequences that deeply affect people's minds. It is, however, crucial to acknowledge that while every war or conflict comes to an end at some point, the battle for the mental health of survivors is a fight that continues long after.

While reading the newspaper in early 2023, I discovered that a survivor of the suicide bombing attacks in Brussels on March 22, 2016 had just asked for euthanasia, a legal procedure in Belgium. Her body had not been injured; she did not suffer from permanent physical injuries. From the outside, she had no visible scars causing her suffering. But she was suffering from deep psychological disorders that she had never been able to overcome. She reported on social media that she could no longer feel safe, that she had frequent panic attacks, that she was afraid in the presence of other people. She eventually attempted suicide twice. As the countless pills she was taking every day were ineffective, she decided that she could no longer live with the psychological trauma that she had had to endure for years.

Huge progress has been made to recognize and understand better the psychological consequences of a trauma, and it is now acknowledged that everyone is at risk in war. The victims who survive face psychological trauma in addition to sometimes permanent physical disabilities. So do their relatives, who witness the suffering of their loved ones and feel unable to help. Their children and even grandchildren, who inherit through epigenetics and social transmission the sequelae of their parents' trauma, suffer as well. Even perpetrators claiming reduced responsibility in an attempt to escape the law may not always avoid the mental torments that could affect their mind. They indeed have to deal with the psychological consequences of what they did or were ordered to do, and may experience trauma, guilt, and shame after the events, which can lead to mental health issues; some even commit suicide.

For example, in Rwanda, with my team we observed a similar prevalence of post-traumatic stress symptoms between survivors and perpetrators.[143] This can be explained by the years spent in overcrowded prisons for perpetrators as well as public blame during the Gacaca courts in Rwanda for what they did, or the fact that they had to flee the country. Some of them also experience feelings of shame and guilt for what they did,[198] and many suffer from substance abuse or anxiety disorder.[21] Several studies have also shown that military veterans suffering from feelings of guilt and shame were more likely to suffer from post-traumatic stress symptoms.[199,200]

The present chapter argues that by recognizing and addressing these issues, by also considering the struggle of assailants, there is a possibility that the cycle of violence can be broken, and future occurrences can be prevented. First, many assailants may not even consider that their mental wellbeing can be affected, as they can be persuaded of the rightness of their actions. Raising awareness of the struggles they may experience afterwards may perhaps prevent some actions from being conducted. Second, deep psychological suffering can be associated with more aggression towards oneself or others. It can also be associated with feelings of revenge that can only contribute to cycles of violence.

As a famous historical example, Germans felt humiliated after World War I, which contributed to feelings of resentment and revenge that helped lay the groundwork for World War II. Many Germans indeed believed that their country had been treated unfairly by the international community, and that the Treaty of Versailles (June 28, 1919) had left them vulnerable to further aggression. Adolf Hitler and the Nazi Party capitalized on these feelings of resentment and humiliation, promising to restore Germany to its former glory and offer revenge against those who had wronged the German people. Hitler's aggressive policies and military conquests ultimately led to the outbreak of World War II, which resulted in the deaths of millions of people and left Germany devastated once again. While the complex causes of World War II cannot be reduced solely to German feelings of humiliation after World War I, it is clear that these feelings played a significant role in shaping German attitudes towards other countries and populations, and led to the outbreak of World War II.

Understanding the psychological effects of perpetrating violence can help in designing appropriate rehabilitation and reintegration programs for these individuals. By doing so, it could increase the chances of their successful reintegration into society and reduce the likelihood of them re-engaging in violent behavior. Peacefulness in the mind is a critical step to ensure peaceful actions in the outside world.

UNDERSTANDING POST-TRAUMATIC STRESS DISORDER

Post-traumatic stress disorder, or PTSD, is a set of reactions that people may experience after a traumatic experience. It does not necessarily develop immediately after the traumatic experience. Usually, the symptoms appear one month after the event, but in some cases, they can also appear months or even years after the event and remain for a long time if not properly handled.

I remember a conversation that I had a few years ago with a researcher from the Dutch Ministry of Defence, at the Brain Research & Innovation Center located in Utrecht. They conduct research on mental health in Dutch military personnel and veterans, and are thus seeing on a daily basis military patients facing mental health issues. The researcher I met told me that it is common for military personnel to develop such mental health issues years, even decades, after the event, sometimes even during retirement. Many veterans may have suppressed their emotions and experiences during their military service, focusing instead on their mission and the needs of their unit. Upon retiring from service, they may find themselves with more time to reflect on their experiences, and may begin to process the emotions and memories they have suppressed. This can be a difficult and painful process, and may lead to the development of mental health conditions.

PTSD diagnosis in adults is based on a range of symptoms, which are typically grouped into four main categories, encompassing various aspects of the disorder. One of the most common is re-experiencing the traumatic event. This can take the forms of flashbacks, nightmares, or repetitive images of painful experiences. People suffering from PTSD will also try to avoid being reminded about the traumatic event. They thus show avoidance and emotional numbing. For instance, they will avoid places or people that recall their experience or will try to stop feeling anything at all, in an attempt to avoid negative thoughts. People suffering from PTSD may also be in a state of hyperarousal, with difficulties relaxing and being frequently in an alert state. They suffer from irritability, insomnia, or angry outbursts.[201] For instance, scientific research has highlighted that many perpetrators of intimate partner violence had previously been exposed to past traumatic experiences themselves.[202] They are also likely to develop severe mental disorders, which correlate with their level of violence towards their partner. People suffering from PTSD may also suffer from a negative alteration of cognition and mood. For example, they can have difficulties remembering some key elements of the traumatic event. They may also have negative thoughts and affects, such as feeling guilty.

PTSD has been extensively studied and researched in psychology. Medicine and neuroscience have also done a lot to increase our knowledge of the symptoms and their underlying mechanisms, allowing us to offer more efficient treatments nowadays. It is important to note that PTSD not only affects mental health. It also affects physical health and emotional health. Individuals suffering from PTSD have reported musculoskeletal pain, as well as cardio-respiratory and gastrointestinal issues to name but a few.[203] It can also lead to self-harming behaviors or destructive behaviors such as drug or alcohol misuse, or even suicide attempts. Furthermore, it can seriously damage personal relationships.

In the case of a war, there are countless situations that can lead to trauma, for victims and assailants. For victims, it can be fearing for one's own life or the lives of loved ones, being separated from one's family, being imprisoned with or without torture, witnessing extreme forms of violence, losing all one's belongings, being raped, or experiencing extreme physical pain. For assailants, it can be killing or injuring others, experiencing postwar guilt, witnessing the pain caused to others, being forced to participate in violent acts, or suffering from the sanctions after a defeat.

This list is of course nonexhaustive, and it only includes examples related to warlike events. Developing trauma is also very frequent after having experienced child abuse, domestic violence, a personal attack, serious health problems, or surviving a natural disaster, to name but a few. Considering the wide range of situations that can lead to trauma and PTSD, 70 percent of the population are likely to experience PTSD at some point in their lives.[204] Moreover, those who have suffered from PTSD may experience a life-long sensitivity to new stressful events. Past research has shown that even after a period of quiescence, a stressful event – even when not related to the initial traumatic event – can reactivate PTSD. For example, a study showed that after the planes crashed into the World Trade Center in the US in 2001, many refugees from South Asia, Bosnia, and Somalia who had seen the television images of the disaster had a reactivation of their PTSD symptoms.[205]

Suffering from post-traumatic stress disorders is devastating for individuals, but also for society. As this section shows, individuals suffering from PTSD have to face a range of damaging symptoms, including intrusive thoughts or memories of the traumatic event, avoidance of triggers that remind them of the trauma, and hyperarousal or an exaggerated fear response. These symptoms can make it difficult to function in daily life, maintain relationships, and hold down a job, and can significantly reduce an individual's quality of life. At the same time, PTSD can also have broader impacts on society, particularly when it affects those in high-risk professions such as military service, law enforcement, or emergency medical services. When individuals who have experienced trauma are unable to access effective treatment for PTSD, they may be at increased risk of substance abuse, domestic violence, and other negative outcomes that can have ripple effects throughout their communities.[206] And it can be difficult for individuals to control the devastating consequences of trauma, because trauma alters both the functioning and structure of the brain.

STRESSFUL EVENTS CHANGE THE BRAIN

Having experienced a traumatic event can change your brain on many levels, be it how you make decisions, how you process what others feel, or even how you subconsciously respond to events happening around you. It is crucial to understand the mechanisms behind these changes if we are to develop efficient treatments.

There are four brain regions that are critical in the development of PTSD: the amygdala, the nucleus accumbens, the hippocampus, and the medial prefrontal cortex[207] (Figure 6.1). When we experience a stressful situation, our organs – mostly our eyes and our ears – collect the information and send it to the amygdala, which is an area of the brain involved in emotional processing.[208] When the amygdala decides that the situation is dangerous, it sends a distress signal to the hypothalamus. The hypothalamus is a critical region in the brain, as it is in charge of sending information to the rest of the body. In the case of a stressful situation, the hypothalamus will send signals through the nerves until they reach the adrenal glands located on the top of your kidneys. Those adrenal glands respond by pumping a specific hormone

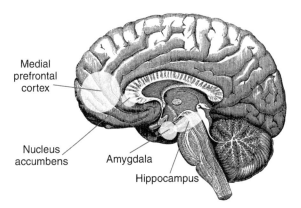

Figure 6.1 Brain regions altered after a trauma. The four key brain regions altered after a traumatic event are the amygdala, the nucleus accumbens, the hippocampus, and the medial prefrontal cortex. Their alterations can lead to PTSD symptoms.

in the bloodstream – adrenaline – which results in several physical changes. This process is why, for example, you will start sweating, breathe faster, or experience a higher heartbeat rate immediately after a stressful event.

The response of our body to a stressful situation is extremely fast and efficient, and we do not even need to process the information consciously for our body to act on its "fight or flight" response. This is a critical mechanism that is largely responsible for our survival as a species.

Research in neuroscience and neurology has illuminated critical information for understanding how stress impacts the brain by changing its neurochemical functioning as well as the brain circuits involved in the "stress response." Past research has shown, for example, that PTSD patients have a decreased threshold for amygdala activations compared to controls without PTSD.[209] In other words, for PTSD patients, any situations can be more easily perceived as potentially threatening. One team of researchers,[210] for instance, recruited two groups of veterans, one with PTSD and the other without PTSD. Participants were presented with both fear and happiness stimuli for a very short period of a few milliseconds. The results indicated that participants suffering from PTSD had a higher activity in the amygdala compared to the participants without PTSD when witnessing the fear stimuli, suggesting that their threshold for considering a situation to be dangerous was reduced. This is why you may see someone overreacting when facing a situation that for you is barely stressful: Their brain does not process the surrounding environment in a regular way.

Amygdala activation and the release of adrenaline is the first step of the stress response process. If the brain continues to perceive the situation as dangerous or threatening, it will then release the corticotropin hormone, which will travel to the pituitary glands located in your brain and trigger the release of the adrenocorticotropic hormone. This hormone travels to the adrenal glands, as well, which then release cortisol.[211]

In the case of a continuous perception of stress or danger, such as may be the case for PTSD sufferers, the body continues to release cortisol. An elevated concentration of cortisol can have a neurotoxic effect on the brain,[212] notably on the hippocampus. The hippocampus is part of the limbic system and plays an important role in the consolidation of information for short-term and long-term memory, in the retrieval of information, and also in spatial memory and orientation.[213] In normal aging, a term that is used to refer to aging without any deteriorative diseases, the hippocampus starts changing after the age of 60 years and its volume is ultimately reduced by less than 1 percent to 2 percent.[214,215] This is the reason why, as they grow older, people start to experience difficulties remembering some events. Elderly individuals are also more at risk of developing PTSD symptoms. As the hippocampal volume decreases with age, this makes elderly individuals more at risk, as the part of their brain helping them regulate memories is already less efficient compared to its younger equivalent.[216] For PTSD patients, it is the result of the sustained neurochemical response to elevated stress.

Indeed, there are several studies using magnetic resonance imaging (MRI) showing that trauma exposure, independent of the presence of PTSD symptoms, is associated with a reduction of the volume of the hippocampus.[217] This may explain why during and after exposure to a traumatic experience, memories are difficult to regulate. They are not processed in a regular way, and the presence of intrusive thoughts, nightmares, or the inability to recall memories are all quite normal.

However, the mechanisms between stress, cortisol, and hippocampus volume may not be perfectly straightforward. For instance, alcohol dependence or major depression can also alter the hippocampal volume and are both very frequent after a traumatic event.[218] Thus, perhaps it is not the trauma itself that causes a reduction of the hippocampal volume, but rather other psychological consequences associated with the trauma. Other studies have even suggested that a smaller hippocampal volume may be a pre-existing trait that predisposes people to PTSD in the case of a traumatic event.[219]

The third key brain region is the medial prefrontal cortex. The prefrontal cortex has already been introduced in Chapter 4 in relation to emotion regulation. The medial part of the prefrontal cortex, specifically, allows us to regulate our behavior, to exert control over our decisions, but also to control anxiety. It plays a key role in the memory of the emotional valence of events and in our fear response.

Managing our emotions involves a good balance between the prefrontal cortex and the amygdala. At the anatomical level, the amygdala and some parts of the medial prefrontal cortex are highly interconnected: The medial prefrontal cortex allows regulation of the activity in the amygdala and, reciprocally, the amygdala modulates the activity of the medial prefrontal cortex.[220]

Several neuroimaging studies have shown that patients suffering from PTSD have structural, neurochemical, and functional abnormalities in the medial prefrontal cortex. Consequently, they are less able to exert control over the emotional processing of fear when it is sent by the amygdala. For example, in some studies, the researchers asked people suffering from PTSD to control their fear response during the presentation of fear-inducing facial expressions[221] or combat pictures or sounds.[222] They observed that the participants had difficulty managing their emotional response to these stimuli, likely because the activity in their medial prefrontal cortex was reduced. Other studies confirmed such results.[223,224] When the medial prefrontal cortex is damaged, the extinction of fear is not appropriately made.

The fourth key brain region impacted after a trauma is the nucleus accumbens (NAcc). It is linked the mesocortical dopaminergic system, which is central to the brain's reward circuit.[225] This is a system that was already mentioned in Chapter 4, when I explained that some prosocial actions can be perceived as rewarding, because they activate neurons in this system that are also involved in the transmission of dopamine, a neurotransmitter linked to reward processing. It has been shown in studies that patients with PTSD have an altered reward processing in the nucleus accumbens compared to healthy controls.[226] Trauma can thus affect dopamine regulation, leading to changes in mood and motivation. This can lead to anhedonia, which is an inability to feel pleasure, in PTSD patients.[227] The nucleus accumbens is also associated with addiction, and its alteration after a trauma also partially explains why people suffering from PTSD display a susceptibility to addictive disorders.

All these studies show that someone suffering from PTSD symptoms may not be able to regulate their reactions as the chemistry, structure, and neural functioning of their brain is altered. It is thus highly important to provide them with the relevant support to help them to overcome their trauma and the damage it has caused.

THE UNSPOKEN STRUGGLE OF COMBATANTS

Indeed, war can have profound psychological effects on all individuals involved, including both assailants and victims. While it is often assumed that those who perpetrate acts of violence are somehow immune to the psychological impact of their actions, research suggests that this is not the case. They can have similar brain alterations at the functional and structural levels as victims.

Current statistics show that military veterans experience a vast range of psychological damage. For instance, past studies have indicated that the prevalence of PTSD in military veterans after wars in Iraq and Afghanistan ranges between 0.6 and 31 percent.[228] The high variability observed could actually be linked to the types of experience of the veterans during war and to the level of combat intensity.[229] Those who have to face higher levels of combat exposure, through sniper fire, firefights or improvised explosive devices, or longer deployments are more at risk of developing PTSD symptoms compared to those working in fortified bases or those associated with the war but not deployed in the field. Suicide rates are also extremely high among military veterans and are considered as one of the leading causes of death in the US military, especially for the youngest, aged 29 or under.

Previous studies have shown that veterans with PTSD also have an alteration in brain regions associated with the development of PTSD symptoms. For example, several studies using neuroimaging methods have shown that military veterans with PTSD symptoms had a reduced volume in the hippocampus compared to healthy controls[230] or compared to military veterans without PTSD symptoms.[231] However, most of the time, the group composed of military veterans also had a history of higher alcohol consumption and differ by several factors from the control groups. Further, up to 20 percent of military veterans have a history of traumatic brain injury,[232] which can be associated with a reduction of the hippocampal volume.[233] Thus, it was not clear if PTSD was the factor that explained the reduced volume in the hippocampus, or if other factors could be the cause.

Uncovering this distinction is not an easy task, but usually to minimize the number of confounding factors in a study where different groups of individuals are compared, the optimal option is to conduct the study on monozygotic and dizygotic twins. Controlling all environmental factors could also be a solution, but hardly realistic as all humans evolve in different and very personal environments. Twins who grew up together have the same early family environment, are likely to have a similar socioeconomic status, and are the same age. The influence of genetics can be relatively well controlled because monozygotic twins are identical twins and share almost 100 percent of their genetic material, while dizygotic twins are fraternal twins that share about 50 percent of their genetic material. Thus, by comparing twins, you can control for a series of factors that can explain differences between two groups of humans.

In an elegant recent study,[234] the authors wanted to understand if the stress of combat exposure was associated with a reduction of the hippo-campal volume, by controlling for a maximum of other confounding factors. The researchers managed to recruit 34 twin pairs that were both working in the military during the Vietnam War, thus ensuring a similar environment overall. However, only one of the twins had been exposed to combat in Vietnam, while the other had not been deployed in the field. The twins also had similar alcohol exposure and childhood trauma. The authors observed that Vietnam combat veterans had a hippocampal volume 11 percent smaller compared to their brother with a history of military service, but without any exposure to combat. Interestingly, the results were similar for both monozygotic twins and dizygotic twins. Such results support the idea that smaller hippocampal volume could not be related to genetics or be a predisposing factor for the development of PTSD.

Another set of studies have shown that the amygdala in military veterans also appears to dysfunction, implying higher fear response. For four years, a team of researchers recruited 200 military currently in service or veterans.[235] All the participants included had been in service since September 11, 2001, and more than 75 percent of them had served in Iraq and/or Afghanistan. They performed structural scans to analyze the volume of the amygdala and compared military with PTSD symptoms to military without PTSD symptoms. The results showed that the amygdala volume was reduced for the group composed of military with PTSD symptoms, compared to those without, after controlling for environmental factors such as depression, alcohol consumption, medication, or PTSD chronicity.

Other studies showed that at the functional level, the activity of the amygdala was also altered in military veterans suffering from PTSD: When observing images of combat or hearing combat sounds, veterans with PTSD had a higher activation of their amygdala compared to healthy controls.[236,237] Further, activity in their medial prefrontal cortex, which helps to control emotional response, was reduced in veterans suffering from PTSD compared to veterans without PTSD when listening to a neutral voice recounting their traumatic experience to them.[223]

As this section shows, military veterans may suffer from PTSD, and several neuroimaging studies have shown that their symptoms can be explained by several brain dysfunctions. In addition to PTSD symptoms, military veterans are at risk of developing a feeling of wrongdoing, a feeling that they did something against their own moral values, and they may develop what are called "moral injuries."

THE MORAL CONSEQUENCES OF WAR

In accordance with international law, Belgian military regulations state clearly that military members must refuse orders if they do not fit in the interest of the service or if they involve committing a crime or delict (Law of May 27, 1870, Chapter IV, Art. 28).* Such regulations are actually present in the juridical system of many different countries worldwide, as it is largely recognized that obeying a superior order is not a defense of a war crime. However, in most cases, orders do not involve a crime or a delict even

---

* In common law jurisdictions, crimes are usually codified in statutes or criminal codes, and include offenses such as murder, robbery, and theft. A delict refers to a wrongful act that causes harm to another person, and is usually the basis for a civil lawsuit seeking damages. Delicts can include a wide range of wrongful acts, such as negligence, defamation, and fraud. It is worth noting that the definitions of these terms can vary depending on the specific legal system in question, and there may be different nuances and interpretations of these terms in different contexts.

though they still involve killing other human beings. In wartime, some acts are authorized even if they may be forbidden in peacetime. Thus, military members must refuse *unlawful* orders, but they cannot disobey *immoral* orders unless they want to be prosecuted by the military court. Military members thus frequently face the very hard task of being obliged to conduct acts that may go against their own moral values because their job implies compliance with given orders.

The concept of "moral injuries" designates military veterans or military still active who have witnessed or perpetrated an act that transgressed their moral values. Some examples involve obeying immoral orders, but they also include accidentally hurting or killing a civilian, or having to transmit an order that would involve killing or hurting a military colleague.

Moral injuries are not a subcategory of PTSD, even though some symptoms may coexist.[238] While the main emotions associated with PTSD are fear, horror, or powerlessness, the main emotions associated with moral injuries are guilt, shame, and anger,[239] which are closely linked to suicide and suicidal ideation in the military.[240] Yet studies on moral injuries in the military have only started recently. In part, this is because recognizing a moral injury in the military was taboo – it involves confessing and admitting psychological weakness, an aspect which is not always looked upon favorably in the military. A second reason that studies on moral injuries have only recently begun is that to preserve positive public opinion, it is not to the advantage of governments to report that they cannot protect the military working for them from physical and psychological damage, especially related to the morality of what they are asked to do.

However, this type of psychological damage is being examined more and more, and is now documented in the scientific literature.

But where do civilians fit in when they participated in mass killings because they fell prey to hateful propaganda and decided to join the movement? To what extent do civilian perpetrators of genocide feel guilt and remorse in the aftermath, and does it change their behavior? A previous study showed that prisoners participating in the Gacaca courts in Rwanda after the genocide reported an increased feeling of personal guilt for what they did.[198] But is this claim of guilt sincere, since expressing guilt was also a prerequisite for earlier release from prison?

The Act of Killing, which is probably one of the most disturbing and disconcerting documentary films ever produced, is nonetheless exceptionally interesting for what it reveals about the guilt and psychology of civilian perpetrators in Indonesia. It was directed by Joshua Oppenheimer and co-directed by Christine Cynn, as well as an anonymous Indonesian, and has received a very high number of awards and nominations. The film retraces a genocide not officially recognized in Indonesia, which resulted in the deaths of about 1,000,000 people belonging to the communist community between 1965 and 1966. But it is not the story itself which is troubling, but rather the way the film retraces this part of history.

The directors of the movie found a former genocide perpetrator, Anwar Congo, and asked him to create a movie with another perpetrator and friend of his, Herman Coto, about what happened and what they did. While facing the camera, Anwar explains and mimes how he used to kill people on the assembly lines without staining his suit. How they raped women and very young girls and how they were trying to be as sadistic as possible while torturing people, such as sticking pieces of wood into their anuses to extract confessions. He even recreates the scenes, sometimes as the perpetrator, sometimes as the victim. He asked villagers and their children to act as if they were going to be killed for the sake of his movie. During the entire documentary, Anwar proudly explains in front of the camera the horrific details of what he did, with a disturbing precision. It was as if Hitler and other Nazi leaders had survived and were proudly re-enacting scenes of the Holocaust in front of the camera. You do not see an inch of remorse, regret, shame, or guilt during most of the documentary.

To gain the trust of the former perpetrators and let them open up freely, Oppenheimer did not interact with them or give opinions despite hearing them proudly talking about the atrocities they conducted. Yet, at the end of the movie, while filming Anwar on a rooftop where he used to torture his victims, Oppenheimer finally makes a comment to him about the fact that he would never know what the real victims were feeling, even if he played the victim himself for some parts of the movie. Victims were scared and knew for sure that their lives would end. They could not just ask the camera to stop what was going on in front of them. Anwar suddenly reports that he does get nightmares from time to time. He eventually vomits on the rooftop after remembering what he did. A tremendous debate has started with my friends and colleagues who have also seen this movie: Does Anwar feel remorse and get the measure of what he did?

This is a very difficult question, and there are almost no elements of an answer currently in the scientific literature, especially when it comes to civilians who agreed voluntarily to participate in a genocide for ideological reasons. After all, providing a reason or a rationale attenuates one's feeling of responsibility for one's actions, and this occurs regularly before, during, and after genocide. Leaders provide explanations for why a part of the population *must* be exterminated. Furthermore, the techniques of moral neutralization used during genocides undoubtedly help people perform terrible acts.[17] In this context, killing, raping, cleansing become actions for the good of the majority, and the people performing such acts might not experience guilt for what they are doing in the moment.

As mentioned at the beginning of this chapter, feeling guilt or shame among assailants can be linked with the development of PTSD.[199] For example, an individual who has been involved in a violent altercation may feel intense guilt or shame about their actions, particularly if they caused harm to another person. If this individual is unable to process or cope with these emotions, they may become stuck in a cycle of avoidance and denial, which can contribute to the development of PTSD. Sometimes, experiencing guilt, as seen in Chapter 4, may lead people to seek repair. When we were in Cambodia, even though none of the former Khmer Rouge interviewed reported having ever hurt anyone, some reported high scores on a scale measuring the strength of their moral injuries regarding what they did during the Khmer Rouge regime. Interestingly, we observed that such scores positively correlated with their willingness to do whatever they could to repair the past.[241] However, every correlation can also be interpreted the other way around. It is possible that the more they are willing to repair the past, the more they suffered from moral injuries.

As this section shows, assailants can indeed suffer from moral harm, from a feeling that they did something they should not have done. But such scientific research is still in its infancy, even though it could have broad societal implications. When individuals are unable to process or come to terms with their actions in the aftermath of a traumatic event, they may be at increased risk of perpetrating further acts of violence or engaging in other harmful behavior. By addressing moral injury and providing support for individuals who have experienced trauma, it may be possible to reduce the likelihood of future harm. This line of research will hopefully be strengthened in the future to bring more pieces of the puzzle into focus.

Even though the focus of this chapter was on people who did commit reprehensible actions – albeit sometimes legal – we should not forget the victims and their families. Although a trauma appears to affect the brains of victims and assailants similarly, past analyses have suggested that symptoms nonetheless differ between civilian populations and trained combatants.[242] While for assailants, feelings of guilt and emotional numbing are more frequent, for the victims, intrusive recollections appear to occur more often. Victims are also more likely to experience psychological damage than assailants. The understanding of the damage caused to victims is thus a necessary step towards obtaining a better overview of the disastrous, but less visible consequences of war. Now we will focus on the targets of the assailants, that is, the victims and their families, who of course suffer from what happened.

PTSD IN WAR-TRAUMA VICTIMS

I will always remember her scream.

It was during one of our stays in Rwanda. We were studying intergroup biases between former genocide perpetrators and survivors, and how such biases extend to the following generations. We had recruited more than 200 individuals and explained to them that they would have to look at pictures of former genocide perpetrators, survivors, or their offspring while we measured their brain activity.

One day, a 47-year-old woman came to participate in the study. She had suffered a lot during the genocide, but she gave her consent to participate in the study after we provided her with the explanation. We then placed the electroencephalogram on her head and began. I had moved into another room to prepare the next volunteer, when suddenly I heard a terrifying scream. A scream of despair that resonated through the entire building. I ran back into the room, where I saw the woman crying and trembling over her entire body. We had just presented her with the first picture of a genocide perpetrator, and her memories from what she had to endure resurfaced. We immediately tried to calm her down and called the associated psychologist.

What we had just witnessed was a classic clinical symptom of post-traumatic stress disorder: the re-experiencing of a traumatic event.

A huge proportion of the participants that we recruited in Rwanda met the criteria for PTSD. We knew that trauma revival could happen and we had specific protocols to follow. In the case of the woman who experienced an intense trauma revival, her strategy for the last twenty-seven years of trying to cope with what happened during the genocide was to systematic-ally avoid crossing paths with former perpetrators. She would also avoid passing some locations, or even avoided tools she associated with the genocide. It is, however, widely known in the scientific community that the avoidance strategy is not good for overcoming a traumatic experience. It prevents one from progressively building a new representation of the memory trace.[243] In addition, the avoidance strategy is not easy in Rwanda. It is a small country and many former perpetrators have been released from prison and are living across the entire country. And, of course, tools used during the genocide can be seen everywhere. Machetes, for instance, were widely used by the perpetrators to attack their victims. They are also commonly used in Rwanda for agricultural purposes so you are highly likely to cross paths with people holding them.

Personally, I can hardly imagine what it would be like to try healing from a trauma while being regularly reminded about the traumatic events you had to endure. In addition, this survivor felt obligated to try to forgive her former aggressors because, as a Christian, she felt that it was her duty. However, because she could not forgive, she was carrying a strong feeling of guilt, thus adding even more psychological damage to her already severe and persistent PTSD symptoms.

As her story shows, trauma and PTSD are complex, and healing can be incredibly difficult depending on circumstances.

War-trauma victims are at a higher risk of developing PTSD than other populations. In 2008, a systematic review was made by two researchers to obtain a global overview of the development and maintenance of PTSD in victims of war and torture. They observed that victims of torture from various nations are very likely to suffer from PTSD, ranging from roughly 50 percent to more than 90 percent. The samples in those studies were very diverse, including, for instance, Vietnamese ex-political detainees[244] and victims of torture in Iran,[245] Bangladesh, Peru, Syria, Turkey, and Uganda.[68] What is noteworthy from a subsequent study is that the circumstances and torture methods differed a lot from country to country. Yet the researchers observed that the prevalence of PTSD was very high in all groups, ranging between 69 and 92 percent.

Such results suggest that while anyone is at risk of developing PTSD, there are risk factors that can be predictive of a higher probability of developing it and of how severe it will be. For example, several studies tend to indicate that a higher number of traumatic events is associated with higher severity of PTSD,[246] a phenomenon known as "building blocks." We observed similar results in Rwanda. The higher the number of stressors our participants had to endure during or after the genocide, the more severe their PTSD symptoms were even twenty-seven years after the event.[143]

Several studies also indicate that gender may be predictive, with women being more at risk of developing PTSD than men.[247] Overall, women are less likely to be on the front lines of combat and one may thus think that they are less exposed to war and its effects. However, women are very frequently the first target of interpersonal violence in wars and are often used as war weapons. They are unarmed, often alone during the conflict, and weaker than men. They are thus easy targets for assailants and are victims of forms of trauma that are more frequently associated with PTSD symptoms. For example, in South Kivu in Eastern Congo, a region plagued by recurrent ethnic conflicts and human rights violations for more than two decades, women have been the victims of sexual abuse and violence conducted by men belonging to small local guerrillas and by the military and police officers who were supposed to protect the local population.[248] They were raped and violently tortured, including, for instance, having their vaginas penetrated with objects such as wood, glass, or guns. It is estimated that at least 40 percent of the women in Kivu have been raped at least once in their lifetime, and more than 72 percent reported that they were tortured during the rape.[249]

Women represent the caste, ethnic identity, or national identity of cultures around the world. By targeting women, raping them, or letting them live with infectious diseases such as HIV, assailants intend to break the identity of the targeted population. Thus, gender-based violence in war has been reported on a massive scale across the world in different cultures and throughout history.

In Rwanda, where many women were raped and left with lifelong diseases during the genocide, rape has been officially recognized as a means of ethnic cleansing.[†] In addition to dealing with the psychological and physical damage associated with the rape, raped women often have to face social exclusion and stigmatization.[250] Unsurprisingly, numbers indicate that these women suffer from severe mental health problems, with between 12 and 76 percent suffering from PTSD, 44–68 percent suffering from depression, substance abuse in 18 percent of the cases, and more than 30 percent attempting suicide, as well as experiencing strong feelings of shame and guilt.[251] And the children born from these rapes are not spared. In Rwanda for instance, they also face stigmatization and have been called "children of bad memories" or even "devil's children."[252,44]

Specific emotions after a traumatic event, including guilt, shame, or a desire for revenge, can also be predictive of the prevalence of PTSD in civilian populations. Guilt has been largely reported among the survivors of the Nazi genocide, where survivors were left wondering, "Why did I survive but not my family?" or "If I had done [this or that], would my loved one still be alive?"[253] Shame is also frequent among survivors of sexually violent trauma. It is common that victims of rape do not talk about what happened to them because they feel ashamed. Experiencing continuous guilt or shame after a traumatic event has been shown to maintain poor mental health and correlates with PTSD symptoms.[254] After a traumatic event, it is also frequent for the victim to feel hostility, anger, or a desire for revenge against their aggressor, which, if sustained over a long period, can also prevent the diminution of PTSD symptoms.[255]

In Cambodia after the defeat of the Khmer Rouge, former victims started to conduct revenge killings, especially against the former Khmer Rouge cadres responsible for the killing of their families,[16] thus becoming perpetrators themselves. In a different context, it has been shown that former Ugandan and Congolese child soldiers displaying post-traumatic stress disorder symptoms were less open to reconciliation and showed more

---

[†] Prosecutor v. Jean Paul Akayesu (1996) Case No. ICTR-96–4-T (International Criminal Tribunal for Rwanda, Trial Chamber).

feelings of revenge,[256] a critical aspect to consider for their reintegration into society. The desire for revenge is an open door to the perpetuation of conflicts across generations, and as a consequence, it enhances the risk of new conflicts with similar dramatic consequences. These psychological wounds must thus be understood and treated, for the sake of everyone.

Although there are recognizable factors that may be predictive of the presence or likelihood of PTSD, it is impossible to know or predict the exact percentage or prevalence of PTSD symptoms among war victims. Studies examining the prevalence of PTSD symptoms greatly vary. Some have taken place in the country where the trauma occurred, others in countries where populations were displaced or found refuge. Some have been conducted by self-report questionnaires and others by interviews. Some have taken place quite rapidly after the traumatic event, while others have evaluated the occurrence or persistence of PTSD symptoms in the long run.

Another important aspect of this ongoing research is that civilian survivors mentioned in the scientific literature are largely non-westerners, while the PTSD scales used were developed by western researchers. Applying a western-based trauma model and declaring the presence of PTSD in people from non-western cultures is questionable. Moreover, people can vary greatly in their psychological response to trauma, with some people being more at risk of developing PTSD symptoms than others. Thus, truly understanding who is at risk of developing PTSD is a hard task. There are also several factors that may play a protective role against the development of PTSD.

THE CONCEPT OF RESILIENCE

While past research essentially focused on the symptoms of trauma, a growing amount of research is now conducted to better understand the protective mechanisms that shield people against the development and persistence of PTSD symptoms after a traumatic experience. This is a phenomenon referred to as "resilience." Resilience allows many individuals to maintain relatively good mental health despite exposure to severe psychological or physical traumatic events. It has been described as the process of adapting well in the face of adversity, trauma, tragedy, threats, or significant sources of stress.[257]

A noteworthy clinical observation has been that some individuals appear to be better shielded to cope with traumatic events, while others cannot get rid of their haunting past. Some people have experienced unbearable atrocities, and yet find the courage to wake up every morning and keep on going. Some may even go back to a relatively normal life.

But why some people are more resilient than others is still a matter of debate in the scientific community. From a neural perspective, resilient individuals might be those who can regulate their emotions in stressful situations or those who have only a limited release of the stress hormone. Individuals who use communication to solve a potential conflict can also be considered as more resilient. But what is crucial to realize is that resilience is not a specific personality trait that some people might have and others not. It is a complex phenomenon that arises depending on the presence of many factors happening before, during, or after the trauma exposure.

In the past, research often only considered the individual dimensions associated with resilience after a trauma, as though the individuals being studied were alone on a desert island. However, it is now well acknowledged that social and environmental factors also play a key role in the prevalence of PTSD symptoms.[258] The possibility of accessing PTSD treatments is obviously a critical factor. After the genocide in Cambodia, for instance, the mental health of survivors was not considered, and the country had no infrastructure, trained medical doctors or psychologists to deal with such issues. For several decades after the Khmer Rouge era, the survivors were thus not able to find mental peace, which also explains why so many survivors still suffer from high PTSD rates.[259] Of the roughly sixty survivors of the Cambodian genocide we met, none had ever seen a specialist in mental health to help them.

The cultural perception of psychology may also add complexity to the idea of mental health accessibility. For example, I met a clinical therapist and professor of psychology at the National University of Battambang who told me that, in Cambodia, many people consider seeing a psychologist to be the purview of "crazy" people, which has been a clear hindrance to getting the help they need.

Poverty may also be a major factor, as lacking physical or financial resources can prevent people from accessing proper support for their mental health. I read a sentence in a paper a few years ago that deeply impacted me:

"... preoccupied with their day-to-day survival, the poor do not have the luxury to revive a past trauma to add to their current frustrations."[260] It is crucial to offer clinical support to everyone, even those who may not ask for help because they just do not have the possibility or time to consider it. Not asking for help does not mean that a person does not need it.

Relatedly, social support helps maintain mental health and can reduce PTSD symptoms. For instance, several studies have shown that people receiving social support from their families, friends, or peers after a traumatic event are less likely to develop PTSD symptoms.[261] But social support is unfortunately far from being guaranteed in many societies worldwide. Imagine a world where victims are condemned to life-long psychological suffering, while their aggressors continue their lives without serving a single day in jail.

Of course, this does not happen everywhere, and lots of progress has been made across the world to protect victims. Yet still, in some societies, victims remain less protected than their aggressors, and this is especially true for women victims of sexual assault. In many places, women who have been raped are considered tarnished and are excluded from their families or community.[262] Some are even forced to marry their rapist – the man who inflicted permanent psychological and physical damage on them. "Marry-your-rapist" laws still allow perpetrators to escape justice in twenty countries across the world,[263] and many young girls and women commit suicide after being forced into such a marriage. And even in the countries that have recently abolished this law, victims of rape still frequently face social ostracization. They find themselves totally isolated while trying to psychologically, physically, and emotionally manage what happened to them.

Studies conducted on war refugees showed that the prevalence of PTSD symptoms can decrease depending on how they are treated. For instance, for Bhutanese refugees displaced in Nepal, a relatively small prevalence rate of 14 percent of PTSD was found, which the authors explain in terms of the positive life conditions in the camps and the high degree of personal support available because entire villages or families were displaced together.[264] The presence of the family helps support the trauma associated with exile. Conversely, in the case of an extended separation, the lack of news from a family can increase stress and reduce hope for the future.[265]

Current research thus strongly supports dismantling policies of splitting up families seeking refuge. Unfortunately, a lot of countries maintain this policy. Under the El Paso program, for example, all migrants crossing the US border without permission, including those seeking asylum, were detained, and criminally charged. Their children, even very young ones, were taken away from them and sometimes sent thousands of kilometers away, without a proper system to facilitate reunification, which was clearly damaging to the mental health of both parents and children. To prevent a lack of support from the populace during his mandate as president, Donald Trump, who initiated this "zero-tolerance policy," depicted the Mexican immigrants as rapists and criminals.[266] This is a typical strategy that makes us more sensitive to outgroup biases, and which is used extensively by some politicians, as we have seen in Chapter 4. By creating fear of an outgroup, he knew that the people would be less inclined to revolt against this terrible act of non-humanity towards migrants and their children.

As this section shows, many factors can explain why some people are more likely to develop PTSD than others. By understanding the factors that protect against PTSD, we can take steps to promote resilience, prevent future trauma, and support individuals and communities in the aftermath of violence and adversity. Some cultural factors can hardly be controlled. However, governments have the power to reduce the struggle of their citizens or of the refugees they welcome, notably by providing support and not splitting families.

CAN THE SEQUELAE OF TRAUMA BE PASSED DOWN THE GENERATIONS?

Unfortunately, trauma does not stop at the level of the individual who directly experienced it but extends to their descendants as well. There is a considerable body of evidence coming from the scientific literature showing that the impact of trauma is passed down from generation to generation, and that the next generation individuals are also affected. The children of trauma victims appear to be less shielded against traumatic events. Indeed, all the current research suggests that our lives are shaped by our parents' experiences, which can alter our physiology and our mental health. Thus, in an attempt to ensure a peaceful future, the youngest generations should also benefit from support to acknowledge their psychological struggle.

In Cambodia, we recruited three generations of individuals – those present during the genocide, the first generation born after the genocide, and the second generation born after the genocide. They all suffered from an equivalent level of PTSD symptoms.[241] Famous studies conducted on Holocaust survivors and their children also showed that when they face a traumatic event themselves, children of Holocaust survivors are more likely to develop PTSD symptoms.[267,268]

It appears that trauma is passed down not only through direct and indirect social transmission, but also through epigenetic transmission. Social transmission of trauma may be related to epigenetic mechanisms in the sense that exposure to trauma can lead to epigenetic changes in an individual, but it is not an epignenetic mechanism in itself. Direct social transmission refers to the stories that children hear from their parents or grandparents, which has been shown to make them suffer from psychological issues.[269] The direct social transmission of trauma has been well documented, for example, among Native Americans. They have suffered throughout their history from many traumatic experiences over successive generations. They have been massacred, they have suffered from genocidal policies, they have died from new diseases brought by the invaders, they have been delocalized many times, their spiritual and religious practices have been prohibited, and Native American children were prohibited from speaking their mother tongue at school.[270] Social transmission is particularly strong in these communities, as they have by tradition extended family and community systems. Further, several movies depicting the massacres, such as some classic westerns in the US, may also involve remembrance of the traumatic experiences.

Indirect transmission refers, for instance, to poor parental mental health, as well as poor parenting styles. As the parents are suffering from the psychological consequences of the traumatic events, they may no longer be able to act as parents towards their children. They may even unconsciously reverse their role in the family and turn to the child to have their emotional needs met. Consequently, the child has to carry the responsibility of the emotional wellbeing of their parents, beyond their own emotional needs. These parentified children lose their childhood, which can affect their mental health as growing adults. Along these lines, a study conducted in Cambodia showed that parents' trauma from during the Khmer Rouge regime involved a frequent role-reversal of parenting and was associated with greater PTSD symptoms in their daughters, specifically.[271]

Epigenetic mechanisms in the transmission of a trauma affect the expression of genes, without altering the DNA structure itself. A growing number of studies on animals have indeed shown that trauma can also leave a mark on an individual's genes, which can be passed down to the next generations. For example, in 2010, a team of researchers studied the extent to which a trauma affects several generations of mice.[272] They made the mothers, isolated from their pups, experience stressful experiences, such as confining them in tubes or dropping them into water.

When the researchers returned the mothers to the cage with their pups, the mothers exhibited altered behavior, frequently ignoring their pups or appearing distracted or frantic. The pups, who did not experience the trauma themselves but observed the behavioral change in their mothers, also started to exhibit altered behavior, similar to that exhibited by their mothers. The researchers then presented the pups to untraumatized females for mating and removed the mothers from the cage to avoid social interference. Critically, the offspring of up to six generations of matings displayed more risk-taking behavior, such as exploring a platform suspended off the ground or not trying to swim faster when dropped in water compared to control mice. This groundbreaking study showed that epigenetics can play a key role in transmitting trauma through generations.

It is, of course, much more complex to control the part played by epigenetic mechanisms and of social transmission in humans than in animals.[273] For obvious ethical reasons, the same experiments cannot be performed on humans: No one can on purpose induce stress with a specific stressor in another person, then force that person to give birth to a child, separating the child from their mother and test their reaction to the stress. Inflicting such psychological pain on animals for science may also be questionable and deeply offend some people's moral values, but that is another debate.

Yet even though the same degree of control cannot be applied, several studies appear to show that the epigenetic transmission of trauma is also observable in humans. In 2014 a team of researchers recruited Rwandan women who were pregnant during the genocide, as well as their children.[274]

They observed that children born to mothers exposed to a traumatic event during their pregnancy and who suffered from PTSD had a higher risk of poor mental health outcomes as adults. The researchers also observed that PTSD in mothers was associated with an alteration in a specific gene associated with the regulation of the stress response – and that the same alteration was found in their children. Interestingly, the researchers also recruited a group of mothers (and children) from the same ethnicity who were pregnant during the same period but not present in Rwanda during the genocide. This alteration was not observable in the latter group.

Paternal trauma, it appears, can also affect children.[275] The researchers of a study recruited thousands of offspring of US Civil War soldiers who had been imprisoned, as well as the offspring of Civil War soldiers who had not been imprisoned after the war. The researchers observed that the mortality rate was higher in the sons of war prisoners compared to those of non-war prisoners.

Another study conducted in 2015 investigated the intergenerational impact of the Holodomor genocide on three generations of Ukrainian families.[276] The Holodomor, which can be translated as "extermination by starvation," was a Soviet-Russian orchestrated genocide conceived to kill ethnic Ukrainians.[277] Organized by Stalin in 1932–1933, it caused the deaths of between 3 and 6 million people. The authors of the study observed that the Holodomor genocide not only impacted the survivors, but also their children and grandchildren. The impact was twofold. Analysis of the emotions of the respondents indicated a high incidence of feelings of horror, fear, mistrust, sadness, shame, anger, stress, anxiety. The reported trauma-caused coping strategies involved the stockpiling of food, reverence for food, overemphasis on food, and overeating. The second and third generations frequently declared that they felt themselves to be in "survival mode," where they experienced a constant need for survival and an inability to enjoy present life.

As this section shows, the descendants of individuals who have experienced a traumatic event are also at risk of developing psychological damage compared to descendants whose parents were not exposed to traumatic events. Untreated mental health difficulties in descendants can contribute to the perpetuation of cycles of violence and conflict; and encourage submissiveness to hateful propaganda seeking revenge for the past.

Interestingly, some studies have shown that the transgenerational effect of trauma can perhaps be prevented, or at least attenuated. We have just seen that it has been repeatedly observed that the offspring of traumatized rats had a pathological reaction to stress. However, other studies showed that when the offspring were placed in an enriched environment, that included food, water, running wheels, and a miniature maze, these effects disappeared.[278,279] These studies thus show the crucial role of environment to cope with stressful events.

WAR, TRAUMA, CONFLICT, WAR, TRAUMA, CONFLICT: AN ENDLESS CYCLE

Conflict is contagious. It is deeply ingrained in human nature to take action against someone in retaliation for an injury. But feelings of revenge can also, in a prolonged way, increase the risk of developing PTSD symptoms.[255] These feelings of revenge can be exacerbated by the lack of justice. In the post-Khmer Rouge years in Cambodia for example, citizens were faced with knowing that former perpetrators were not brought to justice and that, in addition, in many cases they continued to occupy high government positions.[280] After desolation, feelings of wanting revenge frequently emerge. When a desire for revenge is present, it creates an opportunity for conflicts to persist down the generations. It thus increases the likelihood of new conflicts with comparable severe outcomes. It seems like an endless cycle.

This chapter has shown that assailants, as well as victims, can experience severe PTSD symptoms during their lifetime. Engaging in violent acts, even under the justification of obedience to authority, or surviving such acts, can have lifelong consequences for everyone involved, including one's own descendants.

Nobody wins in a war.

However, with the next chapter I plan to bring some glimmers of hope. In the chaos, some ordinary citizens have been able to show their bravery and risked their lives to save individuals who were about to be victims of mass extermination. Those people, even if they are not numerous, are a living example that the endless cycle could stop.

CHAPTER 7

Conclusion: How Ordinary People Stand Up against Immorality

In the darkest night, humanity is hidden.

Jacques Roisin, *Dans la nuit la plus noire se cache l'humanité* [281]

It was early one Sunday morning. I had just returned from Cambodia a couple of days before, still jetlagged and moving into a new house, where we were still finishing the renovation work. Clearly, going to the university on a Sunday morning was the last thing I wanted to do. But I could not miss the opportunity that was presented to me.

I was about to meet Félicien Bahizi, a 50-year-old Rwandan man living in Belgium. He was around 21 or 22 years old when the genocide happened in Rwanda. At that time, he was studying to become a priest at Rutongo, a city located to the north of Kigali, and he was a member of the youth section of the Rwandan Red Cross. Now, almost thirty years later, I was meeting with him to hear his story.

It started on April 7, 1994. The night before, he had returned to his home in Kagano, a township located on the edge of Lake Kivu, for the Easter holidays. On the morning in question, he woke up naturally at 5 a.m. and was about to start a regular day. However, that day was going to change drastically – both for him and the whole country. It was a day that would leave a long-lasting impression on millions of people.

Soon after waking up, Félicien learned about the crash of the plane of President Habyarimana, hit by two surface-to-air missiles as it approached Kigali, killing all onboard. One of his first thoughts was that there would probably be a trial to determine who was responsible for this tragic event. He never considered, however, that it would catalyze a bloody mass killing that would cause the death of about 500,000–600,000 people in just three months.

Later that day, he crossed the path of a group of young men. They were claiming that revenge should be taken against the Tutsis, who they said were responsible for the crash. With their weapons in their hands, they stopped Félicien and asked him if he was a member of the FPR (*Front Patriotique Rwandais* or Rwandan Patriotic Front), a group founded at the end of the 1980s by Tutsi exiles living in Uganda. The group sought to overthrow the Hutu-dominated government of Rwanda. Félicien was afraid, and he denied being associated with the FPR, as indeed he was not. He then immediately went to the presbytery located in Nyamasheke.

The priest talked to him and told him not to go with the others, to not join the groups that were planning to attack the Tutsis. And together, they went to talk to the mayor of the city to ask him to protect the Tutsis who could be attacked. Yet, that same day, Félicien learned that a local Tutsi had been decapitated and that some Hutus were starting to organize themselves into armed militias.

On April 8, tensions rose sharply, but no one could yet predict the scale of the massacre that was coming. Some Tutsis came to take refuge in the enclosures of the parish buildings, thinking that they were just protecting themselves from possible violence. They were far from predicting the unspeakable atrocities, including rape, killing, and torture, that were going to reach them in this space of safety.

Félicien knew a woman, Joséphine, who was responsible for the nutritional center of Nyamasheke. He remembers that she always brought him bread and tea when he was studying at school. On April 9, she told Félicien that she wanted to go back home after stopping by. Félicien tried to discourage her, but she still left. Later, Félicien went to her house with a gendarme to see if she was alright. However, as they entered the house, they made a macabre discovery. The woman had been cut in two. She was not even a Tutsi, but she had the physical characteristics of a Tutsi. It was something that happened frequently during the genocide – some Tutsis who looked like Hutus survived, and some Hutus were killed because they looked like Tutsis. The same thing happened to one of Félicien's cousins.

In the following days, many Tutsis gathered at the parish, and Félicien and the priest tried to protect them. On April 11 and 12, armed militias made several attempts to penetrate the parish to kill the Tutsis hiding inside. Félicien remembers that they were throwing grenades towards them. At one point, a grenade fell right next to him. He thought his last hour was coming, but the grenade never exploded. Eventually, the gendarmes of Nyamasheke came to protect them and succeeded in killing two militiamen. The rest fled.

During the genocide, Félicien tried to help as many Tutsis as possible. He created fake Red Cross armbands and gave them to a refugee team to help with their mission. He participated in the clandestine organization of the evacuation of some Tutsis by boat across Lake Kivu to Bukavu, a city located in the Democratic Republic of Congo. He healed and gave medicines to many people thanks to the nursing training he had received from the Red Cross.

One day, he remembers, he met a young Tutsi mother. She asked him his ethnicity because she found it hard to believe that some Hutus could risk their lives to save Tutsis. She even asked him, "Are you sure you are a Hutu? Check with your parents." How Hutus could risk their lives to save Tutsis seemed totally inconceivable at a time when hatred of the other had reached its peak.

In 2006, Félicien was officially recognized as a *"Juste"* (the French word for "Righteous one") for his actions during the genocide.

At our morning meeting in 2023, I asked him why he thought he had acted as a rescuer at that time. He mentioned the word "instinct" and the fact that for him, all human beings are the same. He said that most human beings need to feel attached to a group, or to a country, but they almost never feel attached to the whole of humankind. He considers that there are no such things as skin color, ethnicity, religion, or countries that separate humans into different groups. People are afraid of the "others," and they stay imprisoned in their own small groups, in their ethnicity, region, or religion. He believes that only education can overcome the human tendency to separate each from the other.

This is also probably why he is now a teacher and tells his story to the youth.

He also added, though, that one of the things he hates the most is injustice. It is probably something that comes from his childhood. His father was a peasant, and the night Félicien was born, a group of bandits attacked them. His father survived, but no justice was served for the victims. Félicien then witnessed too many acts of injustice over the years. He remembered seeing Tutsis abused when he was in the minor seminary, a Catholic institution designed to prepare boys both academically and spiritually for vocation to the priesthood and religious life. At one point, he saw Tutsis in Gisenyi who came for medicine. But instead, they were arrested and mistreated.

Félicien thinks that all these events helped him to develop a strong "spirit of justice." For him, the mass killings in 1994 were a totally unjust act that he could not support. When President Habyarimana was killed, revenge should not have been the response. Justice should have been the response.

When reflecting upon the efficiency of the mass killings that have happened in genocides throughout history, it is often surprising that people managed to survive at all. Some survivors mention chance, others mention "divine intervention." But, more often than not, many owe their lives to the kindness and aid of others, like Félicien. They survived, most likely, because they crossed the path of someone ready to help them in the chaos, whether it was by providing shelter, hiding them from danger, or helping them to escape. These acts of kindness and compassion have been a critical factor in the survival of many individuals.

Heroic acts are generally carried out willingly and despite the risks of sustaining severe physical harm, even to the point of death. But why are some individuals ready to sacrifice their lives to save the lives of others, including complete strangers?

This complex and intriguing question has been explored in a range of different fields, including social psychology, sociology, and neuroscience. This concluding chapter aims to provide a deeper understanding of why some individuals in war and genocides are willing to make the ultimate sacrifice for others, even if they have no personal connection to them.

IDENTIFYING RESCUERS ACROSS HISTORY

Knowing exactly how many people risked their lives to rescue threatened human beings is impossible to quantify. Many died during their rescue efforts or before any official recognition of their actions. Others never publicly mentioned their rescue acts or did not provide the required documentation to be recognized for them. In some cases, the political or social climate makes it difficult to recognize the actions of rescuers, as when there is government censorship or genocide denial, or because the rescuers themselves were members of a persecuted group.

But knowing exactly how many people rescued others is perhaps not the most important thing. After all, saving lives, beyond its quantitative aspect, is a qualitative event. Several studies have tried to evaluate the profile of those who conducted acts of rescue in order to understand better what distinguishes them from others, to understand why those people risked their own lives and safety to help save the lives of people who were targeted for persecution and violence during times of war or genocide.

The first step for such an investigation is to identify those who helped.

In the scientific literature, most of the studies conducted focused on non-Jews who rescued Jews during the Holocaust. This does not, however, mean that rescue acts have not also occurred elsewhere. For instance, studies have highlighted rescuers during the genocide in Rwanda[282,283] and people who helped those persecuted by the military government in Argentina between 1976 and 1983,[284] as well as rescues that occurred during the Armenian genocide, the Bosnian genocide, and the genocide of Native Americans.[285] There is also the famous case of a Soviet naval officer, Vasily Aleksandrovich Arkhipov, credited by the director of the US National Security Archive as "the man who saved the world."[286] When he was on duty during the Cuban Missile Crisis in 1962, his submarine's captain ordered the launch of a nuclear torpedo. This decision required the approval of three senior officers, including Arkhipov. Arkhipov objected to the launch and convinced the other officers to wait for orders from Moscow. If he had not prevented the nuclear attack, a global thermonuclear response could have resulted, destroying large parts of the northern hemisphere.*

Additional examples from other wars and genocides can be read on the webpage of the Gariwo – The Gardens of the Righteous Worldwide[288] – whose purpose is to extend the concept of the "Righteous," first applied to those who saved Jews during the Nazi persecution, to all genocides and crimes against humanity.

Among these, there are several reasons that explain why rescue acts during the Holocaust were the most studied. First, the Holocaust is one of the most largely documented genocides, thus offering a better overview of what happened at this period and the people involved. Second, there were so many people killed or involved in the massacres that, proportionally, more rescuers could emerge. The scientific literature has indicated that many rescue acts took place because rescuers were asked for help by a person in distress.[289] With more threatened human beings, more requests for help could have been made, thus leading to more acts of rescue. Another factor is access to funding, academic resources, and institutional support. For example, universities and research institutions in Europe may be more likely to have the resources and infrastructure to support research on the Nazi genocide and related topics, which could contribute to a higher concentration of studies on rescuers in that region. Cultural differences may also account for the focus on rescuers during the Holocaust, as, in some countries, heroism and altruism may be less celebrated or recognized. And, finally, many rescuers during the Holocaust were officially recognized and awarded in the Yad Vashem program, which facilitated the process of finding them.

Yad Vashem was established by the State of Israel to perpetuate the memory of the six million Jewish victims of the Holocaust. One of Yad Vashem's primary duties is to express gratefulness on behalf of the Jewish people to non-Jewish individuals who endangered their own lives to rescue Jews during the Holocaust. An important element to be considered is that whether or not they succeed in their rescue acts does not

---

* Some elements of the story of Arkhipov have in fact been questioned.[287] Another officer present on that day suggested that it was only the commander who was ready to launch the missile, but that none of the other officers agreed, not only Arkhipov.

matter; what matters is that they tried. Those people were honored with the title "Righteous Among the Nations," as they included people living across Europe.

A series of criteria were established in order to be recognized as Righteous, and one of them is the element of risk. Rescuers during genocides often faced significant risks and challenges. They may have been hunted by authorities or threatened with violence. Rescuers had to be prepared, knowingly and in full conscience, to risk their life or freedom following their rescue acts. In other words, the Righteous are people who, despite all the risks, were ready to save others. In Poland, for instance, posters plastered in major cities, as well as radio messages, warned those who might be tempted to help Jews about the consequences. Such messages clearly indicated that those who admitted a Jew in their home or tried to assist one would be shot.[290] Yet thousands of identified people conducted rescue actions in Poland.[291]

Another criterion involved not being part of the targeted group. In the case of the Yad Vashem program, it mostly meant not being Jewish. Indeed, as discussed in Chapter 4, humans tend to help more victims who are similar to them in regard to ethnicity, attitudes, personality, or cultural background. This partly explains why so few people engage in rescue acts. The Righteous thus transgressed the border of group membership and risked their lives to rescue people they had no religious affinity with.

Among the additional criteria, there had to be no preconditions involved in the rescue acts, such as a monetary reward. Monetary payments have encouraged some people to help, but they are not considered as Righteous given the incentive they accepted in exchange.[292] Being recognized as Righteous also requires one to have never, before or after the rescue event, caused physical harm to Jews or to other nationalities.

The methods of rescue included among the Righteous stories are varied. It could be hiding those who were threatened in secret places or in their homes for an indefinite period, bringing them food, and cleaning up their bodily waste to preserve their dignity. It could also have been helping them to hide their identity and helping them assume a new one, or even helping them flee from an dangerous place.

Dissimulation could be pivotal to the rescue effort. During the Nazi genocide, one form of dissimulation was to be registered as a vital worker for the war industry of Germany. Oskar Schindler is probably the most famous case using this strategy. His story is captured in Steven Spielberg's movie *Schindler's List*. Oskar Schindler was a German industrialist who claimed that the Jews working in his factories were essential to the war effort as they were producing ammunition. In reality, they did not produce a single shell during the whole eight months of the firm's operation. Schindler and his wife, Emilie Schindler, were credited with saving the lives of over 1,000 Jewish men, women, and children during the Holocaust.

Before receiving the title of Righteous, evidence and proof are carefully analyzed by the program to ensure the veracity of these brave actions. So far, 28,217 people have been awarded the title across different countries, whose numbers can be read on their webpage.[291] But comparisons should not be made between countries in terms of numbers. As stated by the Yad Vashem program, these numbers include only individuals officially recognized as such based on the documentation available. Moreover, the implementation of the Holocaust was not the same across all these countries, which may have strongly influenced whether and how rescues were attempted. Still, what these numbers show is that, proportionally to the number of people living in Europe at that time, rescuers are clearly not numerous. Some researchers have estimated that even if they took the highest estimate – 1 million rescuers, which is much larger than the number officially recognized by the Yad Vashem program – it still represents less than 0.5 percent of the population under Nazi occupation.[293]

In Rwanda, two associations – Ibuka and Avega – have similarly started to recognize the *Indakemwa*, or "People with integrity." In 2004, the word "*Juste*" was used to designate "those who helped the Tutsis in the difficult moments of the genocide. " As stated by the associations: "All humanity must know that there were not only genocidaires, but also people who made efforts to protect those who were being hunted."[†] Three criteria were established to receive this honorific title: (1) Having saved at least one Tutsi during the genocide and at the same time never having been involved in reprehensible acts against Tutsis; (2) Having participated in

---

[†] Penal Reform International, 2004, p. 32; PRI, Gacaca Report, November 2004, p. 32.

the Gacaca courts or having contributed to the testimonies after the genocide; and (3) Having been involved in the reconciliation activities in Rwanda. Hundreds of individuals have received the honorific title of "*Juste.*"

Some people acted in other heroic ways, including, for instance, enrolling in resistance organizations. During the Holocaust, those people participated in armed combat, helped to transport food illegally, tried to assassinate Nazis, or bombed the railways.[294] For example, the Danish resistance movement was composed of many people who conducted activities underground, such as spying or sabotaging. These people are not always recognized as rescuers per se, even though they contributed to organized efforts to save lives and defeat perpetrators. The Danish resistance movement as a whole was recognized by the Yad Vashem program as part of the "Righteous Among the Nations," for example, but the individuals who made up its ranks remained unnamed.

For all the rescuers known to us, therefore, there are surely many more whose names and actions are lost to time.

WHO RISKS EVERYTHING TO HELP OTHERS?

In 1988, a couple of researchers, Samuel and Pearl Oliner, conducted a large study on rescuers during the Holocaust, which included 406 rescuers, 126 non-rescuers, and 150 survivors.[293] The Oliners, through their analysis, strongly emphasized the fact that rescuers were very special and out-of-the-ordinary individuals. They put the rescuers on a high pedestal, which can probably be explained by the fact that Samuel Oliner himself was rescued during the Holocaust. He was 10 years old when his family was murdered by the Nazis, but he managed to survive thanks to the help of a Polish Christian woman. The Oliners concluded through their research that rescuers have exceptional moral qualities, a strong commitment to helping others, and were connected to a shared humanity. A shared humanity, in this instance, refers to individuals who do not primarily identify with a specific group of humans. Like Félicien, they believe all humans are equal and should be considered as a whole – as a unique family.

Since the seminal study by the Oliners, many researchers have tried to identify a specific profile associated with rescue acts during wars and genocides.[293] In a study conducted in 2007,[295] a team of researchers observed that rescuers, compared to bystanders, had a higher perceived social responsibility and had a moral reasoning that favored more altruism. They had more empathic concern for others and were more ready to take risks. These results were not influenced by demographic or situational differences. Compassion and empathy for those in need was very high in the sample of the rescuers, even though feeling empathy and compassion for Jews could have resulted in their own death.

These findings resonated with subsequent research elsewhere. In a study conducted in Rwanda in 2018,[296] two researchers interviewed thirty-five people who had been involved in rescue actions in Rwanda. They observed that rescuers reported a sense of common humanity, a sense of moral obligation towards the person in distress, and the fact that they found inspiration in their Christian faith. They said their values and a general moral code provided courage during their rescue acts. In Chapter 1, we saw that religion was mentioned by some interviewees to explain how they stopped taking part in the genocide. But, by the same token, many participated in the genocide despite their religious affiliation. Religion thus does not seem to be a factor that is reliably associated with helping others.

Overall, these studies suggest that it is quite common for the rescuers to report feelings of shared humanity, strong empathy for others, and a high sense of moral responsibility. However, such traits or moral values do not perfectly predict rescue acts. It is also a matter of context.

For example, Lee Ann Fujii, a political scientist, showed that some Rwandans participated both in acts of violence and in acts of rescue during the genocide.[297] Her findings cast significant doubt on the idea that personality is the dominant factor that distinguishes a rescuer from the others. Some researchers thus conducted in-depth interviews in order to better understand the contextual and situational factors that motivated people to engage in rescue acts during the genocide.

In the study conducted in Rwanda in 2018 mentioned above,[296] the researchers further observed that out of all the rescuers they identified, only two acted alone – without specific coordination with other individuals. The coordination was sometimes observed at the family level, but also sometimes with friends or neighbors. For instance, some individuals were hiding Tutsis in their homes and their neighbors stopped armed militias that were approaching. Or some decided as a group to help people hide in churches or to help them cross roads. This result suggests that group influence can have both negative and positive effects. In Chapter 1, we have seen that many former genocide perpetrators reported participating because of group influence. However, as the results of the study suggest, group influence can also have positive effects, such as when a group mobilizes to engage in rescue actions. In this case, individuals who might not have acted alone may be motivated by the sense of collective responsibility and support provided by the group to take action to help others. This shows the complex and sometimes contradictory effects of group influence, which can both facilitate harmful actions and promote prosocial behavior.

The researchers also observed that some people are more likely to engage in rescue acts than others because they are in a situation in which they are able to help. For example, the authors observed that age was critical, as those who engaged in rescue acts were generally older than the general population. The effect of age can be explained by several factors. A first factor to consider is the role of elderly individuals in the Rwandan society, as they are revered and can exert influence within families.[298] Another factor is that before the genocide, some political elites encouraged the formation of young militias to protect the population against "dangerous" Tutsis. The targeted persons for these militias were young men, in their twenties or thirties, without a job or a home.[299] The elderly were thus spared more from the hate propaganda and less present in the armed militias. In a study conducted on Holocaust rescuers,[295] the researchers also observed that rescuers were slightly older than bystanders. They further observed that rescuers had completed more years of education than bystanders. Notably, education may have served as a protective factor against external social influences advocating anti-Semitism at this period.

The researchers of the study conducted in Rwanda also observed that rescuers were more likely to have formal employment. As many acts of rescue took the form of hiding someone in one's home, it involves owning a house and having the corresponding economic status. As those people already had an income and a house, they were perhaps less likely to take part in the group attacks that most of the time ended in looting their victims' house.

However, in Rwanda, many rescuers did manage to hide dozens of people – even when they lived in very small houses. Zura Karuhimbi, a Rwandan woman who managed to save at least eighty persons during the genocide, indicated in an interview by Jacques Roisin, a Belgian psychoanalyst:

> I had Tutsis hidden everywhere in the house, in the small room here, or in that small room there; or even in the ceilings. I can't show the ceiling because the Interahamwe burned my house . . . . Some were hidden below my bed; some were hidden in a tree outside the house . . . . Those hidden under the floor of the house or in the yard, I covered them with leaves and bean peelings . . . . I brought them food and emptied the toilet bucket.[‡ 281]

Zura was a traditional healer, and she managed to rescue and hide dozens of people by masquerading as a witch. She was said to have the *Nyabingi*, an evil force that can cause bewitchment, disease, and death. Each time someone approached, she threatened to use spells against them, which scared the attackers. Zura also appeared to have a sense of shared humanity, reporting in the interview: "As humans, we are all the same, we all belong to the same family" (p. 40).

It also seems that family experience and model were critical. Twenty out of the thirty-five individuals interviewed reported that they had parents or grandparents who had already saved Tutsis during previous periods of violence. Zura explained that during previous wars, her family had already hidden threatened individuals. She reported that her mother told her that she should also save people later (p. 51). This suggests that education and family are two important factors in the transmission of moral values from one generation to the next. In many cultures, parents indeed play an important role in shaping the moral development of their children. They may teach children what is right and wrong, how to treat others with respect and kindness, and other important values that are necessary for living in society.

---

‡ Translated by the author – original texts are in French.

Context and situational factors thus appear to be significant in determining whether some will engage in acts of rescue or not. However, the context does not predict systematically helping behaviors. Not all people having a house or the support of their family will engage in rescue acts. Rescuing behaviors are very complex to study, and in a similar situation, some people will decide to resist orders to hurt part of the population, while others will comply with those orders. Even though past research has documented personality traits, social and situational factors favoring rescue behaviors, some elements are still missing in the equation, which could be critical for developing efficient interventions.

The study of helping behaviors in neuroscience is still in its infancy but can already provide key elements that could be targeted during interventions. Experimental research is relevant to complement the study of helping and resistance because it allows us to perfectly control environmental variables, an aspect that field research could only approximate. For example, even though research has identified that the presence of a supporting group can help people to engage in rescue efforts, members of this supporting "group" will never all be exactly the same. How many people supported the action? Who were those people and their relationship with the rescuer? Such variables can be controlled in a lab context, and thus bring new elements of answer about how such variables influence behaviors and their related mechanisms.

THE NEUROSCIENCE OF COSTLY HELPING BEHAVIORS

The study of rescuers by sociologists and social psychologists taught us that acts of rescue are often made at great personal risk. In neuroscience, several studies have sought to understand the neural mechanisms that underlie prosocial behavior when individuals may choose to help others at a personal cost. Both fields of research are concerned with understanding why and how individuals engage in costly helping behavior, such as acts of rescue. By combining insights from both fields, we may gain a more comprehensive understanding of the factors that drive individuals to engage in rescue behaviors, even when faced with significant personal sacrifices.

In the scientific literature, a typical method used to study helping behaviors is the dictator game. In this game, one player, called the dictator, is given a sum of money (for instance, $10) and has to decide how much of it to give to another player, called the receiver. The receiver has no control at all over the decision and simply receives whatever amount the dictator decides to give. If driven only by their self-interest, players in the role of the dictator should keep 100 percent of the money and give nothing to the other player.

However, laboratory experiments have shown that this does not happen for all dictators. Some share the amount with the receiver. It has, for instance, been shown that only 40 percent of the dictators keep the money entirely for themselves. The others generally share up to 20 percent of the $10 with the receiver.[300] However, these amounts can vary considerably following simple experimental manipulations, and vary greatly from one individual to another.[301]

Using functional magnetic resonance imaging (fMRI), researchers have observed that participants with higher activity in empathy-related brain regions made more donations when playing the role of the dictator, suggesting a key role of empathy.[302,303] Researchers have also observed that higher activity in brain regions associated with empathy predicted more donations specifically to limit the suffering of the other person. Such results suggest that empathy is a strong driver of helping behaviors, despite the personal cost associated with the decision to help.

These conclusions are supported by studies showing a more causal relationship between the neural processing of another's pain and donation by using neuromodulation techniques that are used to increase or decrease the activity of specific brain regions to observe the resulting effects.[§] In 2018,[304] a team of researchers used neuromodulation

---

[§] An important aspect to note is that most of the current neuromodulation techniques, such as transcranial magnetic stimulation (TMS) and transcranial direct current stimulation (tDCS), used in neuroscience research cannot reliably reach deep brain regions. Deep brains regions associated with the emotional component of empathy, for instance, such as the insula and the anterior cingulate cortex, cannot reliably be stimulated. Thus, neuroscientists usually use neuromodulation techniques over brain regions that are located more at the surface of the cortex, but which are known to be functionally linked with the targeted neurocognitive processes. Promising techniques, such as focused ultrasound, are currently being developed and would offer the possibility to reach deeper brain regions, thus leading to new opportunities to significantly improve our understanding of the brain.

techniques in order to modulate the activity of the somatosensory cortex I (SI), a brain region located near the surface of the cortex and linked to the empathy neural network. In their study, the researchers presented another individual to their participants – in reality a confederate of the experimenter – and told them that they could reduce the intensity of pain the person would receive by donating money they could have taken home. That other person was then brought to another room and had their hand swatted with a belt, with increased intensity, which participants could watch through a camera. Behavioral results showed that the more they saw the other person suffering, the more participants donated money to prevent the pain and help that other person. Then, by using neuromodulation techniques, the researchers interfered with the activity of SI, by emitting a weak electrical current. After this interference, participants did not donate as much money to help that other person.

Another team of researchers in 2018,[305] also used the same neuromodulation technique, but stimulated the medial prefrontal cortex (mPFC), a brain region located in the frontal cortex associated with social decision-making and the ability to understand others' states of mind.[306] The participants were led to believe that in each trial, a strong, harmful electrical shock would be delivered to the other person, and that they had a chance to help by giving money. For instance, in some trials they could give up $1.42 of their potential reward money for a 90 percent chance of preventing the shock from being delivered to the other person. The researchers observed that after increasing the excitability of the mPFC, participants gave up money more frequently to prevent the other individual from receiving a shock, confirming a key causal role of this brain region in costly helping.

Another mechanism of interest is a neurochemical called oxytocin, a neuropeptide involved in several prosocial behaviors[307] and linked to empathy.[308] In 2007, a team of researchers used a dictator game and infused their participants with either oxytocin or a placebo.[309] Results showed that participants injected with oxytocin were 80 percent more generous, donating more money than those injected with the placebo. Interestingly, oxytocin also improves helping behaviors in animals. Neuroscience research has shown that helping behaviors are not human-specific and are also observable in other species. For example, in 2015 a team of researchers examined whether rats would help distressed, conspecific rats that had been soaked with water.[310] The researchers observed that rats presented with a distressed cagemate rapidly learned how to open the door to rescue him. Even when they were given the option to open a different door and obtain a food reward, most rats chose to help their distressed cagemate first. In a study published in 2020, the researchers observed that when they were administered oxytocin, rats were faster at helping to free another rat soaked with water – even though they did not know him beforehand.[311]

Empathy does appear to be a critical mechanism associated with helping behaviors, which would be consistent with the reports made by several rescuers indicating that they felt empathy for those in need, despite the dehumanization processes directed towards those people. However, the experimental approach to investigating helping behaviors is frequently made in a context of free decisions, where people do not suffer from additional constraints that could prevent their helping behaviors beyond the financial costs associated with their decisions.

During times of war or genocide, it is typically illegal to help the targeted group, with clear orders from governments sometimes accompanied by elements of coercion. Another experimental approach thus consists in understanding whether the same mechanisms are at play in situations where people both loose a monetary gain and must decide to disobey orders from an authority figure to prevent someone else from receiving pain.

HOW TO MAKE PEOPLE DISOBEY IN A LAB CONTEXT

After years of research on why people commit atrocities when they follow orders, I wanted to develop a novel, but complementary, line of research associated with the neuroscience of how people resist immoral orders. I wanted to understand why some people choose to help despite going against orders.

This may be a very obvious remark, but studying disobedience in an experimental setup actually requires having people disobey orders. While simple in principle, making people disobey my orders was probably the biggest challenge I ever faced when designing experiments.

It is well known in the scientific community that researchers can bias their participants' behaviors in a number of ways, such as by providing clues or hints about what they expect the participants to do or by interacting with the participants in a way that influences their responses. This can occur unintentionally, as the researcher may have preconceived notions about what the results of the study should be or may be unconsciously communicating their expectations to the participants. However, in the study of disobedience, strangely this appears to be less the case. Despite my strong expectation that people would resist orders to hurt another person, I overall largely failed to obtain the expected disobedience.

In the studies I developed with the painful electric shocks, as mentioned in Chapter 2, the disobedience rate was very (very) low. So low that I did not have sufficient trials to perform reliable statistical analyses on disobedience. I thus needed to find a different approach in order to ensure that I would have at least some people resisting my orders to hurt another person. This took me five years, including a systematic analysis of the participants' debriefings about their reasons for obeying my orders, and six experimental studies.[312] During these years of reflection and investigation, several possible solutions emerged, which involved different degrees of resistance to my orders to deliver a painful shock to another person.

I first of all decided that I should distance myself from the participants. In the studies conducted by Stanley Milgram, when the experimenter was not physically present in the same room and gave his orders by phone, disobedience markedly increased.[48] I thus decided, as an overall rule, to always leave my participants alone in the experimental room and to sit in another room, thus increasing physical distance.

In my previous studies, participants had to perform two experimental conditions, one in which I gave them orders and one in which they were free to decide. By reading the debriefings and talking with my participants, I realized that many justified their obedience because there was a condition where they could choose. Some reported explicitly that since they could choose in at least one condition, it was not an issue to follow orders in the other one. I thus considered that, perhaps, removing this free-choice condition and having them only obey my orders would increase disobedience. I thus tested this condition experimentally, by having a group of participants perform the task without a free-choice condition and a group of participants with a free-choice condition. However, results indicated that the presence or absence of a free-choice condition did not statistically influence the prosocial disobedience rate.

As mentioned in Chapter 2, some people explicitly declared that they were happy to make more money for each shock delivered without feeling too responsible as they just had to follow orders. Therefore, a possibility to increase prosocial disobedience would be to remove the financial reward associated with each shock delivered. In one variant of the task, participants received €0.05 for each shock delivered to the victim, while in another variant, they did not receive any financial reward for the shocks. Results showed that people disobeyed about twice as often when they were not given any financial reward compared to when they received €0.05 for each shock. Additional correlations showed that the more frequently people disobeyed my orders, the less they reported being willing to make more money. Such results suggest that providing a form of monetary reward, even one as small as €0.05, prevents people from refusing an order to hurt another person.

However, I was not fully convinced that I had to drop the financial reward to increase prosocial disobedience in my experimental approach. Based on historical examples from the rescuers, helping others always came with a cost or a sacrifice. In the experimental context, the benefit they had to give up was the monetary reward. Removing the reward would reduce the ecology of the task, facilitating the process of disobedience.

An interesting aspect is that some participants justified their obedience by explaining that they wanted to help acquire good data. In the studies I conducted, I observed justifications such as "It felt normal not to bias the study," or "The scientific context provided a legitimacy to the protocol, so I followed orders," or even "I thought that my obedience was crucial for the data of this study." Interestingly, many participants indicated that they obeyed because it was the aim of the study, even if at no point were they told this – especially since I was hoping to obtain some disobedience.

It appears that sometimes, people want to find a justification for their behaviors, and find reasons that have actually never been provided. For instance, in other studies I conducted in Rwanda with a similar protocol, I even made participants sign a document stating explicitly that they were responsible for their own actions and could disobey my orders.[313] Yet almost no one disobeyed and still provided reasons such as "[I did not disobey] because it would interfere with the research. Research results could be inaccurate" or "I did everything that I was supposed to do because it was my responsibility and to not cause any bias in results that will come from this research."

I thus tested whether providing a reason for obedience was associated with a lower disobedience rate. In one variant of the experimental procedure, I provided an explicitly scientific aim for the study. I told my participants that other researchers had observed a specific brain activity in the motor cortex when participants were given instructions. I explained that the present study was a control study to measure different aspects linked to motor activity when they press buttons. To increase the veracity of the procedure, electrodes were also placed on their fingers and connected to a real electromyography (EMG) apparatus to supposedly record their muscle activity. In another variant, I did not provide any aims. Statistical results indicated that participants disobeyed two times less frequently when they were given an objective for the experiment. This finding supported the idea that people will be more obedient when they find or are offered a way to legitimate reprehensible acts.

Another aspect that needed to be addressed was the extent to which the shocks were painful. Even though the shocks were calibrated to be at the pain threshold, they do not cause any permanent damage to the participants for ethical reasons – information that I explain to my participants before starting the study. Participants thus also sometimes explain that they obeyed because the shocks had no lasting effects and were not at the level of atrocious pain. For example, I had reports such as "I knew that the person had chosen a pain threshold that she could tolerate," or "I told myself it is always better to follow orders. I had tested the shocks, and I told myself that following orders would not hurt the other person too much," or even "I knew the pain was only momentary and would not have long-term effects, so it was not that problematic."

However, the pain procedure cannot be changed. When conducting experimental research, we must ensure that potential volunteers are safe and that no physical or psychological damage will be caused to them. Instead, I increased the number of times people received the orders to deliver a shock to another person, from 30 to 64 shocks, to force them to deliver more shocks. My hope was to increase prosocial disobedience.

In the end, across the different variants tested, I obtained a prosocial disobedience rate of approximately 30 percent. This rate was clearly much higher than in my previous studies. I thus decided to use the knowledge acquired in the analyses of the debriefings and across the different experimental variants to study the neural mechanisms associated with resistance to orders to hurt another person.

THE NEUROSCIENCE OF RESISTANCE TO IMMORAL ORDERS

In order to initiate a scientific study associated with resistance to immoral orders, I decided that conducting such research on classic university students in Belgium would not be the most interesting place to start. At that time, I was already considering conducting research activities in Rwanda. In Rwanda, there is indeed great concern regarding obedience to authority since the genocide because many former perpetrators reported that they participated in the genocide because of it. I was also wondering to what extent the existence of family suffering as a result of crimes committed due in part to obedience behaviors would influence submission to immoral orders. For instance, a study conducted in Colombia showed that civilians who saw their families being victimized in armed conflicts were more likely to disobey the main insurgent group.[314]

I thus decided to use my protocol targeting prosocial disobedience on the first generation of Rwandans born after the genocide.[313] I asked for approval from the Rwandan National Ethics Committee and took a flight to Kigali with my portable electroencephalogram and my machine to deliver the shocks.

With my collaborators, I conducted a first study where participants were recruited in pairs, and we followed a quite standard paradigm. One participant was assigned to the role of the "agent" and the other to the role of the "victim." Their roles were reversed at the middle of the experiment. Agents were ordered in 70 percent of the trials to deliver a mildly painful shock to the victim. As I was the experimenter giving orders, I was not present in the same room as them in order to increase physical distance. Participants could hear my (pre-recorded) orders through headphones. Their brain activity was recorded with an electro-encephalogram during the entire experiment in order to study the neural processes associated with resistance to immoral orders.

We tested twenty-four volunteers in this experimental setup. However, while we hoped that several people would disobey orders, we observed that only four participants sometimes disobeyed. Taking a closer look, we realized that prosocial disobedience was even lower, as only one of the four disobeyed in a prosocial way, and only on a single trial. The three other participants disobeyed my orders *not* to deliver a shock to the victim. Despite my order not to, they pressed the shock button in a phenomenon that I call *antisocial disobedience*. With a single trial of *prosocial* disobedience, no statistical analyses were possible.

We thus decided to conduct two other variants: One in which the monetary reward was removed, and one in which we emphasized individual responsibility. In the later variant, we explicitly told participants that they were responsible adults, able to make their own decisions, and that they could disobey my orders. This variant was suggested by our local collaborator, Darius Gishoma, who explained that in Rwanda, obedience to authority is so culturally ingrained that it would be worth explicitly mentioning that aspect to our volunteers.

However, results were still not what we hoped for. In the variant without the monetary reward, 2 participants out of 24 disobeyed my orders to send the shocks, but only on a very few numbers of trials. In the other variant, 3 participants out of 24 disobeyed my orders to send the shocks, but again only on a very few numbers of trials. Even after testing 72 individuals in total, I barely obtained a prosocial disobedience rate of 3.66 percent, which was clearly not sufficient to conduct reliable statistical analyses on prosocial disobedience.

Back in Belgium, I conducted the same three variants on 72 more individuals from the first generation of Rwandans born after the genocide. I wanted to understand if some cultural factors would differ between Rwandans living in Rwanda and those living in Belgium that could explain the low prosocial disobedience rate observed in Rwanda. For people living in a foreign country, an acculturation phenomenon is indeed frequently observed. Acculturation is the process by which individuals or groups adopt the cultural norms and values of a new or different culture while retaining some aspects of their original culture. It frequently happens when someone migrates to another country.[315]

After conducting the same studies in Belgium, I observed that the prosocial disobedience rate across the three variants was 36.26 percent, a rate actually similar to the rate obtained in previous studies on classic university students. And, because the disobedience rate was higher, I was finally able to conduct statistical analyses in order to understand better the mechanisms and factors that lead to more prosocial disobedience.

As empathy was strongly associated with costly helping behaviors in previous studies, I first analyzed the brain activity of my participants when they saw the victim receiving a painful shock on their hand in order to measure their empathy for the pain of others. Consistent with the hypothesis, I observed that the higher their neural response to the victim's pain, the more frequently they resisted my orders to hurt the victim. However, interestingly, this result did not explain the difference observed in Rwandans tested in Belgium and Rwandans tested in Rwanda, as the two groups had a similar neural response to the victim's pain. This suggested that although empathy is a critical determinant for resisting immoral orders, other factors were at play.

Interestingly, I also observed that a specific brain activity linked with the processing of the auditory orders received from the experimenter was associated with prosocial disobedience. When we hear information, our brains process such information at different levels and "decide" how much attention to pay to this auditory information. Here, I observed that the less participants paid attention to the orders of the experimenter, as reflected by a specific brain activity recorded over the frontal lobes, the more they disobeyed orders. This could indicate that disobedience is facilitated when individuals disengage their attention from the orders received by the authority. The results further indicated that this disengagement could be facilitated by a low cultural relationship to authority. As already mentioned, there is a strong cultural relationship to people in authority in Rwanda. This was reflected in our questionnaires as well, where we observed that Rwandans tested in Rwanda scored higher on a scale assessing their deference to hierarchies than Rwandans tested in Belgium. Those scores correlated with the activity of the brain when listening to the orders of the experimenter. Such results indicate that culture can play a significant role in determining resistance to immoral orders. It has been suggested in the literature that in authority-oriented cultures, people are more likely to follow authorities without evaluating the rightness of the actions they propagate.[323] Some authors argue that in such cultures, mass atrocities committed under obedience are more likely to occur. Here, the results obtained suggest that this effect is partly mediated by a greater attention to the words and instructions of authority figures.[313] However, to gain better evidence for the culturation hypothesis a longitudinal study of Rwandan individuals arriving in Belgium, for instance, is necessary.

It is known that humans have a natural tendency to avoid hurting others. This aversion to hurting others is not only reflected by the measurement of empathy, but can also be reflected by another specific neural activity in frontal regions of the brain, the theta activity, which reflects cognitive conflict. Usually, a higher cognitive conflict entails that the selected action was not the most natural one to select compared to the other actions,[316] which is the case when hurting another person.[317] In our study, we observed that participants with the highest theta activity before delivering a shock to the victim were also those who disobeyed the most by refusing to deliver shocks. This result indicates that those with a greater conflict before obeying an order to hurt someone are more likely to disobey such orders in the future.

However, our results also showed that the aversion to hurting others can be attenuated by obtaining a financial reward for the pain inflicted. We indeed observed that individuals scoring high on a scale measuring the importance they gave to money had a more reduced theta activity before delivering the painful shock. This process illuminates how money can reduce prosocial behaviors towards others, by reducing the natural conflict we experience before hurting someone.

Past family experience also partly explained the decision to disobey immoral orders. We observed that the more participants reported on a scale that their family suffered during the 1994 genocide, the more they resisted the immoral orders. A possible interpretation of this effect is that individuals coming from families that were greatly impacted by the genocide would be less likely to perpetrate acts of obedience. We simultaneously observed, however, that a higher level of reported family suffering was also associated with a higher neural response to the pain of others. Other interpretations are therefore possible. On the one hand, it may be the case that a high level of family suffering involved a higher sensitization to the suffering of others,[318] thus leading to more prosocial behaviors. On the other hand, people having a higher neural response to the pain of others could also estimate the suffering of their own family as being higher due to their heightened sensitivity to their suffering. Future research will be necessary to better understand the link between family suffering during a genocide and obedience to immoral orders.

Another recent study also illuminated potential mechanisms involved in resistance to immoral orders.[319] Using the virtual replication of Stanley Milgram's study already described in Chapter 2, the authors scanned the brain of agents delivering the shocks to the avatar, and then used neuromodulation techniques to influence and assess their brain activity. The authors modulated the activity of the right temporoparietal junction (rTPJ), a brain region associated with the ability to understand the states of mind of others.[320] They observed that participants whose brain activity in that region had been reduced decided to hurt the virtual avatar more quickly than when they received a sham stimulation. Such results suggest that an alteration in our ability to understand the state of mind of others can make people less hesitant to hurt another person in a context of obedience.

As this section shows, several neurocognitive processes are at play to help people resist orders received from an authority figure. Empathy plays a key role, but it alone does not determine if someone will engage in acts of disobedience to help another person. However, the current scientific literature in neuroscience on resistance to immoral orders is currently restricted to these two above-mentioned studies, which clearly shows how novel this literature is. Many more studies are expected to narrow the conclusions and the mechanisms associated with resistance to immoral orders.

CONCLUSION

The few studies conducted so far on the neural mechanisms of prosocial disobedience are promising and have started to reveal some key neurocognitive processes, such as empathy, our ability to understand the perspective of others, and the conflict we may experience before carrying out an action with immoral consequences.

But a critical question remains: Why, or how, do these neurocognitive processes appear to attenuate less in some individuals than in others when they receive an order? Why do some people appear to be better shielded against the effect of coercion? The answer is not simple and it involves a confluence of factors, encompassing contextual, social and cultural variables, as well as inherent personality traits. Upcoming research, incorporating diverse populations and neuroscience methodologies, will further elucidate these mechanisms.

Summarizing, the current chapter has highlighted the potential for developing effective interventions to counteract undue submissiveness to unethical commands. As we have observed, ordinary men and women possess the capacity to make different choices, displaying the courage to rescue others. These individuals serve as living examples, illustrating that another choice is possible, and that any person can manifest the strength of human compassion. They signal to perpetrators that there was another path available, one not dominated by blind submissiveness to an authority figure.

Epilogue: A Hopeful Horizon

Recently, while listening to the radio, I have rediscovered a French song, *"Né en 17 à Leidenstadt"* ("Born in 17 in Leidenstadt") by the singer and songwriter Jean-Jacques Goldman. I hadn't heard this song since I was a child and, at that time, I certainly did not understand its meaning. The song, translated into English, goes as follows:

> If I'd been born in '17 in Leidenstadt
> Upon the ruins of a battlefield
> Would I have been better or worse than these men
> Had I been born a German?
> Raised on hate, on humiliation and ignorance
> Nourished by dreams of vengeance
> Would I have had one of those offbeat consciences,
> A simple teardrop amid raging torrents?
> [...]
> We will never know what we're truly made of,
> Hidden behind appearances, is there
> The soul of a hero, or an accomplice or an executioner?
> Either the worst or the best?
> Would we be resisting, or just be another sheep in the herd,
> Judging on more than mere words?

Leidenstadt is the name of a fictitious German city, which means "City of Misery." The author reflects upon what he would have done himself, who he would have become, if instead of being born in 1951 in France of Jewish parents, he had been born in 1917 in Germany and grew up in the post-World War I era, nourished by humiliation and hate messages. Would he have been able to resist the propaganda of the Holocaust and World War II, or would he have been a perpetrator instead?

The general culture may label perpetrators as "psychopaths" because of the horror and incomprehensibility of genocide. People often struggle to understand how anyone could commit such heinous acts. Consequently, they try to find an explanation that seems simple and straightforward, such as labeling perpetrators as "evil" or "monsters." Such a process of categorization and simplification provides a sense of psychological distance and emotional safety, allowing people to avoid confronting the painful realities of genocides.

While it is true that some individuals who commit genocide may exhibit psychopathic traits, such as a lack of empathy and remorse, it is important to understand that genocide is a complex phenomenon with multiple contributing factors. Restricting genocide perpetrators to a simple label overlooks the broader historical, economic, political, and social context that brings people to participate in a genocide or other mass-extermination events. It is fundamental to remember that in the same context and with a similar life history, we never know what we might be capable of.

Taking a neuroscience approach, we have seen throughout the book that several neurocognitive mechanisms are involved in prosocial actions, such as empathy, guilt, and agency. However, we have also seen that many processes at play before and during a genocide can easily blur those mechanisms. For example, genocides often involve hate propaganda, a dehumanization process, and other forms of psychological manipulation that can influence individuals to participate in violence. Genocides are also often the result of long-standing conflicts, of increased categorization of "us" versus "them." These tensions can fuel hatred and violence. Furthermore, we have seen that when people decide to obey the orders of an authority, their prosocial mechanisms are also altered. People experience less empathy for the pain of their victims, they feel less guilty, less responsibility, and less agency – an effect that impacts their ability to take the full consequences of what they are doing.

While it is important to hold genocide perpetrators accountable for their actions, it is also crucial to take a nuanced and interdisciplinary approach to understand the complex dynamics that contribute to the commission of genocide – including unconscious neural activity. We can then use this knowledge to develop interventions that promote empathy, moral courage, and independent thinking. Understanding is the key to preventing.

And especially in times of deep despair, the study of the rescuers who helped those targeted by genocide reminds us that another choice is possible. Regular citizens, like you and me, actively worked to protect and save members of targeted groups during genocides, often at great personal risk. Those people come from diverse backgrounds, with no single factor reliably predicting their actions. Some rescuers were motivated by their religious or moral beliefs, while others were driven by a sense of empathy or a desire to protect. They resisted the dehumanization and demonization of the targeted group, and rather saw them as human beings deserving protection. Whatever guided them, they showed that resisting the influence of propaganda and group pressure is possible. Humans can decide to act ethically and courageously.

As inscribed on the medals given to the Righteous, "Whosoever saves a single life saves an entire universe."

References

1. O. S. McDoom. Contested counting: Toward a rigorous estimate of the death toll in the Rwandan genocide. *Journal of Genocide Research* **22**(1) (2020), 83–93.
2. L. Sillars. *Intended for Evil: A Survivor's Story of Love, Faith, and Courage in the Cambodian Killing Fields.* (Baker Books, 2016).
3. S. P. Singh. Magnetoencephalography: Basic principles. *Annals of the Indian Academy of Neurology* **17** (2014), S107–S112.
4. J. Henrich. *The WEIRDest People in the World: How the West Became Psychologically Peculiar and Particularly Prosperous.* (Penguin UK, 2020).
5. J. J. Arnett. The neglected 95%: Why American psychology needs to become less American. *American Psychologist* **64** (2008), 571–574.
6. S. M. Burns, L. N. Barnes, I. McCulloh, *et al.* Making social neuroscience less WEIRD: Using fNIRS to measure neural signatures of persuasive influence in a Middle East participant sample. *Journal of Personality and Social Psychology* **116** (2019), e1–e11.
7. S. Han & Y. Ma. Cultural differences in human brain activity: A quantitative meta-analysis. *NeuroImage* **99** (2014), 293–300.
8. D. L. Ames & S. T. Fiske. Cultural neuroscience. *Asian Journal of Social Psychology* **13** (2010), 72–82.
9. M. R. Franks. Airline liability for loss, damage, or delay of passenger baggage. *Fordham Journal of Corporate & Financial Law* **12** (2007), 735–752.
10. V. Bondarenko. Your chances of having an airline losing your bag are skyrocketing. *The Street* (2022).
11. M. Sageman. *Understanding Terror Networks.* (University of Pennsylvania Press, 2004).
12. H. Arendt. *Eichmann in Jerusalem: A Report on the Banality of Evil.* (Faber & Faber, 1963).
13. R. J. Lifton. *The Nazi Doctors: Medical Killing and the Psychology of Genocide.* (Macmillan, 1986).
14. K. F. Anderson & E. Jessee (eds.). *Researching Perpetrators of Genocide* (Critical Human Rights). (University of Wisconsin Press, 2020).
15. J. Hatzfeld. *Machete Season: The Killers in Rwanda Speak.* (Macmillan, 2005).
16. L. Sok-Kheang. *Reconciliation Process in Cambodia: 1979–2007: Before the Khmer Rouge Tribunal.* (Documentation Center of Cambodia, 2017).

17. K. Anderson. "Who was I to stop the killing?" Moral neutralization among Rwandan genocide perpetrators. *Journal of Perpetrator Research* **1** (2017), 39–63.

18. L. A. Fujii. *Killing Neighbors: Webs of Violence in Rwanda.* (Cornell University Press, 2010).

19. S. Schaal, R. Weierstall, J.-P. Dusingizemungu, & T. Elbert. Mental health 15 years after the killings in Rwanda: Imprisoned perpetrators of the genocide against the Tutsi versus a community sample of survivors. *Journal of Traumatic Stress* **25** (2012), 446–453.

20. K. Barnes-Ceeney, L. Gideon, L. Leitch, & K. Yasuhara. Recovery after genocide: Understanding the dimensions of recovery capital among incarcerated genocide perpetrators in Rwanda. *Frontiers in Psychology* **10** (2019). doi: 10.3389/fpsyg.2019.00637

21. H. Rieder & T. Elbert. Rwanda – lasting imprints of a genocide: Trauma, mental health and psychosocial conditions in survivors, former prisoners and their children. *Conflict and Health* **7** (2013), 6.

22. D. Southerland. Cambodia Diary 6: Child Soldiers – driven by fear and hate. *Radio Free Asia* (2006). www.rfa.org/english/features/blogs/cambo diablog/blog6_cambodia_southerland-20060720.html

23. P. Clark. *The Gacaca Courts, Post-Genocide Justice and Reconciliation in Rwanda: Justice without Lawyers.* (Cambridge University Press, 2010).

24. S. Straus. How many perpetrators were there in the Rwandan genocide? An estimate. *Journal of Genocide Research* **6** (2004), 85–98.

25. www.newtimes.co.rw/article/6638/National/pastor-showered-with-gifts-for-saving-people

26. R. G. Suny. *"They Can Live in the Desert but Nowhere Else": A History of the Armenian Genocide.* (Princeton University Press, 2015). doi: 10.1515/9781400865581

27. E. A. Caspar. Understanding individual motivations and deterrents: Interviews with genocide perpetrators from Rwanda and Cambodia. *Journal of Perpetrator Research* (2024, in press).

28. P. Verwimp. An economic profile of peasant perpetrators of genocide: Micro-level evidence from Rwanda. *Journal of Development Economics* **77** (2005), 297–323.

29. P. Clark. When the killers go home: Local justice in Rwanda. *Dissent* **52** (2005), 14–21.

30. J. Hatzfeld. *La stratégie des antilopes.* (Éditions du Seuil, 2011), p. 101.

31. J. A. Tayner. State sovereignty, bioethics, and political geographies: The practice of medicine under the Khmer Rouge. *Environment and Planning D: Society and Space* **30** (2012), 842–860.

32. A. L. Hinton. Why did you kill? The Cambodian genocide and the dark side of face and honor. *The Journal of Asian Studies* **57** (1998), 93–122.

33. C. Mironko. Igitero: Means and motive in the Rwandan genocide. *Journal of Genocide Research* **6**(1) (2004), 47–60.

34. C. R. Browning, *Ordinary Men: Reserve Police Battalion 101 and the Final Solution in Poland.* (New York: Harper Collins, 1992).

35. M. Badar. From the Nuremberg Charter to the Rome Statute: Defining the elements of crimes against humanity. *San Diego International Law Journal* **5** (2004), 73 .

36. M. A. King & J. S. King. Führerprinzip. In *The Encyclopedia of Political Thought*, pp. 1406–1407 (John Wiley & Sons, 2014). doi: 10.1002/9781118474396.wbept0396

37. S. M. Moss. Beyond conflict and spoilt identities: How Rwandan leaders justify a single recategorization model for post-conflict reconciliation. *Journal of Social and Political Psychology* **2** (2014), 435–449.

38. E. L. Paluck & D. P. Green. Deference, dissent, and dispute resolution: An experimental intervention using mass media to change norms and behavior in Rwanda. *American Political Science Review* **103** (2009), 622–644.

39. G. Prunier. *The Rwanda Crisis: History of a Genocide.* (C. Hurst & Co, 1998).

40. M. Lacey. A decade after massacres, Rwanda outlaws ethnicity. *The New York Times*, April 9, 2004.

41. A. Mukashema, T. Veldkamp, & S. Amer. Sixty percent of small coffee farms have suitable socio-economic and environmental locations in Rwanda. *Agronomy for Sustainable Development* **36** (2016), 31.

42. L. Waldorf. Ordinariness and orders: Explaining popular participation in the Rwandan genocide. *Genocide Studies and Prevention* **2** (2007), 267–269.

43. J. Hatzfeld. *Dans le nu de la vie. Récits des marais rwandais.* (Média Diffusion, 2009).

44. B. Nowrojee. *Shattered Lives: Sexual Violence During the Rwandan Genocide and Its Aftermath.* (Human Rights Watch, 1996).

45. J. A. Tyner, S. Kimsroy, C. Fu, Z. Wang, & X. Ye. An empirical analysis of arrests and executions at S-21 security-center during the Cambodian genocide. *Genocide Studies International* **10** (2016), 268–286.

46. T. Williams & R. Neilsen. "They will rot the society, rot the party, and rot the army": Toxification as an ideology and motivation for perpetrating violence in the Khmer Rouge genocide? *Terrorism and Political Violence* **31** (2019), 494–515.

47. N. Rafter. How do genocides end? Do they end? The Guatemalan genocide, 1981–1983. In *The Crime of All Crimes: Toward a Criminology of Genocide*, 181–201 (New York University Press, 2016). doi: 10.18574/nyu/9781479814916.003.0012

48. S. Milgram. *Obedience to Authority: An Experimental View.* (Harper & Row, 1974).

49. C. Landis. Studies of emotional reactions. II. General behavior and facial expression. *Journal of Comparative Psychology* **4** (1924), 447–510.

50. J. D. Frank. Experimental studies of personal pressure and resistance: I. Experimental production of resistance. *The Journal of General Psychology* **30** (1944), 23–41.

51. S. E. Asch. Effects of group pressure upon the modification and distortion of judgments. In H. Guetzkow (ed.), *Groups, Leadership and Men: Research in Human Relations*, 177–190 (Carnegie Press, 1951).

52. S. Milgram. Behavioral study of obedience. *The Journal of Abnormal and Social Psychology* **67** (1963), 371–378.

53. Milgram. *Obedience to Authority*, pp. 132–134.
54. T. Blass. The Milgram paradigm after 35 years: Some things we now know about obedience to authority. *Journal of Applied Social Psychology* **29** (1999), 955–978.
55. S. A. Haslam & S. D. Reicher. 50 years of "obedience to authority": From blind conformity to engaged followership. *Annual Review of Law and Social Science* **13** (2017), 59–78.
56. S. A. Haslam, S. D. Reicher, K. Millard, & R. McDonald. "Happy to have been of service": The Yale archive as a window into the engaged followership of participants in Milgram's "obedience" experiments. *British Journal of Social Psychology* **54** (2015), 55–83.
57. L. Bègue, J. L. Beauvois, D. Courbet, D. Oberlé, J. Lepage, & A. A. Duke. Personality predicts obedience in a Milgram paradigm. *Journal of Personality* **83** (2015), 299–306.
58. J. Rantanen, R.-L. Metsäpelto, T. Feldt, L. Pulkkinen, & K. Kokko. Long-term stability in the Big Five personality traits in adulthood. *Scandinavian Journal of Psychology* **48** (2007), 511–518.
59. L. Bègue & K. Vezirian. Sacrificing animals in the name of scientific authority: The relationship between pro-scientific mindset and the lethal use of animals in biomedical experimentation. *Personality and Social Psychology Bulletin* **48** (2022), 1483–1498.
60. M. Michael, L. Birke, & A. Arluke. *The Sacrifice: How Scientific Experiments Transform Animals and People.* (Purdue University Press, 2006).
61. N. Haslam, S. Loughnan, & G. Perry. Meta-Milgram: An empirical synthesis of the obedience experiments. *PLOS One* **9** (2014), e93927.
62. R. A. Griggs & G. I. Whitehead. Coverage of Milgram's obedience experiments in social psychology textbooks: Where have all the criticisms gone? *Teaching of Psychology* **42** (2015), 315–322.
63. Milgram, *Obedience to Authority*, p. 171.
64. M. T. Orne & C. H. Holland. On the ecological validity of laboratory deceptions. *International Journal of Psychiatry* **6** (1968), 282–293.
65. G. Perry. *Behind the Shock Machine: The Untold Story of the Notorious Milgram Psychology Experiments* (New Press, 2013).
66. M. Slater, A. Antley, A. Davison, *et al.* A virtual reprise of the Stanley Milgram obedience experiments. *PLOS One* **1** (2006), e39.
67. D. Baumrind. Some thoughts on ethics of research: After reading Milgram's "Behavioral study of obedience." *American Psychologist* **19** (1964), 421–423.
68. P. A. Moisander & E. Edston. Torture and its sequel – a comparison between victims from six countries. *Forensic Science International* **137** (2003), 133–140.
69. W. H. J. Meeus & Q. A. W. Raaijmakers. Obedience in modern society: The Utrecht studies. *Journal of Social Issues* **51** (1995), 155–175.
70. W. H. J. Meeus & Q. A. W. Raaijmakers. Administrative obedience: Carrying out orders to use psychological-administrative violence. *European Journal of Social Psychology* **16** (1986), 311–324.

71. L. Bègue. & K. Vezirian. The blind obedience of others: A better than average effect in a Milgram-like experiment. *Ethics & Behavior* **0** (2023), 1–11.

72. T. Blass. From New Haven to Santa Clara: A historical perspective on the Milgram obedience experiments. *American Psychologist* **64** (2009), 37–45.

73. E. A. Caspar, J. F. Christensen, A. Cleeremans, & P. Haggard. Coercion changes the sense of agency in the human brain. *Current Biology* **26** (2016), 585–592.

74. B. Gert & J. Gert. The definition of morality. In E. N Zalta (ed.), *The Stanford Encyclopedia of Philosophy.* (Metaphysics Research Lab, Stanford University, 2020).

75. A. Fenigstein. Milgram's shock experiments and the Nazi perpetrators: A contrarian perspective on the role of obedience pressures during the Holocaust. *Theory & Psychology* **25** (2015), 581–598.

76. M. Hopkin. Chimps make spears to catch dinner. *Nature* (2007). doi: 10.1038/news070219-11

77. T. Breuer, M. Ndoundou-Hockemba, & V. Fishlock. First observation of tool use in wild gorillas. *PLOS Biology* **3** (2005), e380.

78. P. Haggard & B. Eitam (eds.). *The Sense of Agency.* (Oxford University Press, 2015).

79. C. S. Mellor. First rank symptoms of schizophrenia: I. The frequency in schizophrenics on admission to hospital II. Differences between individual first rank symptoms. *The British Journal of Psychiatry* **117** (1970), 15–23.

80. C. M. S. D. Sala. Disentangling the alien and anarchic hand. *Cognitive Neuropsychiatry* **3** (1998), 191–207.

81. A. J. Marcel. The sense of agency: Awareness and ownership of action. In J. Roessler & N. Eilan (eds.), *Agency and Self-Awareness: Issues in Philosophy and Psychology,* 48–93 (Clarendon Press, 2003).

82. L. Zapparoli, S. Seghezzi, F. Devoto, *et al.* Altered sense of agency in Gilles de la Tourette syndrome: Behavioural, clinical and functional magnetic resonance imaging findings. *Brain Communications* **2** (2020), fcaa204.

83. M. Carlén. What constitutes the prefrontal cortex? *Science* **358** (2017), 478–482.

84. P. Haggard. Human volition: Towards a neuroscience of will. *Nature Reviews Neuroscience* **9** (2008), 934–946.

85. C. S. Sherrington. The muscular sense. In E. A. Schäfer (ed.), *Textbook of Physiology,* 2: 1002–1025 (Pentland, 1900).

86. A. Sirigu, E. Daprati, S. Ciancia, *et al.* Altered awareness of voluntary action after damage to the parietal cortex. *Nature Neuroscience* **7** (2004), 80–84.

87. M. Desmurget, K. T. Reilly, N. Richard, *et al.* Movement intention after parietal cortex stimulation in humans. *Science* **324** (2009), 811–813.

88. Associated Press. Georgia man wounds mother-in-law after bullet ricochets off armadillo. *The Guardian,* April 14, 2015.

89. J. M. Darley & B. Latane. Bystander intervention in emergencies: Diffusion of responsibility. *Journal of Personality and Social Psychology* **8** (1968), 377–383.

90. 37 who saw murder didn't call the police; Apathy at stabbing of Queens woman shocks inspector. *New York Times*, March 27, 1964, p. 1.

91. K. Kerson. The Kitty Genovese story was the prototype for fake news. *Observer*, January 5, 2017. https://observer.com/author/ken-kurson

92. P. Fischer, J. Krueger, T. Greitemeyer, *et al.* The bystander-effect: A meta-analytic review on bystander intervention in dangerous and non-dangerous emergencies. *Psychological Bulletin* **137** (2011), 517–537.

93. F. Beyer, N. Sidarus, S. Bonicalzi, & P. Haggard. Beyond self-serving bias: Diffusion of responsibility reduces sense of agency and outcome monitoring. *Social Cognitive and Affective Neuroscience* **12** (2017), 138–145.

94. A. Bandura. Selective activation and disengagement of moral control. *Journal of Social Issues* **46** (1990), 27–46.

95. M. Pina e Cunha, A. Rego, & S. R. Clegg. Obedience and evil: From Milgram and Kampuchea to normal organizations. *Journal of Business Ethics* **97** (2010), 291–309.

96. T. Williams, J. Bernath, B. Tann, & S. Kum. *Justice and Reconciliation for the Victims of the Khmer Rouge? Victim Participation in Cambodia's Transitional Justice Process.* (2018). https://edoc.unibas.ch/68564/

97. Ukrainian widow confronts Russian soldier accused of killing her husband. *BBC News*, May 19, 2022.

98. A. P. Brief, J. Dietz, R. R. Cohen, S. D. Pugh, & J. B. Vaslow. Just doing business: Modern racism and obedience to authority as explanations for employment discrimination. *Organizational Behavior and Human Decision Processes* **81** (2000), 72–97.

99. P. Haggard, S. Clark, & J. Kalogeras. Voluntary action and conscious awareness. *Nature Neuroscience* **5** (2002), 382–385.

100. W. H. Meck. Neuroanatomical localization of an internal clock: A functional link between mesolimbic, nigrostriatal, and mesocortical dopaminergic systems. *Brain Research* **1109** (2006), 93–107.

101. P. Nachev, C. Kennard, & M. Husain. Functional role of the supplementary and pre-supplementary motor areas. *Nature Reviews Neuroscience* **9** (2008), 856–869.

102. A. Meyer-Lindenberg, R. S. Miletich, P. D. Kohn, *et al.* Reduced prefrontal activity predicts exaggerated striatal dopaminergic function in schizophrenia. *Nature Neuroscience* **5** (2002), 267–271.

103. F. da Silva Alves, M. Figee, T. van Amelsvoort, D. Veltman, & L. de Haan. The revised dopamine hypothesis of schizophrenia: Evidence from pharmacological MRI studies with atypical antipsychotic medication. *Psychopharmacology Bulletin* **41** (2008), 121–132.

104. N. Akyuz, H. Marien, M. Stok, J. Driessen, J. de Wit, & H. Aarts. Revisiting the agentic shift: Obedience increases the perceived time between own action and results. Preprint (2023).

105. E. A. Caspar, F. Beyer, A. Cleeremans, & P. Haggard. The obedient mind and the volitional brain: A neural basis for preserved sense of agency and sense of responsibility under coercion. *PloS One* **16**(10) (2021), e0258884.

106. S. Karch, C. Mulert, T. Thalmeier, *et al.* The free choice whether or not to respond after stimulus presentation. *Human Brain Mapping* **30** (2009), 2971–2985.

107. E. A. Caspar, S. Lo Bue, P. A. Magalhães De Saldanha da Gama, P. Haggard, & A. Cleeremans. The effect of military training on the sense of agency and outcome processing. *Nature Communications* **11** (2020), 4366.

108. E. A. Caspar, A. Cleeremans, & P. Haggard. Only giving orders? An experimental study of the sense of agency when giving or receiving commands. *PLoS One* **13** (2018), e0204027.

109. C. Peirs & R. P. Seal. Neural circuits for pain: Recent advances and current views. *Science* **354** (2016), 578–584.

110. T. Singer, B. Seymour, J. O'Doherty, H. Kaube, R. J. Dolan, & C. D. Frith. Empathy for pain involves the affective but not sensory components of pain. *Science* **303** (2004), 1157–1162.

111. M. R. Roxo, P. R. Franceschini, C. Zubaran, F. D. Kleber, & J. W. Sander. The limbic system conception and its historical evolution. *The Scientific World Journal* **11** (2011), 2427–2440.

112. H. Meffert, V. Gazzola, J. A. den Boer, A. A. J. Bartels, & C. Keysers. Reduced spontaneous but relatively normal deliberate vicarious representations in psychopathy. *Brain* **136** (2013), 2550–2562.

113. C. Keysers, *The Empathic Brain: How the Discovery of Mirror Neurons Changes Our Understanding of Human Nature.* (Social Brain Press, 2011).

114. G. Rizzolatti, R. Camarda, L. Fogassi, M. Gentilucci, G. Luppino, & M. Matelli. Functional organization of inferior area 6 in the macaque monkey. *Experimental Brain Research* **71** (1988), 491–507.

115. H. Haker, W. Kawohl, U. Herwig, & W. Rössler. Mirror neuron activity during contagious yawning – an fMRI study. *Brain Imaging and Behavior* **7** (2013), 28–34.

116. R. Mukamel, A. D. Ekstrom, J. Kaplan, M. Iacoboni, & I. Fried. Single-neuron responses in humans during execution and observation of actions. *Current Biology* **20** (2010), 750–756.

117. J. Hernandez-Lallement, A. T. Attah, E. Soyman, C. M. Pinhal, V. Gazzola, & C. Keysers. Harm to others acts as a negative reinforcer in rats. *Current Biology* **30** (2020), 949–961.e7.

118. D. Jeon, S. Kim, M. Chetana, *et al.* Observational fear learning involves affective pain system and Cav1.2 Ca2+ channels in ACC. *Nature Neuroscience* **13** (2010), 482–488.

119. B. M. Basile, J. L. Schafroth, C. L. Karaskiewicz, S. W. C. Chang, & E. A. Murray. The anterior cingulate cortex is necessary for forming prosocial preferences from vicarious reinforcement in monkeys. *PLoS Biology* **18** (2020), e3000677.

120. J. P. Demuth, T. D. Bie, J. E. Stajich, N. Cristianini, & M. W Hahn. The evolution of mammalian gene families. *PLoS One* **1** (2006), e85.

121. K. A. Cronin. Prosocial behaviour in animals: The influence of social relationships, communication and rewards. *Animal Behaviour* **84** (2012), 1085–1093.

122. G. Hein, G. Silani, K. Preuschoff, C. D. Batson, & T. Singer. Neural responses to ingroup and outgroup members' suffering predict individual differences in costly helping. *Neuron* **68** (2010), 149–160.

123. J. Decety & J. M. Cowell. Empathy, justice, and moral behavior. *AJOB Neuroscience* **6** (2015), 3–14.

124. P. A. Thoits & L. N. Hewitt. Volunteer work and well-being. *Journal of Health and Social Behavior* **42** (2001), 115–131.

125. E. W. Dunn, L. B. Aknin, & M. I. Norton. Spending money on others promotes happiness. *Science* **319** (2008), 1687–1688.

126. J. Moll, F. Krueger, R. Zahn, M. Pardini, R. de Oliveira-Souza, & J. Grafman. Human fronto–mesolimbic networks guide decisions about charitable donation. *Proceedings of the National Academy of Sciences* **103** (2006), 15623–15628.

127. J. P. O'Doherty, R. Deichmann, H. D. Critchley, & R. J. Dolan. Neural responses during anticipation of a primary taste reward. *Neuron* **33** (2002), 815–826.

128. B. Knutson, C. M. Adams, G. W. Fong, & D. Hommer. Anticipation of increasing monetary reward selectively recruits nucleus accumbens. *Journal of Neuroscience* **21** (2001), RC159–RC159.

129. P. Bloom. *Against Empathy: The Case for Rational Compassion.* (Ecco Press, 2016).

130. E. A. Caspar, K. Ioumpa, C. Keysers, & V. Gazzola. Obeying orders reduces vicarious brain activation towards victims' pain. *NeuroImage* **222** (2020), 117251.

131. G. P. Pech & E. A. Caspar. Does the cowl make the monk? The effect of military and Red Cross uniforms on empathy for pain, sense of agency and moral behaviors. *Frontiers in Psychology* **14** (2023).

132. J. Decety, C. Chen, C. Harenski, & K. Kiehl. An fMRI study of affective perspective taking in individuals with psychopathy: Imagining another in pain does not evoke empathy. *Frontiers in Human Neuroscience* **7** (2013). https://doi.org/10.3389/fnhum.2013.00489

133. R. T. Salekin, C. Worley, & R. D. Grimes. Treatment of psychopathy: A review and brief introduction to the mental model approach for psychopathy. *Behavioral Sciences & the Law* **28** (2010), 235–266.

134. E. Caspar, E. Nicolay, & G. Pech. Volition as a modulator of the intergroup empathy bias. (2024). PsyArXiv Preprints.

135. N. I. Eisenberger, M. D. Lieberman, & K. D. Williams. Does rejection hurt? An fMRI study of social exclusion. *Science* **302** (2003), 290–292.

136. G. Macdonald & M. R. Leary. Why does social exclusion hurt? The relationship between social and physical pain. *Psychological Bulletin* **131** (2005), 202–223.

137. H. Tajfel, M. Billig, R. Bundy, & C. Flament. Social categorization and intergroup behavior. *European Journal of Social Psychology* **1** (1971), 149–178.

138. T. Ito & G. Urland. Race and gender on the brain: Electrocortical measures of attention to the race and gender of multiply categorizable individuals. *Journal of Personality and Social Psychology* **85** (2003), 616–626.

139. D. M. Amodio & M. Cikara. The social neuroscience of prejudice. *Annual Review of Psychology* **72** (2021), 439–469.

140. J. M. Contreras, M. R. Banaji, & J. P. Mitchell. Dissociable neural correlates of stereotypes and other forms of semantic knowledge. *Social Cognitive and Affective Neuroscience* **7** (2012), 764–770.

141. S. Quadflieg & C. N. Macrae. Stereotypes and stereotyping: What's the brain got to do with it? *European Review of Social Psychology* **22** (2011), 215–273.

142. X. Xu, X. Zuo, X. Wang, & S. Han. Do you feel my pain? Racial group membership modulates empathic neural responses. *Journal of Neuroscience.* **29** (2009), 8525–8529.

143. E. A. Caspar, G. P. Pech, D. Gishoma, & C. Kanazayire. On the impact of the genocide on the intergroup empathy bias between former perpetrators, survivors, and their children in Rwanda. *American Psychologist* (2022). doi: 10.1037/amp0001066

144. G. P. Pech & E. A. Caspar. A novel EEG-based paradigm to measure intergroup prosociality: An intergenerational study in the aftermath of the genocide in Rwanda. *Journal of Experimental Psychology: General.* Forthcoming.

145. E. C. Nook, D. C. Ong, S. A. Morelli, J. P. Mitchell, & J. Zaki. Prosocial conformity: Prosocial norms generalize across behavior and empathy. *Personality and Social Psychology Bulletin* **42** (2016), 1045–1062.

146. M. Tarrant, S. Dazeley, & T. Cottom. Social categorization and empathy for outgroup members. *British Journal of Social Psychology* **48** (2009), 427–446.

147. X. Zuo & S. Han. Cultural experiences reduce racial bias in neural responses to others' suffering. *Culture and Brain* **1** (2013), 34–46.

148. B. K. Cheon, D. M. Im, T. Harada, *et al.* Cultural influences on neural basis of intergroup empathy. *NeuroImage* **57** (2011), 642–650.

149. D. de Varennes & N. Podlesny. *A Glimpse of Evil: Part I of a Trilogy.* (HAF Books, 2018).

150. A. Cuddy, M. Rock, & M. Norton. Aid in the aftermath of Hurricane Katrina: Inferences of secondary emotions and intergroup helping. *Group Processes & Intergroup Relations* **10** (2007), 107–118.

151. S. Demoulin, J.-P. Leyens, M. P. Paladino, *et al.* Dimensions of "uniquely" and "non-uniquely" human emotions. *Cognition and Emotion* **18** (2004), 71–96.

152. J.-P. Leyens, A. Rodríguez-Pérez, R. Rodríguez-Torres, *et al.* Psychological essentialism and the differential attribution of uniquely human emotions to ingroups and outgroups. *European Journal of Social Psychology* **31** (2001), 395–411.

153. S. Zebel, A. Zimmermann, G. Tendayi Viki, & B. Doosje. Dehumanization and guilt as distinct but related predictors of support for reparation policies. *Political Psychology* **29** (2008), 193–219.

154. G. T. Viki, D. Osgood, & S. Phillips. Dehumanization and self-reported proclivity to torture prisoners of war. *Journal of Experimental Social Psychology* **49** (2013), 325–328.

155. A. Bandura, B. Underwood, & M. E. Fromson, Disinhibition of aggression through diffusion of responsibility and dehumanization of victims. *Journal of Research in Personality* **9** (1975), 253–269.

156. L. T. Harris & S. T. Fiske. Dehumanizing the lowest of the low: Neuroimaging responses to extreme out-groups. *Psychological Science* **17** (2006), 847–853.

157. J. Vaes, F. Meconi, P. Sessa, & M. Olechowski. Minimal humanity cues induce neural empathic reactions towards non-human entities. *Neuropsychologia* **89** (2016), 132–140.

158. J. Haidt. The moral emotions. In R. J. Davidson, K. R. Sherer, & H. H. Goldsmith (eds.), *Handbook of Affective Sciences*, 852–870 (Oxford University Press, 2003).

159. J. P. Tangney, J. Stuewig, & A. G. Martinez. Two faces of shame: The roles of shame and guilt in predicting recidivism. *Psychological Science* **25** (2014), 799–805.

160. S. G. Michaud & H. Aynesworth. *Ted Bundy: Conversations with a Killer.* (Authorlink, 2000).

161. B. Bastian, J. Jetten, & F. Fasoli. Cleansing the soul by hurting the flesh: The guilt-reducing effect of pain. *Psychological Sciences* **22** (2011), 334–335.

162. R. M. A. Nelissen & M. Zeelenberg. When guilt evokes self-punishment: Evidence for the existence of a Dobby Effect. *Emotion* **9** (2009), 118–122.

163. P. Kanyangara, B. Rimé, P. Philippot, & V. Yzerbyt. Collective rituals, emotional climate and intergroup perception: Participation in "Gacaca" tribunals and assimilation of the Rwandan genocide. *Journal of Social Issues* **63** (2007), 387–403.

164. D. J. Goldhagen. *Worse than War: Genocide, Eliminationism and the Ongoing Assault on Humanity.* (Hachette UK, 2010).

165. R. Zhu, C. Feng, S. Zhang, X. Mai, & C. Liu. Differentiating guilt and shame in an interpersonal context with univariate activation and multivariate pattern analyses. *NeuroImage* **186** (2019), 476–486.

166. N. Mclatchie, R. Giner-Sorolla, & S. W. G. Derbyshire. "Imagined guilt" vs. "recollected guilt": Implications for fMRI. *Social Cognitive and Affective Neuroscience* **11** (2016), 703–711.

167. J. P. Tangney, J. Stuewig, & D. J. Mashek. Moral emotions and moral behavior. *Annual Review of Psychology* **58** (2007), 345–372.

168. Acton, letter on historical integrity, 1887. https://history.hanover.edu/courses/excerpts/165acton.html

169. A. J. King, D. D. P. Johnson, & M. Van Vugt. The origins and evolution of leadership. *Current Biology* **19** (2009), R911–R916.

170. M. Van Vugt, R. Hogan, & R. B. Kaiser. Leadership, followership, and evolution: Some lessons from the past. *American Psychologist* **63** (2008), 182–196.

171. T. A. Judge & J. E. Bono. Relationship of core self-evaluations traits – self-esteem, generalized self-efficacy, locus of control, and emotional stability – with job satisfaction and job performance: A meta-analysis. *Journal of Applied Psychology* **86** (2001), 80–92.

172. T. A. Judge, R. F. Piccolo, & T. Kosalka. The bright and dark sides of leader traits: A review and theoretical extension of the leader trait paradigm. *The Leadership Quarterly* **20** (2009), 855–875.

173. H. N. Southern. Review of *The Spotted Hyena: A Study of Predation and Social Behavior*. *Journal of Animal Ecology* **42** (1973), 822–824.

174. C. Vullioud, E. Davidian, B. Wachter, F. Rousset, A. Courtiol, & O. P. Höner. Social support drives female dominance in the spotted hyaena. *Nat Ecology & Evolution* **3** (2019), 71–76.

175. R. H. Walker, A. J. King, J. W. McNutt, & N. R. Jordan. Sneeze to leave: African wild dogs (Lycaon pictus) use variable quorum thresholds facilitated by sneezes in collective decisions. *Proceedings of the Royal Society B: Biological Sciences* **284** (2017), 20170347.

176. C. A. H. Bousquet, D. J. T. Sumpter, & M. B. Manser. Moving calls: A vocal mechanism underlying quorum decisions in cohesive groups. *Proceedings of the Royal Society B: Biological Sciences* **278** (2010), 1482–1488.

177. H. H. T. Prins. Selecting grazing grounds: A case of voting. In H. H. T. Prins (ed.), *Ecology and Behaviour of the African Buffalo: Social Inequality and Decision Making*, 218–236 (Springer Netherlands, 1996).

178. J. Goodall. The chimpanzees of Gombe: Patterns of behavior. *eweb:64029* (1986). https://repository.library.georgetown.edu/handle/10822/811357

179. R. Wood & A. Bandura. Social cognitive theory of organizational management. *The Academy of Management Review* **14** (1989), 361–384.

180. C. Moore, D. M. Mayer, F. F. T. Chiang, C. Crossley, M. J. Karlesky, & T. A. Birtch. Leaders matter morally: The role of ethical leadership in shaping employee moral cognition and misconduct. *Journal of Applied Psychology* **104** (2019), 123–145.

181. A. Bandura. Toward a psychology of human agency. *Perspectives on Psychological Science* **1** (2006), 164–180.

182. J. D. Ciorciari & A. Heindel. *Hybrid Justice: The Extraordinary Chambers in the Courts of Cambodia*. (University of Michigan Press, 2014).

183. H. Ryan. And then, finally, a judge wrote the shameful end of the Khmer Rouge Tribunal. *JusticeInfo.net* (2022). www.justiceinfo.net/en/87248-finally-judge-wrote-shameful-end-khmer-rouge-tribunal.html

184. Associated Press. No more Khmer Rouge prosecutions, says Cambodia. *The Guardian*, November 18, 2018.

185. *The Last Interview with Pol Pot* (video, English subtitles). (Raudonasis Khmeras, 2014).

186. Profile: Khmer Rouge leaders Nuon Chea and Khieu Samphan. *BBC News*, August 7, 2014.

187. Former Khmer Rouge leader denies role in genocide. *The New York Times*, July 19, 2007.

188. Khmer Rouge leader Nuon Chea expresses "remorse." *BBC News*, May 31, 2013.

189. T. Chy. *When the Criminal Laughs*. (Documentation Center of Cambodia, 2014).

190. W. Kilham & L. Mann. Level of destructive obedience as a function of transmitter and executant roles in the Milgram obedience paradigm. *Journal of Personality and Social Psychology* **29** (1974), 696–702.

191. E. A. Caspar, K. Ioumpa, I. Arnaldo, L. Di Angelis, V. Gazzola, & C. Keysers. Commanding or being a simple intermediary: How does it

affect moral behavior and related brain mechanisms? *eNeuro* **9** (2022). doi: 10.1523/ENEURO.0508-21.2022

192. S. S. Obhi, K. M. Swiderski, & S. P. Brubacher. Induced power changes the sense of agency. *Consciousness and Cognition* **21** (2012), 1547–1550.

193. C. M. Galang, M. Jenkins, G. Fahim, & S. S. Obhi. Exploring the relationship between social power and the ERP components of empathy for pain. *Social Neuroscience* **16** (2021), 174–188.

194. P. Babiak & R. D Hare. *Snakes in Suits: When Psychopaths Go to Work.* (Regan Books/HarperCollins, 2006).

195. H. Cleckley. *The Mask of Sanity: An Attempt to Reinterpret the So-Called Psychopathic Personality* (Mosby, 1941).

196. C. Mynatt & S. J. Sherman. Responsibility attribution in groups and individuals: A direct test of the diffusion of responsibility hypothesis. *Journal of Personality and Social Psychology* **32** (1975), 1111–1118.

197. F. Ciardo, F. Beyer, D. De Tommaso, & A. Wykowska. Attribution of intentional agency towards robots reduces one's own sense of agency. *Cognition* **194** (2020), 104109.

198. P. Kanyangara, B. Rimé, D. Paez, & V. Yzerbyt. Trust, individual guilt, collective guilt and dispositions toward reconciliation among Rwandan survivors and prisoners before and after their participation in postgenocide Gacaca courts in Rwanda. *Journal of Social and Political Psychology* **2** (2014), 401–416.

199. A. H. Jordan, E. Eisen, E. Bolton, W. P. Nash, & B. T. Litz. Distinguishing war-related PTSD resulting from perpetration- and betrayal-based morally injurious events. *Psychological Trauma: Theory, Research, Practice, and Policy* **9** (2017), 627–634.

200. K. Papazoglou, D. M. Blumberg, V. B. Chiongbian, *et al.* The role of moral injury in PTSD among law enforcement officers: A brief report. *Frontiers in Psychology* **11** (2020). doi: 10.3389/fpsyg.2020.00310.

201. American Psychiatric Association, *Diagnostic and Statistical Manual of Mental Disorders: DSM-5-TR.* (American Psychiatric Association Publishing, 2022).

202. J. N. Semiatin, S. Torres, A. D. LaMotte, G. A. Portnoy, & C. M. Murphy. Trauma exposure, PTSD symptoms, and presenting clinical problems among male perpetrators of intimate partner violence. *Psychology of Violence* **7** (2017), 91–100.

203. M. L. Pacella, B. Hruska, & D. L. Delahanty. The physical health consequences of PTSD and PTSD symptoms: A meta-analytic review. *Journal of Anxiety Disorders* **27** (2013), 33–46.

204. C. Benjet, E. Bromet, E. G. Karam, *et al.* The epidemiology of traumatic event exposure worldwide: Results from the World Mental Health Survey Consortium. *Psychological Medicine* **46** (2016), 327–343.

205. J. D. Kinzie, J. K. Boehnlein, C. Riley, & L. Sparr. The effects of September 11 on traumatized refugees: Reactivation of posttraumatic stress disorder. *The Journal of Nervous and Mental Disease* **190** (2002), 437.

206. S. L. Sayers, V. A. Farrow, J. Ross, & D. W. Oslin. Family problems among recently returned military veterans referred for a mental health evaluation. *Journal of Clinical Psychiatry* **70** (2009), 163–170.

207. L. M. Shin, S. L. Rauch, & R. K. Pitman. Amygdala, medial prefrontal cortex, and hippocampal function in PTSD. *Annals of the New York Academy of Sciences* **1071** (2006), 67–79.
208. E. A. Phelps & J. E. LeDoux. Contributions of the amygdala to emotion processing: From animal models to human behavior. *Neuron* **48** (2005), 175–187.
209. A. Gilboa, A. Y. Shalev, L. Laor, H. Lester, Y. Louzoun, R. Chisin, & O. Bonne. Functional connectivity of the prefrontal cortex and the amygdala in posttraumatic stress disorder. *Biological Psychiatry* **55**(3) (2004), 263–272.
210. S. L. Rauch, P. J. Whalen, L. M. Shin, *et al.* Exaggerated amygdala response to masked facial stimuli in posttraumatic stress disorder: A functional MRI study. *Biological Psychiatry* **47** (2000), 769–776.
211. S. A. Lowrance, A. Ionadi, E. McKay, X. Douglas, & J. D. Johnson. Sympathetic nervous system contributes to enhanced corticosterone levels following chronic stress. *Psychoneuroendocrinology* **68** (2016). 163–170.
212. R. M. Sapolsky, H. Uno, C. S. Rebert, & C. E. Finch. Hippocampal damage associated with prolonged glucocorticoid exposure in primates. *Journal of Neuroscience* **10** (1990), 2897–2902.
213. E. Tulving & H. J. Markowitsch. Episodic and declarative memory: Role of the hippocampus. *Hippocampus* **8** (1998), 198–204.
214. N. Raz, U. Lindenberger, K. M. Rodrigue, *et al.* Regional brain changes in aging healthy adults: General trends, individual differences and modifiers. *Cerebral Cortex* **15** (2005), 1676–1689.
215. A. M. Fjell, K. B. Walhovd, C. Fennema-Notestine, *et al.* One-year brain atrophy evident in healthy aging. *Journal of Neuroscience* **29** (2009), 15223–15231.
216. L. K. Lapp, C. Agbokou, & F. Ferreri. PTSD in the elderly: The interaction between trauma and aging. *International Psychogeriatrics* **23** (2011), 858–868.
217. F. L. Woon, S. Sood, & D. W. Hedges. Hippocampal volume deficits associated with exposure to psychological trauma and posttraumatic stress disorder in adults: A meta-analysis. *Progress in Neuro-Psychopharmacology and Biological Psychiatry* **34** (2010), 1181–1188.
218. M.-L. Meewisse, J. B. Reitsma, G.-J. D. Vries, B. P. R. Gersons, & M. Olff. Cortisol and post-traumatic stress disorder in adults: Systematic review and meta-analysis. *The British Journal of Psychiatry* **191** (2007), 387–392.
219. M. W. Gilbertson, M. E. Shenton, A. Ciszewski, *et al.* Smaller hippocampal volume predicts pathologic vulnerability to psychological trauma. *Nature Neuroscience* **5** (2002), 1242–1247.
220. R. Garcia, R.-M. Vouimba, M. Baudry & R. F. Thompson. The amygdala modulates prefrontal cortex activity relative to conditioned fear. *Nature* **402** (1999), 294–296.
221. L. M. Shin, C. I. Wright, P. A. Cannistraro, *et al.* A functional magnetic resonance imaging study of amygdala and medial prefrontal cortex responses to overtly presented fearful faces in posttraumatic stress disorder. *Archives of General Psychiatry* **62** (2005), 273–281.

222. P. Yang, Wu M.-T., Hsu C.-C., & J.-H. Ker. Evidence of early neurobiological alternations in adolescents with posttraumatic stress disorder: A functional MRI study. *Neuroscience Letters* **370** (2004), 13–18.

223. L. M. Shin, S. P. Orr, M. A Carson, *et al.* Regional cerebral blood flow in the amygdala and medial prefrontal cortex during traumatic imagery in male and female Vietnam veterans with PTSD. *Archives of General Psychiatry* **61** (2004), 168–176.

224. L. M. Williams, A. H. Kemp, K. Felmingham, *et al.* Trauma modulates amygdala and medial prefrontal responses to consciously attended fear. *NeuroImage* **29** (2006), 347–357.

225. M. R. Delgado, L. E. Nystrom, C. Fissell, D. C. Noll, & J. A. Fiez. Tracking the hemodynamic responses to reward and punishment in the striatum. *Journal of Neurophysiology* **84** (6) (2000), 3072–3077.

226. U. Sailer, S. Robinson, F. P. S. Fischmeister, D. König, C. Oppenauer, B. Lueger-Schuster, … & H. Bauer. Altered reward processing in the nucleus accumbens and mesial prefrontal cortex of patients with posttraumatic stress disorder. *Neuropsychologia* **46** (11) (2008), 2836–2844.

227. E. A. Olson, R. H. Kaiser, D. A. Pizzagalli, S. L. Rauch, & I. M. Rosso. Anhedonia in trauma-exposed individuals: Functional connectivity and decision-making correlates. *Biological Psychiatry: Cognitive Neuroscience and Neuroimaging* **3** (11) (2018), 959–967.

228. B. C. Kok, R. K. Herrell, J. L. Thomas, & C. W. Hoge. Posttraumatic stress disorder associated with combat service in Iraq or Afghanistan: Reconciling prevalence differences between studies. *The Journal of Nervous and Mental Disease* **200** (2012), 444.

229. B. P. Dohrenwend, J. B. Turner, N. A. Turse, *et al.* The psychological risks of Vietnam for U.S. veterans: A revisit with new data and methods. *Science* **313** (2006), 979–982.

230. M. Vythilingam, D. A. Luckenbaugh, T. Lam, *et al.* Smaller head of the hippocampus in Gulf War-related posttraumatic stress disorder. *Psychiatry Research: Neuroimaging* **139** (2005), 89–99.

231. J. D. Bremner, P. Randall, T. M. Scott, *et al.* MRI-based measurement of hippocampal volume in patients with combat-related posttraumatic stress disorder. *American Journal of Psychiatry* **152** (1995), 973–981.

232. J. C. Chapman & R. Diaz-Arrastia. Military traumatic brain injury: A review. *Alzheimer's & Dementia* **10** (2014), S97–S104.

233. R. E. Jorge, L. Acion, S. E. Starkstein, & V. Magnotta. Hippocampal volume and mood disorders after traumatic brain injury. *Biological Psychiatry* **62** (2007), 332–338.

234. J. D. Bremner, M. Hoffman, N. Afzal, *et al.* The environment contributes more than genetics to smaller hippocampal volume in posttraumatic stress disorder (PTSD). *Journal of Psychiatric Research* **137** (2021), 579–588.

235. R. A. Morey, A. L. Gold, K. S. LaBar, *et al.* Amygdala volume changes in posttraumatic stress disorder in a large case-controlled veterans group. *Archives of General Psychiatry* **69** (2012), 1169–1178.

236. L. M. Shin, S. M. Kosslyn, R. J. McNally, *et al.* Visual imagery and perception in posttraumatic stress disorder: A positron emission tomographic investigation. *Archives of General Psychiatry* **54** (1997), 233–241.

237. A. Pissiota, O. Frans, M. Fernandez, *et al.* Neurofunctional correlates of posttraumatic stress disorder: A PET symptom provocation study. *European Archives of Psychiatry and Clinical Neurosciences* **252** (2002), 68–75.

238. B. T. Litz, N. Stein, E. Delaney, *et al.* Moral injury and moral repair in war veterans: A preliminary model and intervention strategy. *Clinical Psychology Review* **29** (2009), 695–706.

239. A. Nazarov, R. Jetly, H. McNeely, *et al.* Role of morality in the experience of guilt and shame within the armed forces. *Acta Psychiatrica Scandinavica* **132** (2015), 4–19.

240. C. J. Bryan, B. Ray-Sannerud, C. E. Morrow, & N. Etienne. Guilt is more strongly associated with suicidal ideation among military personnel with direct combat exposure. *Journal of Affective Disorders* **148** (2013), 37–41.

241. E. Caspar, G. Pech, & P. Ros. Long-term affective and non-affective brain alterations across three generations following the genocide in Cambodia (under review).

242. D. Meichenbaum, *A Clinical Handbook/Practical Therapist Manual for Assessing and Treating Adults with Post-Traumatic Stress Disorder (PTSD)* (Institute Press, 1994).

243. L. S. Bishop, V. E. Ameral, & K. M. Palm Reed. The impact of experiential avoidance and event centrality in trauma-related rumination and posttraumatic stress. *Behavior Modification* **42** (2018), 815–837.

244. R. F. Mollica, K. McInnes, T. Pham, *et al.* The dose–effect relationships between torture and psychiatric symptoms in Vietnamese ex-political detainees and a comparison group. *The Journal of Nervous and Mental Disease* **186** (1998), 543.

245. S. Priebe & S. Esmaili. Long-term mental sequelae of torture in Iran – Who seeks treatment? *The Journal of Nervous and Mental Disease* **185** (1997), 74.

246. H. Johnson & A. Thompson. The development and maintenance of post-traumatic stress disorder (PTSD) in civilian adult survivors of war trauma and torture: A review. *Clinical Psychology Review* **28** (2008), 36–47.

247. M. Olff. Sex and gender differences in post-traumatic stress disorder: An update. *European Journal of Psychotraumatology* **8** (2017), 1351204.

248. S. Schmitt, K. Robjant, T. Elbert, & A. Koebach. To add insult to injury: Stigmatization reinforces the trauma of rape survivors – Findings from the DR Congo. *SSM – Population Health* **13** (2021), 100719.

249. D. M. Mukwege & C. Nangini. Rape with extreme violence: The new pathology in South Kivu, Democratic Republic of Congo. *PLoS Medicine* **6** (2009), e1000204.

250. A. Schneider, D. Conrad, A. Pfeiffer, T. Elbert, I. T. Kolassa, & S. Wilker. Stigmatization is associated with increased PTSD risk after traumatic stress and diminished likelihood of spontaneous remission – A study with East-African conflict survivors. *Frontiers in Psychiatry* **9** (2018), 423.

251. I. Ba & R. S. Bhopal. Physical, mental and social consequences in civilians who have experienced war-related sexual violence: A systematic review (1981–2014). *Public Health* **142** (2017), 121–135.

252. R. C. Carpenter. *Born of War: Protecting Children of Sexual Violence Survivors in Conflict Zones.* (Kumarian Press, 2007).

253. W. G. Niederland. The survivor syndrome: Further observations and dimensions. *Journal of the American Psychoanalytic Association* **29** (1981), 413–425.

254. J. Leskela, M. Dieperink, & P. Thuras. Shame and posttraumatic stress disorder. *Journal of Traumatic Stress* **15** (2002), 223–226.

255. U. Orth, L. Montada & A. Maercker. Feelings of revenge, retaliation motive, and posttraumatic stress reactions in crime victims. *Journal of Interpersonal Violence* **21** (2006), 229–243.

256. C. P. Bayer, F. Klasen, & H. Adam. Association of trauma and PTSD symptoms with openness to reconciliation and feelings of revenge among former Ugandan and Congolese child soldiers. *JAMA* **298** (2007), 555–559.

257. Resilience. www.apa.org/topics/resilience

258. A. Maercker & A. B. Horn. A socio-interpersonal perspective on PTSD: The case for environments and interpersonal processes. *Clinical Psychology & Psychotherapy* **20** (2013), 465–481.

259. B. V. Schaack, D. Reicherter, & Y. Chhang. *Cambodia's Hidden Scars: Trauma Psychology in the Wake of the Khmer Rouge: An Edited Volume on Cambodia's Mental Health.* (Documentation Center of Cambodia, 2011).

260. B. Münyas. Genocide in the minds of Cambodian youth: Transmitting (hi)stories of genocide to second and third generations in Cambodia. *Journal of Genocide Research* **10** (2008), 413–439.

261. J. Platt, K. M. Keyes, & K. C. Koenen. Size of the social network versus quality of social support: which is more protective against PTSD? *Social Psychiatry & Psychiatric Epidemiology* **49** (2014), 1279–1286.

262. B. Andrews, C. R. Brewin, & S. Rose. Gender, social support, and PTSD in victims of violent crime. *Journal of Trauma Stress* **16** (2003), 421–427.

263. About us. *United Nations Population Fund.* www.unfpa.org/about-us

264. N. M. Shrestha, B. Sharma, M. Van Ommeren, *et al.* Impact of torture on refugees displaced within the developing world: Symptomatology among Bhutanese refugees in Nepal. *JAMA* **280** (1998), 443–448.

265. C. Rousseau, A. Mekki-Berrada, & S. Moreau. Trauma and extended separation from family among Latin American and African refugees in Montreal. *Psychiatry: Interpersonal and Biological Processes* **64** (2001), 40–59.

266. A. Phillips. Analysis. "They're rapists." President Trump's campaign launch speech two years later, annotated. *Washington Post,* June 16, 2021.

267. R. Yehuda, J. Schmeidler, E. L. Giller, L. J. Siever, & K. Binder-Brynes. Relationship between posttraumatic stress disorder characteristics of Holocaust survivors and their adult offspring. *The American Journal of Psychiatry* **155** (1998), 841–843.

268. Z. Solomon, M. Kotler, & M. Mikulincer. Combat-related posttraumatic stress disorder among second-generation Holocaust survivors: Preliminary findings. *The American Journal of Psychiatry* **145** (1988), 865–868.

269. N. C. Auerhahn & D. Laub. Intergenerational memory of the Holocaust. In Y. Danieli (ed.), *International Handbook of Multigenerational Legacies of Trauma,* 21–41 (Springer US, 1998). doi: 10.1007/978-1-4757-5567-1_2

270. R. Thornton. *American Indian Holocaust and Survival: A Population History Since 1492*. (University of Oklahoma Press, 1987).

271. N. P. Field, S. Muong, & V. Sochanvimean. Parental styles in the intergenerational transmission of trauma stemming from the Khmer Rouge regime in Cambodia. *American Journal of Orthopsychiatry* **83** (2013), 483–494.

272. T. B. Franklin, H. Russig, I. C. Weiss, *et al.* Epigenetic transmission of the impact of early stress across generations. *Biological Psychiatry* **68** (2010), 408–415.

273. R. Yehuda & A. Lehrner. Intergenerational transmission of trauma effects: Putative role of epigenetic mechanisms. *World Psychiatry* **17** (2018), 243–257.

274. N. Perroud, E. Rutembesa, A. Paoloni-Giacobino, *et al.* The Tutsi genocide and transgenerational transmission of maternal stress: Epigenetics and biology of the HPA axis. *The World Journal of Biological Psychiatry* **15** (2014), 334–345.

275. D. L. Costa, N. Yetter, & H. DeSomer. Intergenerational transmission of paternal trauma among US Civil War ex-POWs. *Proceedings of the National Academy of Sciences* **115** (2018), 11215–11220.

276. B. Bezo & S. Maggi. Living in "survival mode": Intergenerational transmission of trauma from the Holodomor genocide of 1932–1933 in Ukraine. *Social Science & Medicine* **134** (2015), 87–94.

277. O. Subtelny. *Ukraine: A History*, 4th ed. (University of Toronto Press, 2009).

278. K. Gapp, J. Bohacek, J. Grossmann, *et al.* Potential of environmental enrichment to prevent transgenerational effects of paternal trauma. *Neuropsychopharmacology* **41** (2016), 2749–2758.

279. J. A. Arai, S. Li, D. M. Hartley, & L. A. Feig. Transgenerational rescue of a genetic defect in long-term potentiation and memory formation by juvenile enrichment. *Journal of Neuroscience* **29** (2009), 1496–1502.

280. S. Dicklitch & A. Malik. Justice, human rights, and reconciliation in postconflict Cambodia. *Human Rights Review* **11** (2010), 515–530.

281. J. Roisin. *Dans la nuit la plus noire se cache l'humanité. Récits des justes du Rwanda.* (Les Impressions Nouvelles, 2017).

282. D. Rothbart & J. Cooley. Hutus aiding Tutsis during the Rwandan genocide: Motives, meanings and morals. *Genocide Studies and Prevention: An International Journal* **10** (2016). doi: 10.5038/1911-9933.10.2.1398

283. S. E. Brown. Faith and women rescuers in Rwanda. In S. E. Brown & S. D. Smith (eds.), *The Routledge Handbook of Religion, Mass Atrocity, and Genocide* (Routledge, 2021).

284. J. Casiro. Argentine rescuers: A study on the "banality of good." *Journal of Genocide Research* **8** (2006), 437–454.

285. B. Campbell. Contradictory behavior during genocides. *Sociological Forum* **25** (2010), 296–314.

286. L. Watson. The man who saved the world: The Soviet submariner who single-handedly averted WWIII at height of the Cuban Missile Crisis. *Mail Online* www.dailymail.co.uk/news/article-2208342/Soviet-submariner-single-handedly-averted-WWIII-height-Cuban-Missile-Crisis.html (2012).

287. Cuban Missile Crisis, Russian Submarines – Johnson's Russia List 6–22–02. https://web.archive.org/web/20110530221205/http://65.120.76.2 52/russia/johnson/6320-12.cfm.

288. Gariwo: The Gardens of the Righteous. https://en.gariwo.net

289. F. Varese & M. Yaish. Altruism: The importance of being asked. The rescue of Jews in Nazi Europe. *Rationality and Society* **12** (2000), 307–334.

290. M. Paldiel. The Righteous Among the Nations at Yad Vashem. *The Journal of Holocaust Education* **7** (1998), 45–66.

291. Names of Righteous by country. www.yadvashem.org/righteous/statis tics.html

292. W. M. Landes & R. A. Posner. Salvors, finders, good Samaritans, and other rescuers: An economic study of law and altruism. *The Journal of Legal Studies* 1 (1978), 83–128.

293. S. P. Oliner & P. M. Oliner. *The Altruistic Personality: Rescuers of Jews in Nazi Europe.* (Free Press, 1988).

294. P. Suedfeld & S. de Best. Value hierarchies of Holocaust rescuers and resistance fighters. *Genocide Studies and Prevention* **3** (2008), 31–42.

295. S. Fagin-Jones & E. Midlarsky. Courageous altruism: Personal and situational correlates of rescue during the Holocaust. *The Journal of Positive Psychology* **2** (2007), 136–147.

296. N. Fox & H. Nyseth Brehm. "I decided to save them": Factors that shaped participation in rescue efforts during genocide in Rwanda. *Social Forces* **96** (2018), 1625–1648.

297. L. A. Fujii. *Killing Neighbors: Webs of Violence in Rwanda.* (Cornell University Press, 2010).

298. J. Adekunle. *Culture and Customs of Rwanda.* (Greenwood Press, 2007).

299. H. Nyseth Brehm, C. Uggen, & J.-D. Gasanabo. Age, gender, and the crime of crimes: Toward a life-course theory of genocide participation. *Criminology* **54** (2016), 713–743.

300. R. Forsythe, J. L., Horowitz, N. E. Savin, & M. Sefton. Fairness in simple bargaining experiments. *Games and Economic Behavior* **6** (1994), 347–369.

301. D. Klinowski. Gender differences in giving in the Dictator Game: The role of reluctant altruism. *Journal of the Economic Science Association* **4** (2018), 110–122

302. O. Feldman Hall, T. Dalgleish, D. Evans, & D. Mobbs. Empathic concern drives costly altruism. *NeuroImage* **105** (2014), 347–356.

303. L. Christov-Moore & M. Iacoboni. Self-other resonance, its control and prosocial inclinations: Brain–behavior relationships. *Human Brain Mapping* **37** (2016), 1544–1558.

304. S. Gallo, R. Paracampo, L. Müller-Pinzler, *et al.* The causal role of the somatosensory cortex in prosocial behaviour. *eLife* **7** (2018), e32740.

305. C. Liao, C. Wu, Y. Luo, Q. Guan, & F. Cui. Transcranial direct current stimulation of the medial prefrontal cortex modulates the propensity to help in costly helping behavior. *Neuroscience Letters* **674** (2018), 54–59.

306. C. L. Sebastian, N. M. Fontaine, G. Bird, *et al.* Neural processing associated with cognitive and affective Theory of Mind in adolescents and adults. *Social Cognitive and Affective Neuroscience* **7** (2012), 53–63.

307. I. D. Neumann. Brain oxytocin: A key regulator of emotional and social behaviours in both females and males. *Journal of Neuroendocrinology* **20** (2008), 858–865 .

308. J. A. Barraza & P. J. Zak. Empathy toward strangers triggers oxytocin release and subsequent generosity. *Annals of the New York Academy of Sciences* **1167** (2009), 182–189.

309. P. J. Zak, A. A. Stanton, & S. Ahmadi. Oxytocin increases generosity in humans. *PLoS One* **2** (2007), e1128.

310. N. Sato, L. Tan, K. Tate, & M. Okada. Rats demonstrate helping behavior toward a soaked conspecific. *Animal Cognition* **18** (2015), 1039–1047.

311. A. Yamagishi, M. Okada, M. Masuda, & N. Sato. Oxytocin administration modulates rats' helping behavior depending on social context. *Neuroscience Research* **153** (2020), 56–61.

312. E. A. Caspar. A novel experimental approach to study disobedience to authority. *Scientific Reports* **11** (2021), 22927.

313. E. A. Caspar, D. Gishoma, & P. A. Magalhaes de Saldanha da Gama. On the cognitive mechanisms supporting prosocial disobedience in a post-genocidal context. *Scientific Reports* **12** (2022), 21875.

314. G. Agneman. Conflict victimization and civilian obedience: Evidence from Colombia. HiCN Working Papers (2022).

315. P. Lakey. Acculturation: A review of the literature. *Intercultural Communication Studies* **12** (2003), 103–118.

316. D. M. Amodio, P. G. Devine, & E. Harmon-Jones. Individual differences in the regulation of intergroup bias: The role of conflict monitoring and neural signals for control. *Journal of Personality and Social Psychology* **94** (2008), 60–74.

317. E. Caspar & G. P. Pech. Obedience to authority reduces cognitive conflict before an action. (2024). PsyArXiv

318. R. G. Tedeschi. Violence transformed: Posttraumatic growth in survivors and their societies. *Aggression and Violent Behavior* **4** (1999), 319–341.

319. Y. Cheng, Y.-C Chen, Y.-T Fan, & C. Chen. Neuromodulation of the right temporoparietal junction alters amygdala functional connectivity to authority pressure. *Human Brain Mapping* **43** (2022), 5605–5615.

320. A. K. Martin, K. Kessler, S. Cooke, J. Huang, & M. Meinzer. The right temporoparietal junction is causally associated with embodied perspective-taking. *Journal of Neuroscience* **40** (2020), 3089–3095.

321. L. A. Fujii. The power of local ties: Popular participation in the Rwandan genocide. *Security Studies* **17**(3) (2008), 568–597.

322. Human Rights Watch. Report: www.hrw.org/reports/2003/usa1203/4 .5.htm.

323. E. Staub. Obeying, joining, following, resisting, and other processes in the Milgram studies, and in the Holocaust and other genocides: Situations, personality, and bystanders. *Journal of Social Issues* **70**(3) (2014), 501–514.

Index

mens rea, 94
mice. *See* rats
Milgram, Stanley 12, xii, 21, 57, 60, 70, 75,
    162, 211
military personnel, 108, 170
    junior cadets, 110
    privates, 111
    senior cadets, 111
    soldiers, 101, 139, 193
military veterans, 25, 169, 170, 174,
    177–179, 180
mirror neurons, 117, 119, 120
moral disengagement, 149
moral emotions, 23, 24, 142, 146, 164
moral injuries, 25, 179, 182
movie. *See* documentary/movie
MRI. *See* magnetic resonance imaging
Musekeweya (radio program), x

Nazi leaders
    Eichmann, Adolf, 13, 61, 158
    Hitler, Adolf, 3, 170, 181
Nazi officers. *See* Nazis
Nazi Party. *See* Nazis
Nazis, xii, 3, 12, 27, 28, 42, 52, 100, 135, 170,
    203
neuromarketing, 5
neuromodulation, 133, 208, 209, 218
neuroscience, 4–6, 9, 92, 103, 116, 132, 145,
    171, 207, 210, 214
"New Dawn." *See Musekeweya*
Nuremberg trials, 42

obeying orders, 1, 22, 45, 97, 106–107, 124,
    142, 146, 151
"Only obeying orders." *See* "Just following
    orders"
Oppenheimer, Joshua, 181
ostracization, 144, 186, 189
oxytocin, 209

placebo, 209
Pol Pot. *See* Khmer Rouge leaders: Pol Pot
post-traumatic stress disorder, 170–177,
    184, 185, 191
Prison Fellowship Rwanda, 16, 17, 31
propaganda, xiii, 2, 26, 135, 136, 180, 193,
    205, 220, 222
prosocial disobedience, xiii, 211–218
psychopathic traits, ix, 126, 163
psychopaths, 12, 66, 127, 220
psychopathy. *See* psychopathic traits

PTSD. *See* post-traumatic stress disorder
PTSD symptoms. *See* post-traumatic stress
    disorder

Radio La Benevolencija, x
Radio Télévision Libre des Milles Collines,
    2
rape. *See* sexual assault
rat decapitation study, 59
rats, 120, 135, 192–194
real-time neurofeedback, 129
reconciliation, 16, 17, 44, 186, 203
remorse, 25, 143, 155, 180–182, 221
rescuers, xiii, 199–210, 222
Reserve Police Battalion 101, 41
resilience, 187
resisting immoral orders. *See* prosocial
    disobedience
responsibility, denial, 14, 21, 35, 42, 43, 97,
    101, 102, 154, 169
responsibility, feeling of, 22, 91, 94, 96,
    97, 146, 150, 151, 155, 159, 163–167,
    182
revenge, 14, 15, 24, 169,
    186, 194
reward, xii, 120, 122, 210, 212,
    215, 217
Righteous Among the Nations, xiii, 25,
    200–203, 222
Rizzolatti, Giacomo, 117
robots, 68, 165–167
Roisin, Jacques, 206

S-21. *See* Tuol Sleng
Saloth Sâr. *See* Pol Pot
Schimke, Otto-Julies, 42
Schindler, 202
schizophrenia, 90, 105
self-punishment, 143
sense of agency, 22, 24, 88–91, 93, 100, 121,
    161, 162, 166
sexual assault, 13, 140, 185–189
shame, 169, 180, 181, 186
shared humanity, 203–206
shocks. *See* electrical shock
Singer, Tania, 115
social exclusion. *See* ostracization
South Kivu, 185
spotted hyenas, 148
Srebrenica, 139
Staub, Erwin, x
stigmatization, 186